Grant vs. Lee

Favorite Stories and Fresh Perspectives
from the Historians at Emerging Civil War

Edited by
Chris Mackowski & Dan Welch

The Emerging Civil War Series

offers compelling, easy-to-read overviews of some of the Civil War's most important battles and stories.

Recipient of the Army Historical Foundation's Lieutenant General Richard G. Trefry Award for contributions to the literature on the history of the U.S. Army

Chris Mackowski
Foreword by Gregory A. Mertz

Hell Itself

The Battle of the Wilderness,
May 5–7, 1864

EMERGING CIVIL WAR SERIES

Chris Mackowski and Kristopher D. White

A Season of Slaughter

The Battle of
Spotsylvania Court House,
May 8–21, 1864

EMERGING CIVIL WAR SERIES

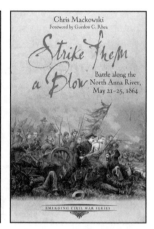

Chris Mackowski
Foreword by Gordon C. Rhea

Strike Them a Blow

Battle along the
North Anna River,
May 21–25, 1864

EMERGING CIVIL WAR SERIES

Daniel T. Davis and Phillip S. Greenwalt

Hurricane from the Heavens

The Battle of Cold Harbor,
May 26–June 5, 1864

EMERGING CIVIL WAR SERIES

Edward S. Alexander

Dawn of Victory

Breakthrough at Petersburg,
March 25–April 2, 1865

EMERGING CIVIL WAR SERIES

Robert M. Dunkerly
Afterword by Chris Mackowski

To the Bitter End

Appomattox, Bennett Place,
and the Surrenders of the Confederacy

EMERGING CIVIL WAR SERIES

**For a complete list of titles in the Emerging Civil War Series,
visit www.emergingcivilwar.com.**

Grant vs. Lee

Favorite Stories and Fresh Perspectives from the Historians at Emerging Civil War

Edited by

Chris Mackowski & Dan Welch

Savas Beatie
California

First edition, first printing

ISBN-13 (hardcover): 978-1-61121-595-3
ISBN-13 (ebook): 978-1-954547-12-4

Library of Congress Cataloging-in-Publication Data

Names: Mackowski, Chris, editor. | Welch, Dan (Educator), editor.
Title: Grant vs Lee : favorite stories and fresh perspectives from the historians at Emerging Civil War / edited by Chris Mackowski, and Dan Welch.
Other titles: Favorite stories and fresh perspectives from the historians at Emerging Civil War | Emerging Civil War (Blog) Description: El Dorado Hills, CA : Savas Beatie LLC, [2022] | Series: Emerging Civil War - anniversary series | Includes index. | Summary: "By the spring of 1864, the Army of the Potomac and the Army of Northern Virginia had become battle-hardened, battle-weary foes locked in an ongoing stalemate. With the presidential election looming in the fall, President Abraham Lincoln needed to break the deadlock and so brought to the east the unassuming "dust-covered man" who had strung together victory after victory in the west: Ulysses S. Grant. "Well," said soldiers in the Army of the Potomac with a grudging respect for their Southern adversary, "Grant has never met Bobby Lee yet." Robert E. Lee and Ulysses S. Grant would come to symbolize the armies they led as the spring campaign got underway, and the clash that began in the Virginia Wilderness on May 5, 1864, turned into a long, desperate death-match that inexorably led to Appomattox Court House eleven months later. The war would come to an end, but at what cost along the way? Grant vs. Lee: Favorite Stories and Fresh Perspectives from the Historians at Emerging Civil War recounts some of the most famous episodes and most compelling human dramas from the marquee match-up of the Civil War-not just the two most successful commanders produced by either side but the two largest and most fabled armies of the war"-- Provided by publisher.
Identifiers: LCCN 2021055449 | ISBN 9781611215953 (hardcover) | ISBN 9781954547124 (ebook)
Subjects: LCSH: Grant, Ulysses S. (Ulysses Simpson), 1822-1885--Anecdotes.
| Lee, Robert E. (Robert Edward), 1807-1870--Anecdotes. | United States.
Army--Biography--Anecdotes. | Confederate States of America.
Army--Biography--Anecdotes. | Generals--United
States--Biography--Anecdotes. | Generals--Confederate States of
America--Biography--Anecdotes. | United States--History--Civil War,
1861-1865--Biography--Anecdotes.
Classification: LCC E467 .G738 2022 | DDC 973.70922--dc23/eng/20211203
LC record available at https://lccn.loc.gov/2021055449

Savas Beatie
989 Governor Drive, Suite 102
El Dorado Hills, CA 95762
916-941-6896 / sales@savasbeatie.com / www.savasbeatie.com

All of our titles are available at special discount rates for bulk purchases in the United States. Contact us for information.

Proudly published, printed, and warehoused in the United States of America.

Table of Contents

List of Maps

Chris Heisey

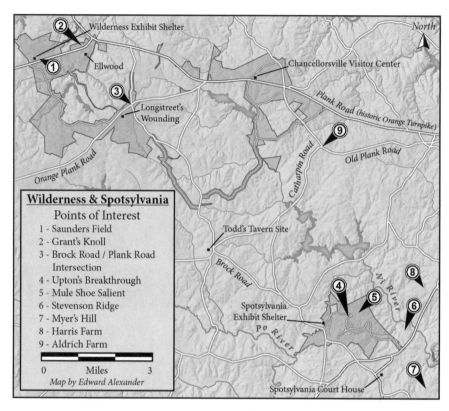

Wilderness Exhibit Shelter

North

Ellwood

Chancellorsville Visitor Center

Plank Road (historic Orange Turnpike)

Longstreet's
Wounding

Catharpin Road

Old Plank Road

Orange Plank Road

Wilderness & Spotsylvania
Points of Interest
1 - Saunders Field
2 - Grant's Knoll
3 - Brock Road / Plank Road
   Intersection
4 - Upton's Breakthrough
5 - Mule Shoe Salient
6 - Stevenson Ridge
7 - Myer's Hill
8 - Harris Farm
9 - Aldrich Farm

0   Miles   3

Map by Edward Alexander

Todd's Tavern Site

Brock Road

Ni River

Spotsylvania
Exhibit Shelter

Po River

Spotsylvania Court House

WILDERNESS & SPOTSYLVANIA (ABOVE) AND PETERSBURG (OPPOSITE)—Particular points of interest discussed in some of the essays are marked on these maps for easy reference. The shaded areas represent property owned by the National Park Service; however, a number of other preservation groups and private entities also own and protect land, historical structures, and other properties associated with the Overland Campaign, the Siege of Petersburg, and the Appomattox Campaign.

From "Point of Interest" 3 (above): Union troops cheer Ulysses S. Grant at the Brock Road/Plank Road intersection. Grant's decision to march south out of the Wilderness, rather than retreat, changed the fundamental dynamics of the war. The fight between Grant and Robert E. Lee would be unlike anything the war had yet seen.

Library of Congress

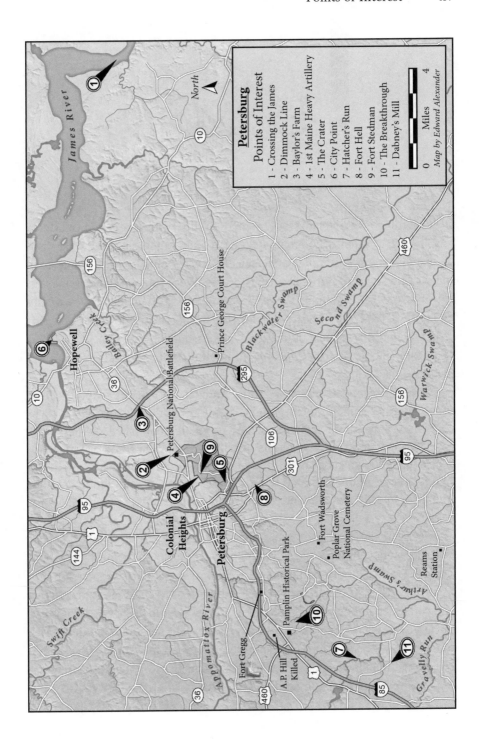

Petersburg
Points of Interest

1 - Crossing the James
2 - Dimmock Line
3 - Baylor's Farm
4 - 1st Maine Heavy Artillery
5 - The Crater
6 - City Point
7 - Hatcher's Run
8 - Fort Hell
9 - Fort Stedman
10 - The Breakthrough
11 - Dabney's Mill

Map by Edward Alexander

Editors' Note

Emerging Civil War serves as a public history-oriented platform for sharing original scholarship related to the American Civil War. The scholarship we present reflects the eclectic background, expertise, interests, and writing styles of our cadre of historians. We've shared that scholarship not only on the Emerging Civil War blog, but also in the pages of the Emerging Civil War Series published by Savas Beatie, in other general-audience and academic publications, at our annual Emerging Civil War Symposium at Stevenson Ridge, on our monthly podcasts, and even through social media.

Our Emerging Civil War 10th Anniversary Series captures and commemorates some of the highlights from our first ten years.

This compendium includes pieces originally published on our blog; podcast transcripts; and transcripts of talks given at the ECW Symposium. It also includes an assortment of original material. Previously published pieces have been updated and, in most cases, expanded and footnoted. Our attempt is to offer value-added rather than just reprint material available for free elsewhere.

Between the covers of this series, readers will find military, social, political, and economic history; memory studies; travelogues; personal narratives; essays; and photography. This broad range of scholarship and creative work is meant to provide readers with a diversity of perspectives. The combined collection of material is *not* intended to serve as a complete narrative of events or comprehensive overview. Rather, these are the stories and events our historians happened to be interested in writing about at any given time. In that way, the collection represents the sort of eclectic ongoing conversation you'll find on our blog.

As a collective, the individuals who comprise ECW are encouraged to share their own unique interests and approaches. The resulting work—and the respectful discussions that surround it—forward ECW's overall effort to promote a general awareness of the Civil War as America's defining event.

Another of ECW's organizational priorities is our ongoing work to identify and spotlight the next generation of "emerging" Civil War historians and the fresh ideas they bring to the historical conversation. (Some of us were "emerging" when ECW started up ten years ago and have perhaps since "emerged," but the quest to spotlight new voices continues!)

Most importantly, it is the common thread of public history and the ideals of interpretation that so strongly tie our seemingly disparate bodies of work together. America's defining event should not be consigned to forgotten footnotes and dusty shelves. As public historians, we understand the resonance and importance history's lessons can have in our modern world and in our daily lives, so we always seek to connect people with those great stories and invaluable lessons. Emerging Civil War remains committed to making our history something available for all of us—writers, readers, historians, hobbyists, men, women, young, old, and people of all races and ethnicities—and by doing so, making it something we can engage, question, challenge, and enjoy.

Please join us online at www.emergingcivilwar.com.

A Note About This Volume:

Grant vs. Lee covers a tremendous amount of ground, but that means there's also a lot of ground we couldn't cover. Many great stories go untold. This collection is intended not as a comprehensive chronicle of the last eleven months of the war but as a sampler of some of our favorite stories from that time period. For reasons of space, we also chose to stick to the main event, as it were, and avoid related side actions like Bermuda Hundred, Yellow Tavern, New Market, Wilson's Wharf, Trevilian Station, Monocacy, or the 1864 Valley Campaign. That's not to diminish the importance of any of those events or the value of the wider context they offer. For more information, we have several relevant titles in the Emerging Civil War Series (see pg. ii).

Acknowledgments

First and foremost, as editors, we'd like to thank our colleagues at Emerging Civil War, past and present. ECW has always been and remains a team effort. We've worked with some wonderful historians, writers, and "emerging voices" over the past decade, and we're proud to show off some of that work here. We are deeply appreciative of the folks who contributed content to this series and to this specific volume.

Thanks, too, to Theodore Savas and his entire team at Savas Beatie, with a special thanks to our editorial liaison, Sarah Keeney. Ted took a chance on us when we were still a young blog, accepting Kris White's pitch for the Emerging Civil War Series. That proved to be a game-changer for us. Together, ECW and Savas Beatie have produced some great work, and we're thankful to Ted for agreeing to help us celebrate ECW's tenth anniversary by allowing us to produce more great work. We thank everyone at Savas Beatie for all they do to support the work of Emerging Civil War.

One of ECW's prime directives is to help our contributors make opportunities for themselves. Edward Alexander's development as a cartographer over the past few years has been a perfect illustration of that guiding principle. We're proud of his work, and we're grateful for the maps he's contributed to this volume. Visit him for cartography services at www.makemeamapllc.com. (And, yes, Edward's "Make me a map" is a reference to Stonewall Jackson's directive to Jed Hotchkiss in March 1862.)

That said, we've been extremely lucky to work so long with cartographer Hal Jespersen, whose maps have been a distinctive part of the Emerging Civil War Series; we're pleased to include some of his maps in this volume, as well.

Sarah Kay Bierle, as ECW's managing editor, manages the content on the blog on a daily basis. Her work made it a lot easier for us to collect the material we've assembled in this volume. Our official un-official archivist, Jon-Erik Gilot, has helped us make it easier to access our past work.

Christopher Kolakowski, as our chief historian, provides overall quality control for our work, offering a soft but firm guiding hand. Dan Davis previously served in that role, and Kris White, as one of our co-founders, originated that role. Our thanks to all three of them for ensuring a high bar for our writers in service to our readers.

Thanks to John Foskett and Patrick McCormick, who both reviewed the text and made valuable suggestions and observations.

And a big thank-you to Chris Heisey for always being willing to contribute *one more* photograph as the design of this book continuted to evolve.

Finally, a special thanks to co-founders Chris Mackowski, Jake Struhelka, and Kristopher D. White, whose brainstorming over beers, cigars, and history led to ECW's creation. To quote Kris's wife, "Not too bad for three idiots sitting on a porch."

*   *   *

Chris: My thanks to Dan Welch for his heavy-lifting on this volume. He's been an apt pupil and fun partner to work with as he learned the editorial ropes. My best of luck to him as he flies out of the nest!

Thanks to Aaron Chimbel, dean of the Jandoli School of Communication, for his ongoing strong support of my work. Thanks, too, to former deans Pauline Hoffmann and Lee Coppola for the similarly strong support they showed during their tenures.

Finally, as always, my thanks to my family, especially my kids, Stephanie, Thomas, and Sophie Marie (my first grandchild!); Jackson; and Maxwell James. Most of all, thanks to my wife and partner, Jenny Ann, who's been by my side through most of this and still hasn't left me on a battlefield yet.

*   *   *

Dan: As always, I'd like to send my continued thanks to Chris Mackowski and Ted Savas for the opportunity to serve as an editor for this series. Their excellent tutelage continues to be a blessing in my own writing and editing.

To all of the contributors to this work, thank you. It has been a true delight to learn from your "emerging voices" and your vast array of knowledge on this period of the war.

Lastly, to my great friends in the field: Billy, Kevin, Mark, Matt, Phill, and Rob. I have learned, and continue to learn, so much from each of you about every facet of public history, the American Civil War, and the Revolutionary War—but perhaps more importantly, the finer points on cigars, beer, and classic outlaw country music.

 Foreword

by Christopher Kolakowski

On April 9, 1864, Lt. Gen. U. S. Grant, commander of all United States Armies, issued his orders for the upcoming Virginia campaign to his principal field force, the Army of the Potomac. Instead of aiming to capture the Confederate capital of Richmond as in so many previous campaigns, hunting and destroying Gen. Robert E. Lee's Confederate Army of Northern Virginia would be army's objective. One year later, Lee's force capitulated to Grant a week after Richmond's fall.

The 1864 battles in Virginia pitted both sides' two great commanders, Grant and Lee, against each other for the first time. Through years of campaigns and victories, both men emerged as exemplars of their respective causes. Their backgrounds presented a considerable dissimilarity: Lee the deep-rooted Virginian versus Grant with his many homes in the Midwest. Lee's long service in the United States Army contrasted with Grant's resignation of his commission in the 1850s. Even in personal appearance, the dapper Lee stood opposite the modest and rumpled Grant. Yet despite their differences, both men compiled admirable combat records in the 24-27 months prior to May 1864.

In the spring of 1864, each side cloaked their champion in the aura of George Washington. In the Confederacy, Lee's army was in a position analogous to General Washington's Continental Army of the War for Independence. Although Confederate arms had sustained many defeats in other theaters, as long as the Army of Northern Virginia stayed in the field there was a hope of Confederate victory and independence. The fact that

General Lee was related to Washington by marriage, and was the son of one of Washington's senior leaders, didn't hurt either.

In Washington, D.C., U. S. President Abraham Lincoln persuaded Congress to recreate the grade of lieutenant general and promoted Grant to that rank. He was only the third officer to hold it, joining George Washington and Winfield Scott (the latter by brevet). This promotion elevated Grant into the pantheon of great American field generals, including General Washington, and doubled down on the idea that Grant was the man to win the war.

The battles in Virginia in 1864 and 1865 involved some of the highest stakes in American military history. In the fighting's background loomed the 1864 U. S. presidential election—the first of its kind in history ever held in the midst of a civil war. Virginia was politically the most important theater of war; battlefield victories by Lee would ruin Lincoln's reelection and give the Confederacy arguably its best chance for negotiated independence. On the other hand, a Lincoln reelection meant prosecution of the war to U. S. victory, followed by a reconstruction involving the abolition of slavery. In short, the very existence and future of the United States rested on the outcome of Grant's operations against Lee.

These outside factors added an edge to the fighting, as both sides strained every sinew toward victory. The 1864-65 Virginia campaigns occurred with a scale and sustained violence unmatched in American military history until World War II and seldom seen since. When Grant's and Lee's forces first met in the Wilderness on May 5, 1864, they did not break contact until Lee's surrender at Appomattox 11 months and 4 days later. In that time, they fought several intense battles, including two of the war's bloodiest; contested numerous skirmishes and other smaller actions; and grappled through nine months of siege that foreshadowed the horrors of World War I fifty years in the future. The intensity and duration of these operations burned into the psyche of the U. S. Army, and Grant's campaigns have since been called the birth of an American Way of War.

Such an eventful period of American military history offers much to teach and inspire. Naturally, it has been a focus of Emerging Civil War's authors, and much of that scholarship is included here. Even at the space of sixteen decades, these stories continue to have power long after the guns have fallen silent.

1. *Photographing Grant vs. Lee*

by Chris Heisey

For more than 30 years, I have been photographing our nation's sacred Civil War battlefields. While I live close to Gettysburg and Antietam and find them endlessly enchanting to photograph, my favorite hallowed fields to explore are the great battlefields of the 1864 Overland Campaign. Monuments sparsely dot the landscape, and suburban sprawl continuously threatens the sanctity of places whose names are seared into all our collective Civil War minds. Immense carnage happened between Fredericksburg and Richmond in that wicked spring and early summer of the war's last year. Whether it be the Wilderness, Spotsylvania, North Anna River, or the environs of Cold Harbor, these fields are remarkably beautiful and peaceful today, yet if you still yourself long enough there is a foreboding sense of dread that still lives here in in the heart of Virginia.

Some time ago, I got a voicemail message that changed my life in a good manner. "The call," as my family called it, came from Gordon Rhea, who inarguably remains the preeminent historian of the Overland Campaign. Gordon has authored five full book studies on the fighting between the war's two great generals: Ulysses S. Grant and Robert E. Lee.

After a few days of touring the battlefields with Gordon and a few veteran National Park Service historians, I went from an almost novice student of these pivotal battles to having a more modest grasp of what happened over this roughly 50-mile stretch of Central Virginia. "Have at it, Chris," Gordon told me. Shoot what you want and when you want over the next year, he said, and we will assemble a book called *In the Footsteps of Grant and Lee.*

Grant's relentless flanking maneuvers and Lee's masterful defensive retreats make this campaign fascinating to study as a chess match. But in my year of visiting nearly every square mile of this campaign, what struck me most about this ultimate turning point of the war is the uncanny endurance and fortitude of the common soldier in the ranks for both the blue and the gray. Many of these soldiers were hardy veterans of many other great battles, but even more were raw recruits drafted to replace the dwindling ranks of both the Union Army of the Potomac and the Confederate Army of Northern Virginia. For many, these battles would be their first and last fighting.

Whether I shot battlefields on frosty mornings when the temperature was

two degrees on a December morning at Saunders Field in the Wilderness or on a day that exceeded one hundred degrees at Cold Harbor's Garthright House, I was always reminded of the conditions these mostly still boys fought in. There is no escaping the eeriness of the Mule Shoe at Spotsylvania in the mist of dawn in May where the fighting raged all day long. There are places in the Confederate works where men died stacked five deep, so deadly was the carnage in the mud-filled trenches.

It was one of the best years of my life shooting these battlefields, rivers, and swamps. I found a sort of peace at Widow Tapp Farm that awed me as autumn's splendor surrounded me in a spectrum of color. Whenever I return to these moving sites, I remember the privileged project that changed me as a photographer. Never do I take beauty for granted any more, nor do I fail to appreciate our hallowed grounds that so many preservationists have fought to save so that we all can better recall and and ponder the immensely important issues that the 1864 Overland Campaign ultimately decided.

But most importantly, through the camera's lens I learned the importance of not forgetting the day-after-day horror that the blue and the gray who fought for Grant and Lee endured those many years ago.

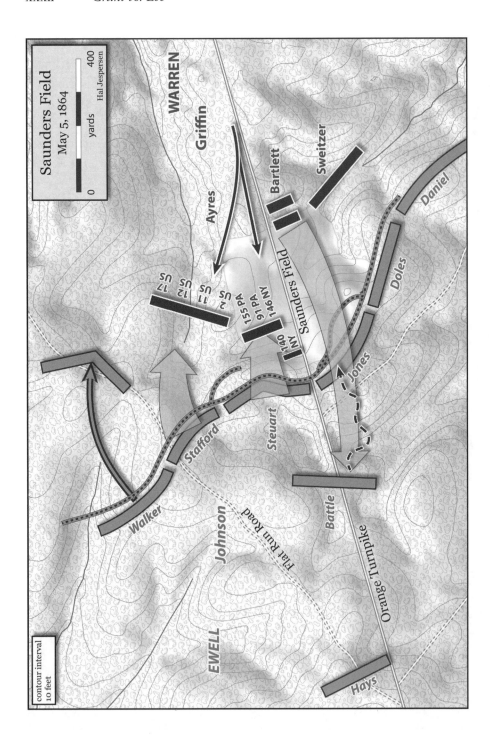

Saunders Field
May 5, 1864

0   yards   400

Hal Jespersen

contour interval
10 feet

WARREN

Griffin

Ayres

Bartlett

Sweitzer

Daniel

17 US
12 US
11 US
2 US
155 PA
91 PA
146 NY
140 NY

Saunders Field

Doles

Jones

Steuart

Stafford

Walker

JOHNSON

Flat Run Road

EWELL

Battle

Orange Turnpike

Hays

"Goodbye from Your Soger Boy: One Last Letter Before the Wilderness

by Sarah Kay Bierle

Point of Interest #1 on the map on pg. xiv.

*Originally published as a blog post
on Emerging Civil War on May 1, 2019*

Sometimes he signed his letters "with affection" or "good-night" or "good-bye." Sometimes he wrote his full name, other times just initials, sometimes with the familiar name to his family and friends: "Will." Most of his correspondence went to his younger sister "Jennie" and was addressed to the family home in Sebec, Maine. Will had left home in August 1862 when he was eighteen, enlisting in the 20th Maine Regiment, Company B.[1] He had already survived long months of campaigning and camp life, had fought at Gettysburg, and had been one of the fortunate ones to recover from dysentery and a lengthy hospital stay.

On May 3, 1864, twenty-year-old Private William P. Lamson wrote his

---

1 William P. Lamson, edited by Roderick M. Engert, *Maine To The Wilderness: The Civil War Letters of Pvt. William Lamson, 20th Maine Infantry* (Orange, VA: Publisher's Press, 1993), 9.

OPPOSITE: SAUNDERS FIELD—On the north side of Saunders Field, Ayres' brigade split when faced with Confederate fire from multiple angles, dilluting the power of its attack. On the south side of the field, Bartlett's brigade broke through the Confederate line, but regiments became isolated from each other in the thick foliage and had to either retreat or fight their way out. Sweitzer's brigade could offer little support because it, too, was tangled in the foliage.

sister a brief letter, just another in the series of correspondence that had traveled between Virginia and Maine in the past two years. If he had premonitions about his fate in the coming battle, he did not tell sixteen-year-old Jennie.

> Camp Near Culpeper, Va.
> May 3rd, 1864, evening
> Dear Sister,
>
> I expect that before you receive this we will be across the Rapidan and no knowing how much farther. We came about 4 miles on Sunday and today 5 or 6.
>
> I know Wm. C. Brown as well as anyone else in this Co. He is a drummer now. I should advise you not to answer that advertisement in the Observer for letters, or any other. The one you speak of was from one of the teamsters who don't amount to much anyway. When you answer advertisement you needn't write to me – They only want letters for sport or they can't get anybody to write that knows them.
>
> I came by that "Miss Terius" honestly, but don't understand how it ever came on our doorstep at home.
>
> It's late and I must close. Give love to all.
>
> We'll soon be in business.
>
> Good bye from your soger boy,
> Will[2]

Parts of Will's letters are cryptic to modern readers, though they would have made perfect sense to Jennie. She seems to have asked for advice about writing to other soldiers, and here her older brother advises her to be wary of the guys who just wanted entertainment by writing to impressionable girls. He takes a protective stance even though he is hundreds of miles away.

Will mentions a mystery letter that had been delivered to home instead of him, but either did not know the details of its origins or did not feel it necessary to explain to his sister. Throughout the previous months, Will had repeatedly asked for information about "the girls" back home, but did not seem to single out one particular lady, casting doubt that this is a reference to a beginning romance.

Militarily, Will does not reveal much. Common soldiers did not attend war councils and were not informed of the campaign plans. Like his comrades, he knew battles were ahead, but certainly not the details or order of march beyond his brigade. Will correctly surmises that they would cross the Rapidan River.

On the night of May 3, 1864—probably just hours after he signed and sealed the letter for Jennie—the 20th Maine marched to the riverbank and, the following morning, crossed at Germanna Ford. Part of General Joseph Bartlett's brigade, General Charles Griffin's division, V Corps, Army of the Potomac, the regiment headed into the Wilderness.

On May 5, Confederates noticed Union pickets near Saunders Field, and Lt. Gen. Richard S. Ewell's Rebels hastily constructed trenches (some can still be seen today) and barricades from tree branches. While the soldiers skirmished, the generals decided. Major General George G. Meade ordered Maj. Gen. Gouverneur K. Warren's V Corps to attack at Saunders Field, but Warren took a long time to get the troops into position.

Private Will Lamson and his comrades in the 20th Maine found themselves in the second line of battle.[3] Pressured by Grant and Meade, the V Corps commander ordered an assault by General Griffin's division without waiting for support to arrive via the traffic jammed Wilderness roads. By the time the 20th Maine soldiers reached the edge of the open field, the first line of battle ahead of them was already about halfway across.

Plunging forward, the regiment ran through a firestorm of bullets, but forced the Confederates to abandon their position. Enthused, the Union men pressed forward through the trees to another clearing—only to halt in horror. The 20th Maine got flanked and suffered from intense Confederate fire. Captain Walter Morrill, commander of Company B, rallied his men and other broken units, managing to briefly halt the Confederate counterattack, giving others time to retreat.[4] This Union attack ultimately failed, though, and the battered regiments fell back, ending one short chapter in the Wilderness's bloody and intense history.

---

3   John J. Pullen, *The Twentieth Maine* (Mechanicsburg, PA: Stackpole Books, 1957), 184.

4   Ibid., 187.

Will made this charge with the 20th Maine. But it is unclear how far he went or if he fought in Company B's defense. At least 85 men were killed, wounded, or missing from the regiment after this charge and retreat.[5] Will Lamson was one of the fallen.

According to family records and stories, Will died on May 5, 1864—the same day as the attack on Saunders Field. Regimental records suggest he was badly wounded, captured by Confederates, and died shortly after. One comrade later informed the family that he had last seen Will lying under a tree, wounded.[6] Will's body was never identified or recovered; perhaps he is buried in the Wilderness or in an unmarked grave in Fredericksburg National Cemetery. In the family plot in Maine, a memorial gravestone has been added.

Will Lamson's last letter to his sister is a reminder of young soldiers far from home. He did not detail a campaign or tell her about boiling coffee. He tried to give brotherly advice. Will knew that "business" (battle) loomed, but he addressed it casually to avoid worrying Jennie. He usually downplayed dangers and battles to her, always trying to shield or protect her from his experiences.

Will's final moments or hours went unrecorded. The day Jennie received news of her brother's death also went unrecorded. However, based on evidence through years of letters, it does not seem wrong to suppose that if he was conscious, Will thought about home and about Jennie. He may have hoped Jennie would never know the details about the ending of his life; let her remember him as the soldier brother who wasn't afraid and who had marched off to war in '62. Pain, danger from blazing flames, and a deep consciousness of being alone without comrades likely marked the end of his life.

It was late. He had to go. Loving thoughts struggled to hold him longer, for more moments of living. But "business" was over. Somewhere, not far from Saunders Field in the dense Virginian Wilderness, Will Lamson—the "soger boy"—had to say a final goodbye to all that he loved and held dear.

---

5   Ibid., 191.

6   Lamson, 98.

Re-Crossing Saunders Field

by Sarah Kay Bierle

Point of Interest #1 on the map on pg. xiv.

Originally published as a blog post at Emerging Civil War on March 10, 2021

Unless you're walking a loop trail on a battlefield or have a vehicle waiting to pick you up, there's a pretty good chance you'll have to walk back the way you crossed a field. For many battlefield visits, I focus on "the attack route," and I don't care much about the return trip to the parking areas. That started to change as I studied the battle of New Market and found some poignant descriptions of the Virginia Military Institute cadets walking back over the fields and positions they had fought through, looking for fallen comrades. There is history to explore in the land of attacks when you "about face" for the return walk. Then, the footsteps to follow lead through the history of a repulse or over the ground of a victorious charge's aftermath.

Sometimes, I have tried to explore the return experience and look for the possible or recorded locations of field hospitals or first-aid stations. How far did the wounded have to go? Or if it's ground where there was a military retreat, I want to see how that might have looked. Did the troops find any shelter in the topography on their return? Was it an orderly retreat that could have taken advantage of any land features (if they exist) or was it a broken retreat with every man for himself?

These thoughts came to mind when I walked through the south side of Saunders Field on the Wilderness Battlefield. I wanted to look at the topography from a Union perspective in both attack and retreat, though I had had to see it in reverse order. I parked in one of the pull-offs on Hill-Ewell Drive, walked around the earthworks, and headed into the field from the Confederate position. For the trip across, I stayed closer to the tree line than the road (Route 20/Orange Turnpike), and I noticed that the land closer to the road could have been more suitable for attack. That was the area Union Brig. Gen. Joseph Bartlett used for his attack which briefly broke through the Confederate lines on May 5, 1864. When I reached the far side of the field, I marched back closer to the road and to the earthworks (which I went around instead of over).

While it was interesting and insightful to see the attack route from the Union perspective, I kept thinking about the retreats through Saunders Field. Walking alone in the open space and seeing how artillery and rifle fire easily swept most of the field sent shivers up my spine. There's little effective cover, which could be frightening enough in an attack but must have been absolutely terrifying when those battle lines broke and the soldiers tried to dash across the open ground to cover in the opposite tree line.

Captain Judson of the 83rd Pennsylvania Regiment, which was in Bartlett's 3rd Brigade in Maj. Gen. Charles Griffin's 1st Division of the V Corps, described his regiment's attack across the field as swift and effective. However, the brigade got disorganized and when the Confederates rallied and brought in reinforcements, the tide turned:

> our brigade alone with both flanks exposed and without any support. It was now the Johnnies' turn to come . . . and right well did they improve the opportunity. Every man saw the danger, and without waiting for orders to fall back, broke for the rear on the double quick. The rebels, in their turn, commenced yelling and sending minies after us, killing and wounded many of our men. . . . We ran almost every step of the way back, and when we got there we laid down on our backs and panted like so many hounds which had just come in from a ten hours' chase after a gang of foxes."[1]

1   A. M. Judson, *History of the 83rd Regiment Pennsylvania Volunteers*, (Erie: B.F.H. Lynn Publishers, 1881), 94. Accessed through archive.org https://openlibrary.org/works/OL228078W/History_of_the_Eighty-Third_Regiment_Pennsylvania_Volunteers?edition=historyofeightyt00judso

The May 28, 1864, issue of *Harper's Weekly* featured an image of Bartlett's brigade—including the 20th Maine—advancing across Saunders Field. *Harper's Weekly*

Others recrossed Saunders Field wounded. Theodore Gerrish, a soldier in the 20th Maine Regiment—also in Bartlett's brigade—wrote about his personal retreat in his chapter about *The Wilderness in Army Life*, which was published in 1882:

It is impossible to describe the sensations experienced by a person when wounded for the first time. The first intimation I had that I was wounded was my falling upon the ground. My leg was numb to my body, and for a moment I fancied that my foot had been carried away; but I soon learned the true condition of my situation. Our regiment was rapidly retreating, and the rebels as rapidly advancing. The forest trees around me were on fire, and the bullets were falling thick and fast. If I remained where I was, the most favorable result that I could hope for was captivity, which, in reality, would be worse than death by the bullet on the field.

I stood up, and, to my joy, found that my leg was not entirely useless. I could step with it, and so long as it remained straight I could bear my weight upon it, but when bent at the knee it refused to bear me up, and I

Bartlett's brigade advanced across the southern portion of Saunders Field (from left to right in the top photo). As the brigade neared the Confederate line beyond the crest of the hill (directly forward in the above photo), the topography shielded them from fire, helping the Federals sustain enough momentum to break through. *Sarah Kay Bierle*

would fall to the ground. Under existing circumstances I determined to retreat. I threw off all my baggage and equipments, and turned my face toward the line of breastworks, which we had that morning built. Fear lent wings to my flight, and away I dashed. Frequently my wounded leg would refuse to do good service, and as a result I would tumble headlong upon the ground, then rising, I would rush on again, and I doubt if there has been a champion on the sawdust track in Maine for the last five years who has made such a record of speed as I made on that retreat through the

Wilderness. In my haste I did not keep so far to my right as I should have done, and consequently was obliged to cross the lower end of the field over which we had made our charge. It was a sad spectacle, that lonely field in the forest. Here and there a wounded man was limping painfully to the rear; dead men, and others wounded too severely to move, were scattered thickly upon the ground.[2]

Fighting continued to rage around and through Saunders Field over the next hours, with more regiments attacking and retreating. On the opposite side of the Orange Turnpike, some retreating soldiers ran holding their metal canteens to the back of their heads in a small attempt at protection. Regiments became completely disorganized. Some soldiers lay down behind dead horses or piled into the field's small gully in an effort to get out of the line of fire and find protection.

Perhaps it's not glamorous to look at a field from the perspective of chaotic retreats, but it is part of the military history and the saga of the human will to survive. And when we choose to see a piece of battlefield from that perspective, perhaps we are closer to understanding the destruction and the panic of war than in the pursuit of the footsteps that broke through the lines with no time to stop for fallen comrades. A retreat through the eyes of history and in the words of the participants brings different words to the pages and different emotions to the forefront, and whether an attack field was recrossed swiftly in retreat or more slowly looking for the fallen, there is a confrontation of the sobering effects of that "glorious charge" of a prior time.

---

2   Theodore Gerrish, *Army Life: A Private's Reminiscences of the Civil War*, (Portland: Hoyt, Fogg & Donham, 1882), 166-167.

A Daring Dash in the Wilderness

by Chris Mackowski

Point of Interest #1 on the map on pg. xiv.

Originally published as a blog post at Emerging Civil War on January 12, 2016

One of my favorite stories from the battle of the Wilderness is a small tale of derring-do passed along by Theodore Gerrish of the 20th Maine. The event took place on the afternoon of May 5, 1864.

After his brigade's initial assault across Saunders Field stalled and the men retreated, Gerrish spotted an officer he assumed to be his brigade commander, Brig. Gen. Joseph Bartlett, who unexpectedly found himself in a tight spot:

[A] Union officer . . . also came out into the field, not twenty rods from the rebel line. He was on horseback; not a staff officer was with him; his uniform was torn and bloody; blood was trickling from several wounds in his face and head. . . . The rebels saw him, the moment he emerged from the forest, and called upon him to surrender, while a wild yell rang along their line as they saw their fancied prize.

But they did not know the man with whom they had to deal. Shaking his fist at them in defiance, he put spurs to his horse and dashed away. He was a target for every rifle in the rebel line. Five hundred guns were pointed at him, and five hundred bullets whistled around him, the enemy pursuing as they fired. It was a brilliant ride for life. . . .

Over one-half the distance across that field had been passed, and yet . . . [a] deep ditch must be crossed before they could gain the cover of the forest. . . . The horse and rider evidently saw the obstacle at the same moment and prepared to meet it. Firmly the rider sat in his saddle, and gathered the reins of his horse with a firm hand. I never beheld a nobler spectacle than that presented by the gallant steed—his nostrils dilated, his ears pointed forward, his eyes seeming to clash with the fire of

Brig. Gen. Joseph Bartlett. *Library of Congress*

conscious strength as he made the fearful leap. For a moment I thought they were safe, but rebel bullets pierced the horse, and turning a complete somersault he fell stone dead, burying the rider beneath him as he fell.

Again the rebels cheered and rushed on, but to my surprise, the officer, with the assistance of a few wounded soldiers, extricated himself from his dead horse, ran across the edge of the field, and made his escape."[1]

---

1   Theodore Gerrish, *Army Life: A Private's Reminiscences of the Civil War* (Portland, ME: Hoyt, Fogg & Donham, 1882), 168-9. Gerrish wrote his account as a single paragraph, but I've broken it up here for easier reading.

U. Grant the Butcher?

by Chris Mackowski

Point of Interest #2 on the map on pg. xiv.

*Originally published as a blog post at Emerging Civil War
on May 6, 2014*

Although saddled with the reputation of "Grant the Butcher," Ulysses S. Grant was hardly unmoved by the butchery around him. An incident in the Wilderness, relayed by Grant's chief of staff, Brig. Gen. John Rawlins, to biographer Maj. Gen. James Wilson (Federal cavalryman and friend of Grant), speaks volumes.

On the evening of May 6, Grant received news about the attack on Maj. Gen. John Sedgwick's VI Corps, holding the Federal right flank. "[A]fter he had asked such questions and given such orders as the emergency seemed to call for," Wilson wrote, "he withdrew to his tent and, throwing himself face downward on his cot, instead of going to sleep, gave vent to his feelings in a way which left no room to doubt that he was deeply moved."[1]

Rawlins and other witnesses "had been with [Grant] in every battle from the beginning of his career, and had never before seen him show the slightest apprehension or sense of danger; but on that memorable night in the Wilderness it was much more than personal danger which confronted him. No one knew better than he that he was face to face with destiny, and there was no doubt in their minds that he realized it fully and understood

---

1   James Harrison Wilson, *The Life of John A. Rawlins: Lawyer, Assistant Adjutant-General, Chief of Staff, Major General of Volunteers, and Secretary of War* (New York: Neal Publishing, 1916), 216. Wilson recounts the story as told to him by Rawlins.

After the difficult first day at Shiloh in 1862, Grant looked ahead to the next day: "Whip 'em tomorrow," he said. Two years later in the Wilderness, he showed that same sense of calm resolve, although subordinates knew Grant felt the strain of much higher stakes. *Campaigning with Grant*

perfectly that retreat from that field meant a great calamity to his country as well as to himself. That he did not show the stolidity that has been attributed to him in that emergency but fully realized its importance is greatly to his credit."[2]

The "stolidity" Wilson referred to was an account of the evening written by Grant's aide, Col. Horace Porter. When news of the attack came, Porter reported that he looked in Grant's tent "and found him sleeping as soundly and peacefully as an infant." When Porter relayed news of the attack, he claimed Grant's "military instincts convinced him that it was a gross exaggeration, and as he had already made every provision for meeting any renewed attempts against the right, he turned over in his bed, and immediately went to sleep again."[3]

Wilson takes issue with Porter's account: "Many misleading accounts have been given to the world in regard to Grant's bearing when the news of [the]

2   Ibid., 217.

3   Horace Porter, *Campaigning with Grant* (New York: Century Co, 1897), 71.

disaster and capture reached him. He has been reported as having remained unmoved and unshaken throughout the excitement which followed."[4]

Porter himself offers an account of his own that underscores Grant's aversion to butchery. During a meeting with Maj. Gen. George Meade during the battle, "[it] was noticed that he was visibly affected by his proximity to the wounded, and especially by the sight of blood. He would turn his face away from such scenes, and show by the expression of his countenance, and sometimes by a pause in his conversation, that he felt most keenly the painful spectacle presented by the field of battle. Some reference was made to the subject in camp that evening, and the general said: 'I cannot bear the sight of suffering.'"[5]

Porter backs up this observation with another anecdote from later in the campaign. On May 18, after ordering a major attack at Spotsylvania, Grant rode from his headquarters to watch the progress. Along the way, he passed a number of wounded men lying along the roadside awaiting medical transport. One man in particular caught Grant's eye. "The blood was flowing from a wound in his breast, the froth about his mouth was tinged with red, and his wandering, staring eyes gave unmistakable evidence of approaching death," Porter recalled.

Just then, a staff officer dashed by at full gallop, splashing a mass of black mud on the wounded man's face. Grant, who saw the whole thing, reigned in his horse and prepared to dismount to "bestow some care upon the young man." Porter beat him to it, wiping the man's face clean—but soon the wounded man "breathed his last."

Continuing onward, Grant kept an eye out for the staff officer, "as if he wished to take him to task for his carelessness." Porter noted:

> There was a painfully sad look upon the general's face, and he did not speak for some time. While always keenly sensitive to the sufferings of the wounded, this pitiful sight seemed to affect him more than usual.[6]

---

4   Wilson, 215.

5   Porter, 64.

6   Porter, 123-4.

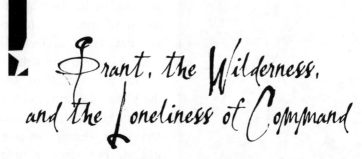

Grant, the Wilderness, and the Loneliness of Command

by Christopher Kolakowski

Point of Interest #2 on the map on pg. xiv.

Originally published as a blog post at Emerging Civil War on November 18, 2016

On the evening of May 6, 1864, Lt. Gen. U.S. Grant considered the day's events. The battle of the Wilderness had just ended its second day, and Grant's forces had been beaten and battered in a way he'd never seen. Both his flanks had been driven in, and panic had set in among some of the Army of the Potomac's officers. The fate of the 1864 Overland Campaign hung on what Grant decided to do next.

That evening, Grant retired to his tent for what Bruce Catton called "an unpleasant ten or fifteen minutes." Some of his staff heard him thrashing around. He was wrestling with the lonely weight of command and staring into the abyss of failure.[1]

It is almost a cliché to say "it is lonely at the top." But there are times when a person is leading an organization or an enterprise (military or civilian) that everything rides on what he or she chooses to do in response to events not breaking favorably. Such times take the full measure of a leader, and their character, values, and vision.

In his tent, General Grant underwent just such a test. It is impossible to

---

1   Bruce Catton, *Grant Takes Command* (New York: Little, Brown, 1968), 179-201.

In the Wilderness, Ulysses S. Grant sat like the calm eye at the center of the Federal storm—but internally, he felt the tempest deeply.
Library of Congress

know exactly what went through his mind in this most human and naked of moments, but others who have faced similar situations offer clues to his struggle.

On May 25, 1940, General the Viscount Gort stood before a map in his French headquarters trying to decide whether to use his last reserves to attack or shore up failing defenses as German troops hammered his men from three sides. He knew that 250,000 men of the British Expeditionary Force (BEF), Britain's only major field army, depended on him making the right decision.

Colonel Gerald Templer, one of Gort's intelligence officers, saw him at the map and later described the scene:

> I then walked in, to see Gort standing in a very typical attitude—with his legs apart and hands at his back. He was staring—quite alone—at a series of maps of Northern France and the Channel ports, pinned together and covering the wall of his small room . . . wrestling with his God and his duty at a moment of destiny. It was only later that I realized he was, at that precise point in time, making the decision as to whether to bring the remains of the BEF out through Dunkirk . . . all my heart went out to him in his loneliness and tribulation.[2]

Gort's example shows how his test looked from the outside. But the next example gets inside the commander's head.

---

2   J. R. Colville, *Man of Valour: Field Marshal Lord Gort V.C.* (London: Collins, 1972), 215-217. The quote comes from page 216.

On March 5, 1944, Lt. Gen. William Slim stood at an Indian airfield with a group of officers. Thousands of men and dozens of planes and gliders stood poised to launch Operation Thursday, the largest airborne attack of World War II to that point. Plans called for night landings on three drop zones deep inside northern Burma.

An hour before the planes were to take off, a jeep raced up and deposited an intelligence officer with new photos of the landing zones. One was blocked with logs, but the reason was unknown; the other zones were clear. Was this an ambush? Nobody was sure, and there was no time to investigate. Postponement was not an option; they had to go that night or cancel. "The decision is yours," said Maj. Gen. Orde Wingate, Thursday's commander, to Slim.

"I knew it was," recalled Slim a dozen years after:

> Not for the first time I felt the weight of decision crushing in on me with an almost physical pressure. The gliders, if they were to take off that night, must do so within the hour. There was no time for prolonged inquiry or discussion. On my answer would depend not only the possibility of a disaster with wide implications on the whole Burma campaign and beyond, but the lives of these splendid men, tense and waiting around their aircraft. At that moment I would have given a great deal if Wingate or anybody else could have relieved me of the duty of decision. But that is a burden the commander himself must bear.[3]

Such moments as these become defining. Leaders need strong character, values, and vision to succeed; those without one or more of these attributes almost always fold under the pressure.

All three men above met the test. Grant came out of his tent and issued orders to prepare for a march to Spotsylvania. Gort decided to defend and march to Dunkirk and evacuation. Slim directed the operation to proceed under a modified plan, which proved successful.

---

3   William Slim, *Defeat Into Victory: Battling Japan in Burma and India, 1942-1945* (New York: Cooper, 2000), 260-262.

"The" Turning Point of the War: The Wilderness, Not Gettysburg

by Chris Mackowski

Point of Interest #3 on the map on pg. xiv.

Originally published as a blog post at Emerging Civil War on July 4, 2013

Working at the Wilderness today, I couldn't think of a better place to be sitting in the wake of the Gettysburg sesquicentennial. Why? Well, while throngs of people stare at the bronze tablet by the copse of trees along Gettysburg's Cemetery Ridge, I'm hanging out on the battlefield where the war's most significant turning point really took place.

The war really had many "turning points" (see our ECW book *Turning Points of the American Civil War* from Southern Illinois University Press for a run-down). But here in the Wilderness, where Lt. Gen. Ulysses S. Grant chose to go to the left and the south around Gen. Robert E. Lee's army on the evening of May 7, 1864, the very nature of the entire war changed.

Lee's victory at Chancellorsville in May 1863 represented the true high-water mark of the Confederacy. After Chancellorsville, Lee never again achieved a major offensive battlefield victory. Nineteenth century historian John Bachelder, who chronicled the battle after the war, made the shrewd choice to frame Gettysburg as the high-water mark—an inspired bit of marketing genius but one that bore very little weight as truth at the time. (This idea is explored in detail in Tom Desjardin's must-read book *These Honored Dead*.)

Like "high-water mark," "turning point" is another term frequently used to succinctly frame the meaning of Gettysburg in a convenient way. But Gettysburg can only be seen as a turning point in the context created by Grant's decision to fight it out across the line through Virginia the following summer. "There will be no turning back," Grant had said when he launched the campaign.

Had Grant turned back after coming to grief in the Wilderness, then the Wilderness would have been just one more in a string of Union losses. Similarly, that decision would have made Gettysburg just another Confederate loss (some

At the Brock Road/Plank Road intersection, Grant knew a move toward Chancellorsville would have been seen by his men as a retreat, while a move toward Spotsylvania Court House would signal "onward." That road led him inexorably to Appomattox Court House eleven months later. *Chris Mackowski*

argue the *only* Confederate loss) in the ongoing back-and-forth between the two armies.

It was Grant's determination to press the issue southward rather than retreat and resupply, refit, and reinforce—as all previous Union commanders had done after taking a hard knock from Lee—*that* was the game-changer. His intent was to shift the strategic objective of the war. Gone were the days of "On to Richmond." Lee's army instead became the objective, and if he could not score a decisive knock-out, then he would grind down Lee's army by attrition. It was grim arithmetic, but Grant knew that the North had more men, more material, more resources, more money—more everything—and he intended to bring all the weight of it to bear and not let up the pressure.

Grant certainly didn't win in the Wilderness, but by pressing on he certainly made sure everyone knew he didn't consider himself the loser, either. "I propose to fight it out along this line if it takes all summer," he famously said at Spotsylvania. Lee's inability to stop him from doing so means that Grant retained the strategic initiative all summer long—and in that context, Grant was clearly the winner during the tactical stalemates of the Overland Campaign.

The Brock Road/Plank Road intersection, then, represents the war's real turning point—because at that intersection there was, quite literally in Grant's view, no turning back. Instead, he headed left and south in the first of a series of similar left-and-south maneuvers that finally led across the James River and settled into the siege of Petersburg.

John Bachelder worked hard to shape Gettysburg into the turning point of the war because that narrative reinforced the narrative of the war he himself had constructed through his own history. It was truly an act of genius—a "self-fulfilling prophecy," Desjardin has called it. The Wilderness, by contrast, had no self-serving champion to push an agenda—only a dust-covered man from the West, determined to change the very nature of the war.

A Grand Charge:
Emory Upton's Assault
on the Mule Shoe Salient

by Daniel T. Davis
Point of Interest #4 on the map on pg. xiv.

*Originally published as a two-part series on Emerging Civil War
on May 10, 2015*

A small group of officers stood at the tree line. To their immediate front, resting across an open field lay fresh mounds of earth: earthworks constructed by Confederate infantry. Each man studied the ground intently, some conversing in hushed tones. Others stood silently, chewing on cigars, taking in the scene before them. Cautiously, as the conversations dissipated, they began to make their way back to their own picket line. One man lingered while the others left his side. Colonel Emory Upton stood by himself for a few moments, taking a last few mental notes on the enemy lines. Turning, he walked back to rejoin his comrades.[1]

Upton hailed from the Empire State. After attending Oberlin College in the winter of 1854-55, he entered West Point in June 1856. He graduated in May 1861, ranking eighth in a class of forty-five. Upton saw action at

---

1   United States War Department, *The War of the Rebellion: A Compilation of the Official Records of the Union and Confederate Armies,* 70 vols. in 128 parts (Washington D.C.: Government Printing Office, 1880-1901), Series I, volume 36, part 1, 667 (hereafter cited as *O.R.*).

It takes a bold man of vision to pull off a cape. Such was Col. Emory Upton. The gloves add an extra touch. *Library of Congress*

the battle of First Manassas as an aide-de-camp to Brig. Gen. Daniel Tyler. Slightly wounded during the fighting, Upton took over command of Battery D, 2nd U.S. Artillery in August. He served in this capacity through the Seven Days' battles in the spring of 1862. During the Maryland Campaign, he commanded the Artillery Brigade in the First Division of the VI Corps. Following the battle of Antietam, Upton received the colonelcy of the 121st New York Infantry.

One soldier wrote of Upton, "In discipline he was strict but just. In administration he was efficient. In action he was prompt. In danger he was cool. . . . [U]nder no circumstances did he show fear or lack of decision. To these admirable qualities of an officer, he was strictly temperate, and decidedly religious in his conduct. He was not ashamed to keep a well-worn Bible on his desk." Upton, the consummate professional, "drilled the regiment diligently. . . . [U]nder his regime the improvement of the regiment was rapid and the officers and men caught the enthusiasm of their leader and became ambitious to become a model regiment. It was no wonder that the regiment soon became known as 'Upton's Regulars.'"[2]

The regiment engaged in minor skirmishing at Fredericksburg, but experienced heavy fighting at the battle of Salem Church during the Chancellorsville Campaign in May 1863. In early November, Upton, along with his "Regulars," executed a successful assault on a Confederate position at Rappahannock Station. This attack brought Upton into the

2   Isaac O. Best, *History of the 121st New York State Infantry* (Baltimore: Butternut and Blue, 1996) 29, 33-34.

spotlight as one of the more aggressive commanders in the Army of the Potomac. It ultimately earned him command of the Second Brigade, First Division of the VI Corps. The "Regulars" were one of four regiments that made up this command.

Around midnight on May 3, 1864, the Army of the Potomac, under the direction of Lt. Gen. Ulysses S. Grant and Maj. Gen. George G. Meade, roused itself from its encampments in Culpeper County and marched toward the Rapidan River. This movement opened the spring campaign against Gen. Robert E. Lee and the Army of Northern Virginia. Lee countered, catching Grant and Meade in a tangled second-growth forest known as the Wilderness. The engagement stopped the Federals in their tracks. Positioned on the Union right, Upton's brigade saw fighting on both days of the battle. Rather than withdraw and regroup, Grant decided to swing south, beyond Lee's right toward Spotsylvania Court House. Whoever held this hamlet could access the main road leading to the Confederate capital of Richmond.

Grant began pulling out of the Wilderness on the night of May 7. After a long march in which the Confederates narrowly won the race, Confederate infantry engaged the lead elements of the Potomac army west of the Court House the following morning. Throughout the day, both sides rushed more troops onto the field. Late that evening, Upton and his men participated in an assault on the Confederate right. Before they could reach their objective, gray reinforcements arrived and quickly repelled the Union onslaught.[3]

On the morning of May 9, a Confederate sharpshooter killed VI Corps commander Maj. Gen. John Sedgwick. Sedgwick's death created a void in the chain of command. Major General Horatio Wright took over for Sedgwick while Brig. Gen. David Russell succeeded Wright.[4] Russell had served in the Mexican American War and, by 1864, had established himself as a reliable officer. He also recognized Upton's skill at leading men on the battlefield. Russell had overseen Upton's assault at Rappahannock Station, and the two men had quickly developed a strong working relationship.

The men of the VI Corps engaged in light skirmishing for much of May 9. Throughout the day, Grant focused his attention on attacking the Confederate left. Lee shifted troops to meet the Federal threat. Grant

3   *O.R.* 36, 18-19, 665-666.

4   *O.R.* 36, 19.

Confederates "couldn't hit an elephant at that distance," said John Sedgwick—who unfortunately found out they *could* hit a major general. Sedgwick's death on May 9 triggered a command shuffle at exactly the time Federals were hoping to shake things up along the VI Corps' front. Sedgwick's replacement, Maj. Gen. Horatio Wright, would find himself facing a steep learning curve. *Emerging Civil War*

abandoned the effort the following day for what appeared to be a promising opportunity. He incorrectly surmised that Lee had weakened his lines to reinforce his left, particularly the sector in front of Wright. Grant ordered an assault for 5 p.m. that evening. Orders probably came down from Wright late in the morning, directing Russell to begin preparing for the attack. To lead it, Russell had the perfect subordinate in mind—his most aggressive officer, Emory Upton.

Russell likely began planning the assault some-time that morning with the assistance of Wright's chief of staff, Lt. Col. Martin McMahon. With the details worked out, Russell directed McMahon to send for Upton. Meeting with Upton, McMahon asked for his opinion after he handed the infantry commander a list of twelve regiments from the corps. Upton responded with a resounding approval of "splendid," and McMahon informed Upton that he would lead them later that day in an attack.[5]

Toward the middle of the afternoon, Russell, Upton, and each of the regimental commanders made their way through the lines to the edge of

5   Best, 135.

While Emory Upton gets the credit for the May 10 breakthrough against the Mule Shoe Salient, the planning of Lt. Col. Martin McMahon (left) and Brig. Gen. David Russell (right) contributed to the assault's success. *Library of Congress/Library of Congress*

a wood to scout the enemy position.[6] They were led by a young engineer, Capt. Ranald MacKenzie. Russell dispatched MacKenzie, a West Point graduate in the Class of 1862, to select a location where Upton's regiments could hit the Confederate line. Earlier in the day, Union infantrymen had captured a portion of the Confederate skirmish line that fronted a Georgia brigade under Brig. Gen. George Doles. Doles failed to reestablish the line, thus allowing MacKenzie and Upton to get a full view of his defensive alignment. From their vantage point, the officers looked to their right and could see a sharp swale, which partially shielded them from Smith's battery of the Virginia Light Artillery (part of the Richmond Howitzers battalion). The swale butted against a gentle ridge to their front, which in turn blocked their view of the Confederates to the right of Doles, the Stonewall Brigade commanded by Brig. Gen. James Walker. The swale, along with the ridge, would provide ample cover for the attacking Federals as they moved across the open field toward the Confederate line.

6   *O.R.* 36, 667.

With the location chosen, the group withdrew. Upton and his men faced a formidable task. The Confederates had spent the better part of the previous two days strengthening their position. "His entrenchments were of formidable character with abatis in front and surmounted by heavy logs, underneath which were loopholes for musketry," Upton recalled. "There were also traverses at intervals along the entire work. About 100 yards to the rear was another line of works, partly completed and occupied by a second line of battle."[7]

Doles held a section of the Confederate position known as the "Mule Shoe Salient." Deriving the name from its distinctive shape, the salient jutted out from the main Confederate line. While vulnerable to attack from three directions, the breastworks that made up the Mule Shoe were the strongest yet encountered by the Union army. Construction began by digging a ditch five to six feet deep, with the dirt thrown up in front. Logs reinforced the earthen wall. About six to twelve inches above the embankment, a "head log" protected the soldiers and provided an opening from which they could fire on an attacker. Every ten to twelve feet, traverses protected defenders from enfilading fire. Ten to fifteen yards in front of the trenches, branches, their ends sharpened were pointed toward the attacking enemy.

The execution of Upton's assault against these formidable works would revolutionize warfare in Virginia.

*   *   *

The men from New York, Pennsylvania, Maine, Wisconsin and Vermont milled about the clearing in the middle of the afternoon. A cool spring breeze rustled the leaves on the trees around them. Some talked, while others smoked or chewed on hardtack or quietly read. While they passed the time in different ways, each man shared one thing in common: they made up the twelve regiments of Upton's assault column. Altogether, they numbered around 5,000.[8]

Upton reflected on what he had observed of the Confederate position as

---

7   *O.R.* 36, 667.

8   John M. Lovejoy, "Spotsylvania: A Sketch of the Grand Charge of the 12 Regiments on the 'Angle'" *National Tribune,* May 26, 1887.

he walked back through the woods to his men, joining up with them near their rendezvous point at the Scott/Shelton House. The enemy fortifications had impressed him. He realized his success hinged on a critical factor: getting his men across the open field to the Confederate line while maintaining enough momentum to pierce it. Allowing his men to stop and return fire would slow the advance, incur costly casualties, and reduce his men's effectiveness when and if they reached their objective. Upton decided to form his regiments in a three-by-four column formation. He also ordered that no one was to discharge their weapon until they reached the gray army's works.[9]

Although the column assault gave Upon an advantage, the concept also came with disadvantages. Such a compact formation was susceptible to enemy fire. MacKenzie's eye for terrain, however, benefited Upton. The swale in front of Doles's line and the abutting ridge would protect the men from Confederate artillery on their right and infantry on their left. Upton hoped to reduce the impact of frontal fire by pushing his men across the open field and capturing the position as quickly as possible. Accordingly, Upton directed his officers to encourage the men by continuously yelling "Forward."[10]

Support also played a critical element in the assault. Upton intended to capture part of the Confederate position and then hold it long enough for additional troops to move up and exploit the breach. Curiously, Upton's support came in the form of a II Corps division led by Brig. Gen. Gershom Mott. Mott received orders to strike the Mule Shoe several hundred yards east of Upton's point of attack.

At the Scott/Shelton House, Upton's regiments unslung their knapsacks and relieved themselves of any accoutrements that would make noise or weigh them down during the charge. "A wood-road led from our position directly to the point of attack," Upton wrote:

> The column of attack was formed in four lines of battle, four regiments being on the right and eight on the left of the road. The regiments on the right moved up the road by the right flank, those on the left by the left flank, each regiment lying down as soon as in position. The lines were arranged from right to left as follows: First line, One Hundred and Twenty-

9   Ibid.

10   Ibid.

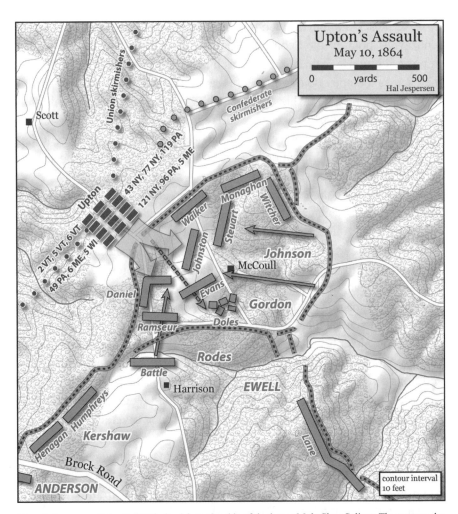

UPTON'S ASSAULT—Doles Salient bulged from the side of the larger Mule Shoe Salient. The topography in the area offered Federals the best opportunity to get close to the Confederate line without being detected. Upton organized his men into a heavy fist and punched through.

first New York, Ninety-Sixth Pennsylvania, and Fifth Maine; second line, Forty-Ninth Pennsylvania, Sixth Maine and Fifth Wisconsin; third line, Forty-Third and Seventy-Seventh New York and One Hundred and Nineteenth Pennsylvania; fourth line, Second, Fifth and Sixth Vermont. No commands were given in getting into position. The pieces of the first line were loaded but not capped; bayonets fixed. The One Hundred and Twenty-first New York and Ninety Sixth Pennsylvania were instructed, as soon as the works were carried, to turn to the right and charge the battery. The Fifth Maine was to change front to the left and open an enfilading fire to the left upon the enemy. The second line was to halt at the work and open fire to the front if necessary. The third line was to lie down behind the second and await orders. The fourth line was to advance to the edge of the woods, lie down and await the issue of the charge.[11]

Moving to only a couple hundred yards from their objective, Upton ordered his men to halt, lay down, and await the word to begin the assault. Prior to the attack, Union batteries opened a bombardment to pave the way for the infantry. All seemed ready.

However, events on other parts of the field soon unraveled Upton's plans.

Earlier that afternoon, V Corps commander Maj. Gen. Gouverneur Warren appealed to George Meade to attack at 4 p.m. ahead of schedule. Confederates in front of Warren easily repulsed the assault. Warren's premature effort prompted the Union high command to change the time for Upton's attack from 5 p.m. to 6 p.m. In a massive oversight, no one thought to inform Gershom Mott. Thinking that he was advancing in conjunction with Upton, Mott went forward against the tip of the Mule Shoe Salient only to have his men beaten back by artillery fire. Additionally, no one informed Upton of Mott's failed attempt.

At 6:10 p.m. on May 10, 1864, Upton's men stepped off.

"The lines rose, moved noiselessly to the edge of the wood, and, with a wild cheer and faces averted, rushed for the works," Upton wrote:

> Through a terrible . . . fire the column advanced, quickly gaining the parapet. Here occurred a deadly hand-to-hand conflict. The enemy, sitting in their pits, with pieces upright, loaded, and with bayonets fixed, ready to impale the first who should leap over, absolutely refused to yield the ground. The first of our men who tried to surmount the works, fell, pierced through the head with musket-balls; others, seeing the fate of their comrades, held their pieces at arm's-length and fired downward; while others, poising their pieces vertically, hurled them down upon their enemies, pinning them

11   *O.R.* 36, 667.

to the ground . . . the struggle lasted but a few seconds. Numbers prevailed, and, like a resistless wave, the column poured over the works.[12]

Upton's charge shattered the Confederate line. Doles's Georgians ran for the rear while the 5th Maine turned and quickly drove in the left two regiments of the Stonewall Brigade. Turning to their right, the 121st New York and the 96th Pennsylvania neutralized Smith's battery. These regiments were joined by the 49th Pennsylvania and the 6th Maine who quickly moved up into the breach.

Although Upton punched a hole in the Confederate defenses, he had stirred up a hornet's nest. A number of Rebel brigades responded to the attack: North Carolinians under Brig. Gens. Junius Daniel and Stephen Ramseur, Alabamans under Brig. Gen. Cullen Battle, Georgians under Brig. Gen. Clement Evans, Virginians under Brig. Gen. William Witcher, elements of the Stonewall Brigade and a mixed brigade commanded by Brig. Gen. George "Maryland" Steuart combined to pinch off the Federals within the salient and slowly drive them back.

Upton hurried back to the tree line to bring up the Green Mountain Boys only to discover the Vermonters had already entered the fight. Drawing his men back to the first line of works, Upton eventually withdrew to the safety of the Union lines.

Despite the repulse, Upton's performance impressed Grant and other Union officers. The army as an institution adopted the column assault as the unofficial tactic when attacking a fortified position. For example, two days later, Grant sent Maj. Gen. Winfield Scott Hancock's II Corps against the Mule Shoe in a larger version of Upton's assault. Hancock also enjoyed initial success until Confederate counterattacks drove him back in savage fighting. On May 18, Grant once again sent Hancock forward in column against "Lee's Last Line" along the Brock Road. At Cold Harbor on June 1, Upton (now a newly-promoted Brigadier General) led the 2nd Connecticut Heavy Artillery in an assault using tactics similar to those he had formulated at Spotsylvania. In the great Union attack at Cold Harbor on June 3, elements from the Army of the James, along with Brig. Gen. John Gibbon's II Corps division, copied Upton's tactics in their assault. Finally, on April 2,

12   *O.R.* 36, 668.

1865, the VI Corps stormed the Confederate lines at Petersburg. Upton's tactics came to define offensive operations for the Army of the Potomac for the remainder of the war in Virginia.

Upton's story, though, is a tragic one. From 1870 to 1875, he served as Commandant of Cadets at West Point. Throughout the rest of the decade, he traveled extensively, studying the armies of Europe and Asia. He also authored new manuals and treatises on military tactics and organization. These accomplishments covered up his personal struggles. After suffering from the mental and emotional anguish of losing his wife in 1867 and struggling with his own physical health,

A monument to Upton was dedicated in May 1994, paid for by a descendant of a corporal from the 49th Pennsylvania. The reverse side depicts the Confederate defenders. *Chris Mackowski*

Upton took his own life on the night of March 14, 1881. He is buried in Fort Hill Cemetery in Auburn, New York.

Today, a simple, solitary monument rests at Spotsylvania in the field that Upton's regiments crossed to reach Doles's line. It commemorates the Union and Confederate soldiers who fought at the Mule Shoe during Upton's Charge. In a larger sense, it commemorates a man who overcame the earthworks of the battlefield but could not breach the bastions of his own soul.

Music on the Spotsylvania Earthworks

by Kevin Pawlak

Point of Interest #4 on the map on pg. xiv.

Originally published as a blog post at Emerging Civil War on May 11, 2019

By May 11, 1864, Ulysses S. Grant's Virginia campaign had been underway for one week. The men of both armies went through the blazing inferno of the Wilderness only to find themselves now huddled behind substantial earthworks ringing the landscape around Spotsylvania Courthouse.

On the evening of May 10, Union soldiers led by Col. Emory Upton led a narrow but dense assault against the Confederate earthworks at a stretch of the line that has since become known as Doles's Salient, named for the Confederate commander in that sector, Brig. Gen. George Doles. While Upton's assault did not permanently pierce the enemy lines, it ushered in one of the most horrific moments of the Civil War on May 12: the battle at Spotsylvania's Bloody Angle. But all of that was still in the future. For now, the men that participated in Upton's charge on both sides vainly tried to come to grips with their experiences of the previous week.

When Upton's attack concluded in the evening hours of May 10 and the Federals pulled back to their own works, the field in front of Doles's Salient was littered with the dead and wounded. The wounded, abandoned in their places, "sounded all night with their cries and groans," recalled one Union officer. Another Federal, no doubt emblematic of so many other tired and exhausted soldiers seeking to come to terms with their experiences of the last week, "sat down in the woods and as I thought of the desolation and misery about me, my feelings overcame me and I cried like a little child."

Behind the Confederate earthworks, the survivors faced the disturbing reality of examining the field of dead and wounded laid out before them. "The situation was a sad one," remembered a survivor in the 44th Georgia Infantry. A Confederate band gathered behind the earthworks and struck up the solemn tune, "Nearer My God to Thee," a solemn reminder to all within earshot of their own mortality.[1]

One Union band within earshot responded to its Confederate counterpart with the "Dead March." The Confederates answered back with a jollier tune, "The Bonnie Blue Flag," capped by a resounding rebel yell. "The Star Spangled Banner" wafted back from the Federal lines, followed by their own cheers and yells. Finally, the Confederate band played "Home Sweet Home." When the instruments fell silent, men on both sides cheered tremendously before all ultimately fell silent.

The Confederate band's choice of "Nearer My God to Thee" is especially poignant. It struck a chord that the United States and the Confederate States had reached by this point in May 1864 as battles spread from the tangled woodlots of Virginia to the Shenandoah Valley to the hills of Georgia and beyond. The war had taken a new turn and would bring many more men nearer to their maker before it was over.[2]

---

1   "Nearer My God to Thee" is a well-known hymn written in 1841 by British actress Sarah Flower Adams. Legend has it that the hymn was played by the RMS *Titanic*'s band as the ocean liner sank in the North Atlantic in April 1912. Never confirmed, the legend posits that the ship's band played to calm the nerves of the ship's passengers as the vessel went down. Perhaps the Confederate band at Doles's Salient intended that same effect on the listening soldiers.

2   Gordon C. Rhea, *The Battles for Spotsylvania Court House and the Road to Yellow Tavern, May 7-12, 1864* (Baton Rouge, LA: Louisiana State University Press, 1997), 174-177.

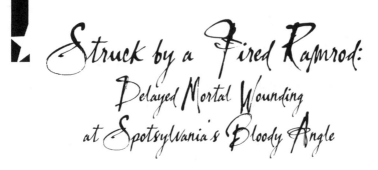

Struck by a Fired Ramrod: Delayed Mortal Wounding at Spotsylvania's Bloody Angle

by Edward Alexander

Point of Interest #5 on the map on pg. xiv.

Originally published as a three-part series on Emerging Civil War in November 2018

"This has been a Sabbath to me," wrote Surgeon George T. Stevens, 77th New York Infantry, to his wife Harriet on Thursday evening, August 4, 1864. "No day since the campaign commenced last May has seemed like Sabbath before, but this has been more than usually a day of rest and a day of solemnity with us."[1] Stevens, with the rest of the VI Corps, was camped in Maryland at the time, sent north from Petersburg to Fort Stevens to help repulse Jubal Early's offensive against the national capital. The Union soldiers now enjoyed their bloodless respite away from the Army of the Potomac, which had been locked in continual combat from the Wilderness to Petersburg. Tragedy managed to still strike along the Monocacy River valley, the repercussions finally manifesting themselves from a unique wound sustained nearly three months earlier at Spotsylvania. Major William Ellis, a friend of the New York surgeon, had been found dead in his tent from no noticeable cause.

---

1   George T. Stevens to "My Darling Hattie," August 4, 1864, Wiley Sword Collection at Pamplin Historical Park.

William Ellis was born on July 17, 1842 in Brantford, Canada West—present-day Ontario. His father, Alexander Ellis, died in 1854, leaving William to provide for his mother Catharine. The next year, at the age of fifteen, William enlisted into British service in the 100th (Prince of Wales's Royal Canadian) Regiment of Foot and was soon promoted to color sergeant in the 22nd Regiment of Foot. When the Civil War broke out, William bought his discharge from the British army and traveled to his mother's home in Buffalo, New York. There in the summer of 1861 he enlisted into the 49th New York Infantry.[2]

A former "Foot" soldier in the Royal Canadian Army, William Ellis emigrated to Buffalo, New York, so he could enlist in the Union army. He became the unfortunate victim of an unusual wounding at Spotsylvania's Bloody Angle. *New York State Military Museum*

His previous military service merited the nineteen-year-old a position as second lieutenant. Sergeant Alexander H. McKelvy recalled, "I do not know whether [Ellis] raised any men or not, but there was a camp rumor afloat among the men that he had taken some sort of leave from one of Her Majesty's rifle regiments in Canada in order to see service in the war between the states." The next year Ellis received promotions to captain in January and major in December. His experience and pompous attitude impressed his comrades. Surgeon Stevens referred to him as "the dashing, impetuous young fellow who used to ride his horse so furiously." McKelvy commented on Ellis's exploits inside and outside of the encampment, "It was his great delight to break loose from the monotonous round of camp life and go on a scouting trip beyond the lines in pursuit of adventure and

2   John M. Priest, ed. *Turn Them Out to Die Like a Mule: The Civil War Letters of John N. Henry, 49th New York, 1861-1865* (Leesburg, VA: Gauley Mount Press), 1995, 204.

pleasure, for it was rumored that he was not averse to the charms of the fair sex. He was always well mounted and . . . he rode a powerful black horse, fleet of foot, and able to extricate his daredevil master from any difficulty he might plunge into."[3]

Ellis became a popular figure in camp. His various exploits invariably produced frequent gossip. "It is said that Major Ellis who had just returned from a visit to Canada was also married in his absence," wrote a member of the 49th in March 1863.[4] Later testimony would suggest it was just a rumor, but Scott Valentine, a contributing editor of *Military Images*, profiled William Ellis in the magazine's Spring 2014 issue after finding a carte de viste of Ellis, upon the reverse side of which the flirtatious major had signed, "I kiss your hand."[5]

The New York major also won the approval of his commanders and fellow officers, serving at the head of the regiment several times when his superiors went on medical or personal furlough. A newspaper correspondent with the regiment claimed that Maj. Gen. John Sedgwick, commanding the VI Corps, had declared shortly before his untimely death that Ellis "was the best fighting officer in his corps."[6] Sedgwick's death on May 9, 1864, and the Wilderness wounding of Brig. Gen. George W. Getty, at the helm of the division to which the 49th New York belonged, shuffled the VI Corps' high command during the Overland Campaign. Brigadier General Horatio G. Wright took over the corps, promoting Brig. Gen. David A. Russell to lead the 1st Division. Brigadier General Thomas H. Neill also moved up to take command of Getty's 2nd Division, leaving his 3rd Brigade under the leadership of Col. Daniel D. Bidwell, the original commander of the 49th New York. Lieutenant Colonel George W. Johnson now led that regiment.

---

3   "Sergeant Alexander H. McKelvy's Report of His Capture by the Confederates, September 17, 1863," in Frederick D. Bidwell, ed. *History of the Forty-ninth New York Volunteers* (Albany, NY: J.B. Lyon Company, 1916), 105' Stevens, August 4, 1864, PHP.

4   John N. Henry to "My Dear Wife," March 16, 1863, in Priest, *Turn Them Out to Die Like a Mule*, 177-178.

5   Scott Valentine, "A Conspicuous Target: Major William Ellis, 49th New York Infantry, at the Bloody Angle," in *Military Images*, vol. 32, no. 2 (Spring 2014), 52.

6   "From the Forty-ninth Regiment," *Buffalo Daily Courier*, May 17, 1864. A Massachusetts captain agreed that Ellis "was one of the best officers in our corps." Mason W. Tyler to parents, August 4, 1864, in William S. Tyler, ed. *Recollections of the Civil War with Many Original Diary Entries and Letters Written from the Sear of War, and with Annotated References* (New York: G.P. Putnam's Sons, 1912), 262.

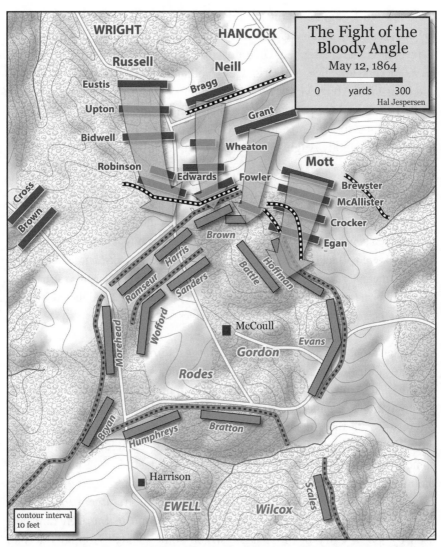

THE FIGHT OF THE BLOODY ANGLE—The 49th New York, part of Bidwell's brigade, was among Wright's VI Corps reinforcements sent in as part of the Federal assault's second wave. The first wave, comprised of Hancock's II Corps troops, punched a hole in the Confederate line in much the same way Emory Upton's colum punched through two days previously. Wright's men were tasked with exploiting the breakthrough, but Confederate reinforcements flooded into the breach at the same time.

During the infamous morning of May 12th, Bidwell sent his former regiment and the 77th New York to support Oliver Edwards's brigade, who in turn had advanced to assist the II Corps as its determined assault against the Spotsylvania "mule-shoe salient" bogged down. Together the two New York regiments hit the left-side face of the salient, just north of the spot that Col. Emory Upton had targeted with an attack two days prior. Brigadier General Stephen D. Ramseur's North Carolinians opposed the New Yorkers' advance, and Brig. Gen. Nathaniel H. Harris's Mississippians and Brig. Gen. Abner M. Perrin's Alabamians, reinforcements from Lt. Gen. A. P. Hill's Third Corps, soon threw their weight into the combat. The New Yorkers clung to their position just outside of the Confederate earthworks, dubbed the "Bloody Angle." Surgeon Stevens recalled after the war:

> A breastwork of logs separated the combatants. Our men would reach over this partition and discharge their muskets in the face of the enemy, and in return would receive the fire of the rebels at the same close range. Finally, the men began to use their muskets as clubs and then rails were used. The men were willing thus to fight from behind the breastworks, but to rise up and attempt a charge in the face of an enemy so near at hand and so strong in numbers required unusual bravery. Yet they did charge and they drove the rebels back and helf the angle themselves.[7]

Occasional charges and countercharges throughout the long day of combat did little to break the locked stalemate. At some point during this chaotic back-and-forth phase the Canadian major was wounded in an unconventional manner. Sergeant George N. Galloway, 95th Pennsylvania Infantry, wrote that "during one of the several attempts to get the men to cross the works and drive off the enemy," Ellis "excited our admiration" as he mounted the parapet in advance of the brigade, before he "was shot though the arm and body with a ramrod."[8] Sergeant McKelvy afterward recalled that Ellis was wounded "while leading the regiment in a daring charge on the enemy's works. He was hit with one of the iron ramrods, used by the infantry in those days, which some excited Confederate had neglected to remove from his rifle barrel before firing. This rammer passed

7   George T. Stevens, *Three Years in the Sixth Corps: A Concisce Narrative of Events in the Army of the Potomac, from from 1861 to the Close of the Rebellion, April, 1865* (Albany, NY: S.R. Gray, 1866), 334.

8   G. Norton Galloway, "Hand-to-hand Fighting at Spotsylvania," in *The Century Illustrated Monthly Magazine*, vol. 34, no. 2 (New York: The Century Co., June 1887), 306.

Major William Ellis and the 49th New York Infantry advanced across this ground toward the Bloody Angle on May 12, 1864. *Edward Alexander*

through the major's left arm and bruised his chest severely."[9]

The New Yorker's gallant action before his wounding was noticed by now-Brig. Gen. Upton, who had just been promoted for his audacious and innovative attack two days earlier. Upton singled Ellis out for praise when writing the May 12th section of his Overland Campaign report. "By their gallant conduct excited the admiration of all," Upton wrote, noting, "the country can ill afford to lose two such officers."[10]

Ellis was evacuated to a hospital in Fredericksburg, where Surgeon Stevens examined the injury and found the ramrod "passed through the left arm and then bruised the side near and a little below the heart." The major

9   A.H. McKelvy, "Forty-ninth New York Volunteers," in New York Monuments Commission for the Battlefields of Gettysburg and Chattanooga, ed. *Final Report on the Battlefield of Gettysburg*, vol. 1 (Albany, NY: J.B. Lyon Company, 1902), 390.

10   Emory Upton to Henry R. Dalton, September 1, 1864, in *The War of the Rebellion: A Compilation of the Official Records of the Union and Confederate Armies*, 128 vols. (Washington, DC, 1880-1901), Series 1, vol. 43, pt. 1, 669. Hereafter cited as *O.R.* Major Henry P. Truefitt, 119th Pennsylvania Infantry, who was killed at the Bloody Angle, was the other officer Upton mentioned.

"suffered fearfully from the effects of the bruise in the side," and the surgeon afterward claimed, "I supposed at the time that his heart was injured."[11] Surgeon William W. Potter, a friend of Ellis's who was serving with the II Corps' 57th New York Infantry, however, saw the major and noted that his wound "is not reported as dangerous."[12] After being stabilized, Ellis was sent onward to Washington to continue his recuperation. Soon thereafter he received a thirty-day furlough and returned to Buffalo to recover, arriving at the city on May 25th. "It is to be hoped that he will recover from his injuries while among friends," the *Buffalo Daily Courier* expressed.[13] "He is able to be about," wrote the *Buffalo Evening Post*, "and anticipates a speedy cure."[14] A prominent local judge later testified that he hosted William at his home frequently during his medical leave and that the soldier's painful wounds produced occasional spasms.[15]

Only partially recovered from his injury, Ellis departed from home on June 17th to rejoin his unit. In his absence the Army of the Potomac had fought its way from Spotsylvania to Petersburg, via the North Anna River, Totopotomoy Creek, and Cold Harbor. Rejoining the VI Corps, Ellis received a new assignment as inspector general on Brig. Gen. David A. Russell's 1st Division staff. Surgeon Stevens wrote that Ellis's supposedly less taxing change of assignment nevertheless resulted in the officer performing "a great deal of labor as provost marshal and in many other capacities."[16] He further elaborated:

11   Stevens, August 4, 1864, PHP.

12   William W. Potter, "Three Years with the Army of the Potomac—A Personal Military History," in *Buffalo Medical Journal*, vol. 68, no. 1 (August, 1912), 15.

13   "Personal," *Buffalo Daily Courier*, May 27, 1864.

14   "Home Again," *Buffalo Evening Post*, May 26, 1864.

15   Isaac A. Verplank, Statement, June 28, 1865, in William Ellis Pension, Case Files of Approved Pension Applications of Widows and Other Veterans of the Army and Navy Who Served Mainly in the Civil War and the War With Spain, compiled 1861-1934, Record Group 15, National Archives.

16   "Gone to the Front," *Buffalo Evening Post*, June 23, 1864. Stevens, August 4, 1864, PHP. Hospital Steward John N. Henry noted that Ellis returned earlier than the rest of the Overland Campaign casualties, writing on the 29th, "None of our wounded officers have returned but Major Ellis." John N. Henry to "My Dear Wife," March 16, 1863, in Priest, *Turn Them Out to Die Like a Mule*, 374.

Returning to his command before he had fully recovered, he was advised by medical officers not to attempt any severe duty. But being detailed to the staff of General Russell, commanding the First Division, he at once resumed active military duties. On these recent marches, the major, weary of inaction, had taken command of a body of men who acted as additional provost-guard to the division. In this position he had exhibited his usual energy, though it was thought by some he executed his duties with too great severity. Ever since receiving his wound, he had complained of severe neuralgic pain in the region of the heart.[17]

Other friends in the army, like William Potter, noted, however, at the beginning of July that Ellis "was, as usual, looking well." A week later Potter visited the 49th New York and took supper with Bidwell. Ellis called on him while the surgeon was there and the two snuck away to view a carriage that Ellis had stashed away in the woods after capturing it. While admiring the prize, orders arrived at Russell's headquarters to prepare to leave for Maryland to repulse Jubal Early's offensive. "Ellis was in great glee over the prospect, and flew around to make preparations for the transfer of the troops to their new field;" recalled Potter, "so I hastily bade him good-bye, but never saw him afterwards."[18]

Two VI Corps divisions immediately sailed north for the capital. There they beat back the Confederate invasion at Fort Stevens on July 11-12, during which Lt. Col. George W. Johnson, commanding the 49th New York, was mortally wounded. For a short time, the VI Corps chased Early through Maryland before settling into place near the Monocacy battlefield. There they enjoyed their break from combat, trenches, and the uninviting southern soil.

Adjutant Theodore F. Vaill recalled that his Connecticut VI Corps regiment "encamped on the 3d of August on the north bank of the Monocacy, about four miles south of Frederick City. It was the pleasantest camping ground we had ever seen. The clear, sparkling river ran along the lower edge of it, and the surrounding woods abounded in saplings, poles and brush, for which soldiers can always find so many uses. Regular camp drills were

17   Stevens, *Three Years in the Sixth Corps*, 334.

18   William W. Potter, "Three Years with the Army of the Potomac—A Personal Military History," in *Buffalo Medical Journal*, vol. 68, no. 2 (September, 1912), 83-84.

instituted, company and battalion drills ordered, and things began to assume the appearance of a stay."[19] "All are well in the regiment," wrote Surgeon Stevens about the 77th New York. "We have a lovely situation here among the mountains, with the purest of air and of water, and if we can only stay here, we shall recruit [recover, recuperate] wonderfully. I am feeling a great deal better already, & expect to be as strong & well as ever in a day or two."[20]

Major Ellis meanwhile retired to his tent on the night of August 3, telling Stevens, the surgeon recalled, that his "pain was slightly more acute than usual" though he was "in his accustomed health." The next morning Ellis waved his servant out of the tent for a moment and when the man returned, he was shocked to find the major dead.[21]

Ellis's unexpected passing was immediately misdiagnosed by many. "They supposed it must be heart disease," wrote Massachusetts Capt. Mason Tyler.[22] Rumors quickly spread through the Union camps. Sergeant Cyrille Fountain chronicled in his diary, "This morning Major Elles of the 49th N.Y. Vols dropt down dead from his char. The Drs. called it hart desease."[23] The first Buffalo newspaper to report the death meanwhile assumed "it is supposed that he was killed in an effort to drive the rebels out of Maryland."[24]

Upon hearing the news, Stevens and Dr. James Hall proceeded at once to Russell's headquarters where the general insisted on an immediate autopsy. In the presence of twenty of his professional colleagues, Stevens examined the body and found that lingering effects of the Spotsylvania wound had killed Ellis, concluding, "A sharp splinter of bone from one of the ribs was found with its acute point piercing vital organs."[25]

Stevens further described his findings in his letter to his wife: "I made

---

19   Theodore F. Vaill, *History of the Second Connecticut Volunteer Heavy Artillery. Originally the Nineteenth Connecticut Vols.* (Winsted, CT: Winsted Printing Company, 1868), 89-90.

20   Stevens, August 4, 1864, PHP.

21   Stevens, *Three Years in the Sixth Corps*, 385.

22   Mason W. Tyler to parents, August 4, 1864, in Tyler, *Recollections of the Civil War*, 262.

23   Cyrille Fountain, Diary, August 4, 1864, in Donald Chipman, ed. "An Essex County Soldier in the Civil War: The Diary of Cyrille Fountain." *New York History* (July, 1985), 303.

24   "Death of Major Ellis," *Buffalo Daily Courier*, August 6, 1864.

25   Stevens, *Three Years in the Sixth Corps*, 386.

the examination and found that the ramrod had split a splinter of bone from one of the ribs, and that splinter, as sharp as a needle, had been piercing & irritating the internal organs ever since he was wounded. Abscesses had formed & broken in the spleen & the diaphragm had been haggled through, and finally the splinter had pierced the lung & had killed him instantly." The surgeon preserved parts of the rib and diaphragm for medical study and noted Ellis's physical toughness. "It is wonderful that during the month he had been on duty he had made no complaint of pain," he wrote, "although his countenance showed constant suffering."[26]

Just as the misinformed rumors of heart disease had earlier, the full coroner's report now evidently spread through the ranks with remarkable speed and detail. Corporal John F. L. Hartwell, 121st New York, wrote a detailed summary the next day to his wife. "He was shot with a ramrod which shattered a rib, a piece of the bone could not be extracted & it remained loose on the inside. Yesterday morning this bone in contact with his liver or heart & caused almost immediate death, his body was sent immediately north."[27]

While the medical professionals examined the corpse, Russell set his own staff to work in preparing an elaborate funeral procession. The entire 1st Division turned out as the fallen officer's remains were carried to a train bound for New York. "It was the most impressive and grand pageant that I ever witnessed," recalled Stevens. "I have often seen military displays on a far larger scale, but nothing to compare with its solemn sublimity." Ellis's body was wrapped in a silken flag and laid in state next to Russell's headquarters in a large tent draped with the national colors. The 49th New York marched past, unarmed, as mourners and formed next to the tent in two ranks facing each other. Chaplain Winthrop H. Phelps, 2nd Connecticut Heavy Artillery, offered a brief sermon, deemed "very appropriate and impressive" by Stevens.[28]

Meanwhile, all of Russell's division formed in two parallel lines of

---

26   Stevens, August 4, 1864, PHP.

27   John F.L. Hartwell to "My Dear Wife," August 5, 1864, in Ann Hartwell Britton and Thomas J. Reed, eds. *To My Beloved Wife and Boy at Home: The Letters and Diaries of Orderly Sergeant John F.L. Hartwell* (Madison, NJ: Fairleigh Dickinson University Press, 1997), 266.

28   Stevens, August 4, 1864, PHP.

battle, eighty paces part and facing each other.[29] When Phelps concluded his sermon, Ellis's remains were "inclosed in a rude coffin, wrapped in the flag under which he had so often fought," and placed in an ambulance draped with a flag and the major's hat, coat, and sword. With a mournful dirge providing the solemn musical accompaniment, the ambulance passed in front of its escort who stood at present arms. The escort then reversed their arms and marched slowly in front of the ambulance, which was followed in turn by Ellis's horse, saddled and bridled but riderless. The band followed, still playing their dirge.[30]

Slowly the large procession passed through the sunbrowned ranks of the division, twin lines stretching a third of a mile, where all stood at "present arms" with uncovered heads. Each regiment lowered their colors in honor as the ambulance passed. The 49th New York fell into line behind the ambulance, followed by Russell, his division staff, and those of the various brigades, all bearing their own flags. "A large concourse of officers, personal friends of him whose remains were thus honored," accompanied the procession, as did many from the 2nd Division to which the 49th belonged. After passing down the length of the line the column sped up its pace and marched three miles to the train station at Buckeyestown. Following a short service the coffin was loaded on the cars bound for Baltimore, then Buffalo.[31]

In his letter that day, Stevens supposed "that friends at home would hardly think that firearms, military parade, bands of music, & muffled drums were best calculated to produce solemnity on a funeral occasion, but I can not conceive a more deeply solemn show than that which we have witnessed this morning. Indeed, it seems to me that for any grand display in which an impression is to be produced, whether for the brilliant gayeties of a Fourth of July, or the mournful rites of a funeral, nothing can compare with a military parade."[32]

A newspaper correspondent meanwhile observed, "The funeral service was one of the most imposing ever witnessed in the Army of the Potomac. . . .

29   According to various sources, either a heavy artillery regiment or four companies of the 121st New York were detailed as an escort.

30   Stevens, *Three Years in the Sixth Corps*, 387.

31   Ibid., 386-387.

32   Stevens, August 4, 1864, PHP.

Major Ellis was one of the most popular men in the corps. He was beloved by both officers and men, to whom he had endeared himself by his unassuming demeanour and great bravery. To his immediate associates his loss is irrepairable, by whom, together with his numberless friends in the Sixth corps, his death will long be regretted."[33] Captain Elisha H. Rhodes, whose writings are popularly consulted by modern historians, simply noted, "Major Ellis, a Division staff officer, died yesterday from the effects of wounds received at Spottsylvania. The entire Division was under arms and saluted the remains as they were bourne past our lines."[34]

Many of the soldiers also participated in special religious services that day as part of a proclamation by President Lincoln calling for a Day of National Humiliation, Fasting, and Prayer. "Attended in an open field where the sun was hot enough to melt almost anything down," wrote Corporal Hartwell. He expressed resentment toward the special treatment for the officer. "A great parade was made over him, more than would have been shown a whole brigade of private soldiers if all died at once."[35] Others deemed such displays appropriate, given the major's reputation. "Such men deserve the honor which our heroic people are ever willing to aware to merit and patriotism," stated the *Buffalo Advocate*. "Thus our brave men go forth, gallant in spirit, fired with the best and loftiest inspirations to fight and die for their native land."[36] With the benefit of hindsight after the war, Adjt. Vaill realized the elaborate display represented more than just the loss of Ellis. The military parade occurred during a time of respite "after so many officers and men had been buried without funeral, coffin, shroud, or audible word of prayer."[37]

Perhaps, indeed, the funeral was the soldiers' first real opportunity to take time to reflect on the massive amount of blood shed within the VI Corps

33   "The Late Major Ellis," unidentified newpaper article, New York State Military Museum and Veterans Research Center.

34   Robert Hunt Rhodes, ed. *All for the Union: The Civil War Diary and Letters of Elisha Hunt Rhodes* (New York: Vintage Civil War Library, 1992), 169.

35   John F.L. Hartwell to "My Dear Wife," August 5, 1864, in Britton and Reed, *To My Beloved Wife and Boy at Home*, 266.

36   "Honor to the Brave Dead," *Buffalo Advocate*, August 11, 1864.

37   Vaill, *History of the Second Connecticut Volunteer Heavy Artillery*, 90.

over the last three months—at the intersection of the Brock Road and Orange Plank Road as well as during Gordon's flank attack at the Wilderness; during Upton's assault and at the Bloody Angle at Spotsylvania; the June 1st attack at Cold Harbor; the brief stay in the Petersburg trenches which included the outright capture of several Vermont regiments abandoned without support at the Weldon Railroad; the desperate struggle to delay the Confederate invasion at Frederick City; the unnerving test protecting the national capital under the eyes of the president.

Along the tranquil banks of the Monocacy River the VI Corps at last exhaled. The coffin that passed through their ranks on August 4th did not just carry Ellis's body but that of thousands of brothers-in-arms whose lives had been lost without time enough to properly mourn. Even the body of the beloved "Uncle John" Sedgwick was unable to receive an appropriate send-off after the major general's death at the hands of a Confederate sharpshooter on May 9th. Just twenty-four hours later, one-third of the corps was tasked under Upton to carry out one of their most dangerous assignments of the war.

Sergeant McKelvy detailed the 49th New York's casualties during the first eight days of the Overland Campaign, "During this week of fighting at the Wilderness and Spotsylvania, the regiment lost 231 in killed and wounded out of the 384 officers and men who crossed the Rapidan on May 5th. Of this number, 89 were killed or mortally wounded. Ten officers were killed and four wounded."[38] William F. Fox wrote in his *Regimental Losses in the Civil War*, "At Spotsylvania the [49th] regiment behaved with especial gallantry, its percentage of loss in that battle being a remarkable one."[39]

Within days of Ellis's death, Maj. Gen. Phil Sheridan arrived to guide the VI Corps and the newly organized Army of the Shenandoah into its namesake region in an incredibly successful campaign. The terms of service for the 49th New York expired on September 17th, but four consolidated companies of reenlisted New Yorkers composed a battalion that remained active in Virginia through the end of the war. They joined Sheridan for his

---

38   McKelvy, "Forty-ninth New York Volunteers," 390.

39   William F. Fox, *Regimental Losses in the American Civil War, 1865-1865* (Albany, NY: Albany Publishing Company, 1889), 197.

victories in the valley which further depleted the leadership in Wright's corps. Emory Upton was wounded and David Russell was killed on September 19 at Third Winchester. The fighting one month later at Cedar Creek claimed the life of the 49th's first commander, Daniel Bidwell, then leading the brigade. The corps rejoined the Army of the Potomac at Petersburg in December and played an important role in the final campaign. One week before Confederate surrender at Appomattox, Lt. Col. Erastus D. Holt, the new commander of the 49th, was also mortally wounded, shot by a Confederate picket while the corps formed overnight for their decisive charge that broke through the lines at Petersburg on April 2nd. "The Forty-ninth suffered a severe and unusual loss in the number of its field officers," noted William Fox.[40]

The 49th New York's adjutant, 1st Lt. John P. Einsfeld, accompanied Ellis's body to Buffalo. Upon arrival, eight members of the Veteran Reserve Corps escorted the remains from the Erie Railway station to Catharine Ellis's home. Funeral services were held on Thursday, August 11, at the Church of the Ascension. The *Buffalo Daily Courier* eulogized the fallen:

> In the death of Major Ellis, the country has lost one of the noblest of its defenders. All who knew him concur in eulogy of the chivalry, the lofty patriotism, the noble manliness which marked his character. He was indeed a good and true knight, sans peur et sans reproche [without fear and without reproach]; as tender and faithful in his discharge of duty as a son and brother as in his military capacity he was brave and soldierly. At one of the battles of the Wilderness he was shot through the arm with the ramrod of some rebel soldier's gun, the strange missile at the same time inflicting a severe blow on his side near the heart. He came home on a furlough, but, anxious to be with his regiment, returned to the field before he had fairly recovered. In the absence from the regiment of both Col. Bidwell and Lieut. Col. Johnson, the command of the 49th devolved upon him, and it is believed that over exertion in front of Washington gave a fatal character to the stroke received near his heart. 'For such choice souls earth has no price, no mart.'[41]

---

40   Fox, *Regimental Losses in the American Civil War*, 197.

41   "The Late Major Ellis," *Buffalo Daily Courier*, August 9, 1864.

Company D of the 74th New York Infantry escorted the major's body to Forest Lawn Cemetery where it was finally laid to rest. "A braver, purer heart has not been laid beneath the Lawn's green sod."[42]

For two decades after William Ellis's death, his story was concluded for all but his mother. The already-widowed Catharine began the process in late August 1864 of obtaining a pension for her own support. The fifty-year-old woman secured testimony from several of William's former comrades who stated that the deceased officer had sent large sums of his army wages home to care for his mother. Catharine herself testified. "That from the time he [William] was sixteen years old up to the time of his death he has contributed to my support all his earnings except what was absolutely necessary for his own support and that

William Ellis's plot at Forest Lawn Cemetery in Buffalo has two stones: the original cross erected by his family and a government headstone marking his Federal army service. The family monument makes note that Ellis "died in camp Aug. 4, 1864, of wounds recieved in the battle of the Wilderness." *Mike Erb*

what he has contributed to my support has been necessary and that I have relied upon his assistantance to enable me support myself."[43]

The major's story was reopened in the 1880s. George N. Galloway,

42   "Funeral of Major Ellis," *Buffalo Daily Courier*, August 13, 1864.

43   William S. Bulls, Statement, May 12, 1865, Theodore P. Samo, Statement, May 12, 1865, and Catharine Ellis, Statement, June 28, 1865, William Ellis Pension, NA.

veteran of the 95th Pennsylvania Infantry, began writing extensively about his wartime experiences.[44] His articles appeared as a brief regimental history and in the pages of the *Philadelphia Weekly Times* and *Century Magazine*, the latter of which was republished as *Battles and Leaders of the Civil War*. Galloway's articles focused on the Overland Campaign and triggered a wave of responses from Confederates. Private Thomas T. Roche, 16th Mississippi, wrote an article about the Bloody Angle for the *Philadelphia Weekly Times* in which he noted three instances of observing bravery displayed by Union officers who were ultimately shot by the southerners. For the last encounter, Roche wrote:

> Suddenly, a large, fine-looking officer, whom I think was a captain, stepped briskly forward and came upon the works, remarking, "Well boys, I suppose you have all surrendered!" Receiving a negative reply, he asked for the commanding officer. Major Council, of the Sixteenth, stepped up and said: "I am, sir." When the officer again remarked, "Well sir, I suppose you have all surrendered?" Major Council replied, "No, sir; we have not surrendered, but consider yourself a prisoner."

> Then the officer boldly and firmly answered, "I'll die first!" and turning on his heel slowly and deliberately attempted to return to his own lines, as coolly as though there was no enemy in ten miles of him. He was repeatedly called on to halt or he would be shot, but he paid not the slightest attention, when some one shot him. He fell about thirty paces in front of our works. The courage and daring of this brave but rash man I think has never been equaled during the war. Will some of the Federal survivors at that point give his name? For one who could be so insensible to fear should have his name inscribed in the temple of fame. Probably Mr. Galloway recollects the incident, as he says that his (Upton's) brigade occupied the position. Many of the Mississippians, and none more than the writer, regretted the fate of that brave spirit. But after learning our weaknesses on the right it would have been self-destruction to have permitted him to return to his

---

44   In 1895, Galloway would be awarded the Medal of Honor for his demonstration of extraordinary heroism at Alsop's Farm at Spotsylvania on May 8, 1864, when he voluntarily held an important position under heavy enemy fire.

own lines. When the fatal shot was fired it was the signal for the musketry to break forth in all its fury, which never ceased till next morning.[45]

Galloway read this account and responded, "The gallant officer to whom Mr. Roche referred was doubtless Major Ellis of the Forty-ninth New York. His arm was pierced and badly bruised with a ramrod, shot away either in the exciting moment of loading and firing, or in a spirit of haste to get a quick shot at one offering so good a target." However, the Pennsylvanian claimed that Ellis was "shot upon the parapet of the Confederate works, and there was not at that time so great a space as that alluded to by Mr. Roche."[46]

The Mississippian's account also did not match earlier descriptions, but he did provide two other instances that could perhaps reference the New York major's mortal wounding, writing, "At 9 o'clock A.M. the Federals made a second charge and advanced in fine style until near the works, when they began to waver, but their officers undaunted, sprang forward with sword in hand, actually springing upon our works, cheering and imploring their men to follow them, when the brave fellows were shot down. Such examples are seldom equaled for courage and daring. I heard several of our men say on that day that it was a pity to sacrifice the lives of such gallant men." Roche also claimed that at 9:30 when "the Federals made their third desperate charge on our front... two gallant Federal officers seized a stand of colors, one a large blue starry flag and the other the Stars and Stripes, and calling on their men to follow their colors, sprang upon our works and while in the act of planting them in the embankment were shot off."[47]

Though the exchange between the Pennsylvanian Galloway and the Mississippian Roche could not definitely place the timing and condition of the New York major's wounding, Galloway's 1887 article in the *Century Magazine* caught the eye of Richard T. Owen, a former second lieutenant in the 12th Mississippi Infantry, Harris's Brigade. After reading about the unusual nature of Ellis's wound, Owen set about tracking down a former

---

45   Thomas T. Roche, "The Bloody Angle. A Participant's Description of the Fiercest Combat of the War," *Philadelphia Weekly Times*, September 3, 1881.

46   G. Norton Gallway, "Annals of the War, Chapter of Unwritten History: Capture of the Salient," *Philadelphia Weekly Times*, November 18, 1882.

47   Roche, "The Bloody Angle," *Philadelphia Weekly Times*, September 3, 1881.

comrade, Sergeant John G. Darrah (or Derrah). It took him some time, but eventually he determined a New Orleans address and wrote:

Well, old fellow, I have found your ramrod, or at least the one you shot at the Yanks in the battle of Spottsylvania Courthouse; just as you caught that minie ball in the head. If you remember just before you fell you loaded your gun with one of the loose ramrods lying around and remarked to me that you had been in every battle our regiment had been in up to that time, and had fired as often as any one else, but you never knew that you had killed any of the enemy and that if one of them was found with a ramrod in him he was your man. You were struck just as you fired your gun.

In looking over an account of the battles of the wilderness campaign under Grant, published in the June number of the *Century Magazine* of 1887, I find in the description of the federal historian of the Sixth Corps that just in front of the 'bloody angle' at the point occupied by Harris and McGowan's brigades, Major Wm. Ellis of the Forty-ninth New York Volunteers, was killed by a ramrod piercing his breast and right arm. Of course it brought to my mind the scenes enacted on that bloody day, and which I would not forget were I to live a thousand years. On reading it I remarked to a friend that I intended hunting you up and letting you know the result of your last shot. I want you to write and let me know if you recollect the incident, as you were 'knocked out of the box' so completely at the time I doubted your recollecting the conversation with me.[48]

The *New Orleans Times-Picayune* published the letter on March 23, 1890. Soon other newspapers ran the thrilling story, including the *St. Louis Post-Dispatch* under headline, "His Last Shot. An Incident at Spottsylvania Recounted by a Confederate Soldier." A resident of the city, Mrs. A.F. Fay, read the article and forwarded it home to her brother, Joseph E. Rogers, a former private in Ellis's regiment living in Chautauqua, New York. Rogers responded directly to the editor of the *Post-Dispatch* to correct him that Ellis had not been instantly killed and Darrah would have to look elsewhere for his ramrod:

---

48   "A Witness of Death. The Story of a Ramrod Fired by a New Orleans Confederate During the War," *New Orleans Times-Picayune*, March 23, 1890.

I was somewhat amused in reading in your paper of March 23 an account
of "His Last Shot," a letter by Mr. Owen, the dashing young Lieutenant,
who belonged to the famous Twelfth Mississippi Volunteers, to John G.
Darrah of New Orleans, who was in the same company, telling him that
he had found his ramrod, which was his last shot at Spottsylvania, and
that Maj. Ellis of the Forty-ninth New York Volunteers was killed with
it. I beg leave to correct that statement. I happened to be there, and was
shot through and through at Spottsylvania and I was with Maj. Ellis in the
Lincoln Hospital, and in the same ward in Washington. He was wounded
with a ramrod, but it did not kill him. He pulled it out of his side and sent
it back where it came from. After his recovery from this wound he joined
his regiment and died at the battle of Fort Stevens, August 4, 1864. Please
give this room in your paper, as I should like to have Mr. Owen know that
he has not found his ramrod.[49]

Rogers's version of the story incorrectly claimed that Ellis died in that
later battle outside of Washington, though it provided the sensational detail
that Ellis returned the ramrod "where it came from." The editor of the *Post-
Dispatch* meanwhile called on the home of Mrs. Fay for more detail. She
incorrectly identified the wounded officer as Daniel Bidwell and spoke more
of her brother Joe Rogers's experience:

I wish I could tell you more about this incident, but I married nearly
twenty years ago and have not lived at my old home since, so I do not
know much about these incidents of the war which my brother has told at
home. I remember his speaking of this, however, but I do not recall any
more than that an officer of the regiment was shot with a ramrod. I was
under the impression that it was Col. Bidwell. My brother was wounded at
Spottsylvania and received there a wound that has made him quite noted in
Washington. From the effects of it he lost three inches of his backbone, and
the Pension office in Washington has pronounced him the worst wounded
man in the United States who stands on both feet. He can walk without a
cane, but he cannot bend over or do any work on account of this wound.

49   "The Story of a Ramrod. Sergt. Darrah Fired It at the Federal Forces. It Struck Maj.
Ellis, Who Drew It from His Side and Returned It to the Confederate Side—How the History
of That Ramrod Has Come to Light," *St. Louis Post-Dispatch*, April 6, 1890.

He received his wound about the same time that the officer was shot with the ramrod and, as he says, they went to the hospital together.[50]

A moderate combing of regimental and newspaper records revealed no further information about Ellis's wound, but several modern sources reference the story. Historian Wiley Sword first identified the letter Stevens wrote to his wife on August 4, 1864. He included a vignette on the major's service through the pain in *Courage Under Fire: Profiles in Bravery from the Battlefields of the Civil War*:

> Yet the pain threshold varies from person to person, as evidenced from confronting a dentist's drill or playing injured in a sporting event. That some individuals have been able to rise above extreme pain and perform effectively is food for thought. Is it courage of the mind, or endurance of the body? Is there a method, or is it a matter of will? To tough it out may involve a matter of seconds, minutes, or hours. But protracted endurance of extreme pain is a matter of dire experience, and in the case of a few individuals, it involves the height of courage, both physical and mental... Ellis had endured what they supposed others could not, and continued to do hard, active duty. Given a hero's funeral in which the entire division participated, Ellis was later laid to rest in New York, the victim of a bizarre wound and fate, but one of the nation's most profound if unheralded heroes: a man whose courage extended far beyond the ordinary through the threshold of pain to a level that few could even imagine.[51]

Formal memorialization of the 49th New York's service at Spotsylvania meanwhile occurred in October 1902. A thousand Union veterans traveled to Fredericksburg that month as part of a Grand Army of the Republic reunion. Fifty former members of the 49th New York had a special reason for their attendance. On October 9, they dedicated a monument to those who died at the Bloody Angle. Captain French W. Fisher and nine other men spoke before the veterans and their guests ate lunch and toured the

---

50   "The Story of a Ramrod," *St. Louis Post-Dispatch*, April 6, 1890.

51   Wiley Sword, *Courage Under Fire: Profiles in Bravery from the Battlefields of the Civil War* (New York: St. Martin's Press, 2007), 99-101.

The 49th New York's monument was the first of three regimental monuments that would eventually be erected at the Bloody Angle. Monuments to the 15th New Jersey and 126th Ohio would come later. *Fredericksburg and Spotsylvania National Military Park*

battlefield. According to historian Don Pfanz, "The speakers addressed themes common at such events: the history of the regiment, the sacrifice of those who fought, and the reconciliation between North and South."[52]

The regiment erected a twelve-foot-tall monument just ten feet north of the Bloody Angle. It cost $500 to construct the granite shaft and base, adorned by the VI Corps' Greek Cross at the top of all four sides and with four granite cannonballs resting at the top. The names of five officers and thirty-four enlisted men scroll down the north side of the monument. Only those killed in action are listed, so Ellis's name was not included. "49th N.Y. Inf'y 3d Brig. 2d Div. 6th Corps. Held this position May 12, 1864" faces south. If the monument fell in that direction it would land inside the Confederate lines, near, perhaps, where Ellis received what eventually proved to be his fatal ramrod wound.

---

52   Donald C. Pfanz, "History through Eyes of Stone," revised September 2006, FRSPNMP.

The 23rd USCT at Spotsylvania

by Steward T. Henderson

Point of Interest #9 on the map on pg. xiv.

Originally published as a blog post at Emerging Civil War on May 15, 2014

At the beginning of the Overland Campaign, the 23rd Regiment United States Colored Troops (U.S.C.T.) was an infantry regiment in the 4th Division of the independent IX Army Corps. This regiment became the first black regiment to fight in directed combat against the Army of Northern Virginia. This happened 150 years ago today, on May 15, 1864.

The 23rd was organized at Camp Casey, Virginia—in the area of where the Pentagon is today—on November 23, 1863 until June 30, 1864. The unit consisted of freed and escaped slaves, plus a few freedmen. Some of the men that we know who escaped and came back as members of the 23rd USCT were Peter Churchwell, Andrew Weaver, and Abraham Tuckson. These men escaped from the vicinity of Fredericksburg, Virginia.

In January 1864, Maj. Gen. Ambrose E. Burnside was asked to reorganize his IX Corps. He asked for and was granted permission by Secretary of War Edwin Stanton to form a division of "colored troops." The 4th Division of the IX Corps would consist entirely of black troops fighting for the Union and would be commanded by Brig. Gen. Edward Ferrero. The regiments were divided into two brigades: the first brigade was made up of the 27th, 30th, 39th, and 43rd USCT, while the second brigade was comprised of the 30th Connecticut Colored Infantry (only 4 companies), 19th, and 23rd U.S.C.T. Later in May, the 30th Connecticut was merged into the 31st U.S.C.T., which had joined the second brigade. In late June, the 28th and 29th U.S.C.T. regiments were added to the second brigade. These regiments came from across the north, from Illinois to Connecticut, and across the east from New York to Virginia. There are anecdotes that when the entire division was at Petersburg, their relatives who had escaped slavery saw other relatives in different units—a homecoming of sort to these men.

When the 4th Division left Camp Stanton in Annapolis, Maryland, they paraded in front of President Abraham Lincoln and Burnside in Washington, D.C. The 23rd joined the division when they marched across the Potomac River into Virginia.

Sergeant Nimrod Burke originally came from Prince William County, Virginia, but his family had been freed and moved to Ohio. In 1861, Burke was a teamster and scout for the 36th Ohio infantry. In 1864, he joined the 23rd U.S.C.T. and was promoted to sergeant. His picture is widely circulated—in some cases, as an unidentified soldier. His family now has a website devoted to him.

Burke is just one of many of the soldiers in the 23rd who were from Virginia. We have traced men back to the city of Fredericksburg and the counties of Caroline, Culpeper, Fauquier, Orange, Prince William, Rappahannock, Spotsylvania, and Stafford. Many of these men broke free from slavery during the Union occupation of Fredericksburg from April to early September 1862, when more than 12,000 slaves escaped their "masters." These men fled bondage only to come back and fight with the United States Colored Troops—many of them with the 23rd U.S.C.T.

They were sent to Manassas and arrived there by train on May 1, 1864. General Burnside ordered General Ferrero to practice his troops "at target and drill." On May 4, the division marched to Warrenton Junction.

On May 5, Ferrero wanted to rest his men since they had marched more than 30 miles in 24 hours. However, as soon as Burnside heard about the fighting in the Wilderness, the 4th Division was told to move immediately. On May 6, they crossed Germanna Ford and were ordered to report to Maj. Gen. John Sedgwick of the VI Corps. Two regiments were ordered to guard the ford and the rest were deployed to the right of the VI Corps. After Confederate Maj. Gen. John B. Gordon's flank attack broke the VI corps, the 4th Division was ordered down the Plank Road to guard wagon trains.

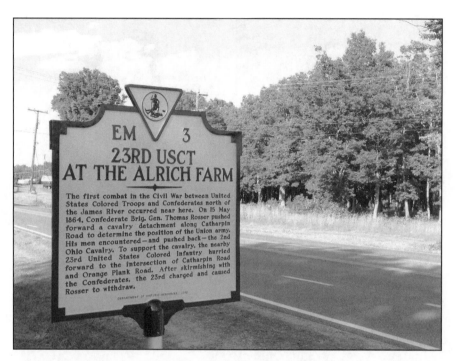

EM ▽ 3

23RD USCT
AT THE ALRICH FARM

The first combat in the Civil War between United States Colored Troops and Confederates north of the James River occurred near here. On 15 May 1864, Confederate Brig. Gen. Thomas Rosser pushed forward a cavalry detachment along Catharpin Road to determine the position of the Union army. His men encountered—and pushed back—the 2nd Ohio Cavalry. To support the cavalry, the nearby 23rd United States Colored Infantry hurried forward to the intersection of Catharpin Road and Orange Plank Road. After skirmishing with the Confederates, the 23rd charged and caused Rosser to withdraw.

DEPARTMENT OF HISTORIC RESOURCES, 2012

Installed for the Sesquicentennial of the battle of Spotsylvania Court House, a state historical marker commemorates the first action by black soldiers on the Fredericksburg-area battlefields. The engagement took place well to the rear of the Federal army's main position at Spotsylvania but close to the Chancellorsville battlefield. *Chris Mackowski*

From May 7 until the end of the battle of Spotsylvania Court House, the 4th Division guarded and escorted wagon trains behind the lines and to the Belle Plain depot. On May 12, they took Confederate prisoners back to the rear. A famous *Harper's Weekly* sketch shows black soldiers guarding captured Confederate generals "Allegheny" Johnson and "Maryland" Steuart. These soldiers would have been from the 4th Division of the IX Corps.

During the battle of Spotsylvania Court House, the 23rd U.S.C.T. was at the Chancellorsville ruins, guarding wagon trains on May 15, 1864, when the 2nd Ohio Cavalry asked for assistance. The Ohioans were being attacked by Brig. Gen. Thomas Rosser's Confederate Cavalry Brigade. Ferrero marched the 23rd at the double-quick to the intersection of the Catharpin and Old Plank roads.

"It did us good to see the long line of glittering bayonets approach,

Edward Ferrero (left) may have been the prewar dance instructor, but Thomas Rosser (right) did the dancing when he wrote his official report of their encounter. Rosser refused to admit his men had been bested by black soldiers. *Library of Congress/Emerging Civil War*

although those who bore them were Blacks," one Buckeye wrote, "and as they came nearer they were greeted by loud cheers."[1]

The 23rd USCT formed a battle line and fired on the Confederate cavalry and drove them away. They became the first African American soldiers to fight in "directed combat"—that is, intentionally—against the Army of Northern Virginia. They were cheered by the white soldiers of the 2nd Ohio, who now knew these black soldiers would fight against the Confederates.

Ferrero wrote this report of this engagement and sent it to Brigadier-General John Rawlins, General Grant's Chief of Staff:

HDQRS. FOURTH DIVISION, NINTH ARMY CORPS,
Miller's House, on Plank Road east of Alrich's, May 15, 1864

GENERAL: I have the honor to report that at 12:30 p. m. this day the Second Ohio cavalry, stationed at Piney Branch Church, were compelled

---

1   Quoted in Gordon Rhea, *To the North Anna River: Grant and Lee, May 13-25, 1864* (Baton Rouge: LSU Press, 2000), 106.

to fall back, being attacked by superior forces, consisting of one brigade of cavalry, with two pieces of artillery. I immediately ordered the Fourth Division in readiness, and marched the Twenty-third U. S. Colored Troops to support the cavalry. On arriving at Alrich's, on the plank road, I found the Second Ohio driven across the road, and the enemy occupying the cross-roads. I ordered the colored regiment to advance on the enemy in line of battle, which they did, and drove the enemy in perfect rout. Not being able to pursue with infantry, the Second Ohio formed and gave chase to Piney Branch Church, which they (the Second Ohio) now occupy. All quiet elsewhere. Our loss amounted to about 8 or 10 wounded. The enemy lost some 5 horses killed. I have changed my position to a more secure one, to protect the trains and roads leading to the army. I have since learned from one of my scouts that Hampton's brigade is in full retreat, in perfect disorder, toward Todd's Tavern.

I am general, very respectfully, your obedient servant,
EDW. FERRERO,
Brigadier-General, Commanding.[2]

Rosser, on the other hand, mentioned the engagement in his report only briefly and, even then, he neglected to mention that he had encountered black troops.

The 23rd U.S.C.T. and the 4th Division would fight on throughout the rest of the Civil War. Their most famous battle was in Petersburg at the battle of the Crater on July 30, 1864. The 23rd suffered the most casualties of all of the black regiments in the battle.

In December of 1864, all of the black regiments in the Army of the Potomac and the Army of the James were assigned to the XXV Corps—the largest grouping of African American men in the Civil War. Those men would fight at Petersburg, Richmond, and all the way to Appomattox Court House. After the war, the XXV Corps was sent to Texas with Maj. Gen. Philip Sheridan. The 23rd was mustered out on November 30, 1865.

2   *O.R.* 36, Pt. 1, 989.

From Spotsylvania's Eastern Front

by Chris Mackowski

Points of Interest #6, #7, and #8 on the map on pg. xiv.

Originally published as a blog post at Emerging Civil War on May 20, 2019

On May 20, 1864, Lt. Gen. Ulysses S. Grant began his withdrawal from Spotsylvania Court House, swinging once more around Gen Robert E. Lee's right flank and moving south. I want to share a writing project I did in my capacity as historian-in-residence at Stevenson Ridge, a historic property owned by my wife's family on the eastern edge of the Spotsylvania battlefield. To recap the anniversary of the two-week battle, I wrote a day-by-day account of the battle for Stevenson Ridge's blog, focusing on action that took place on the oft-overlooked eastern front of the battlefield along the historic Fredericksburg Road (modern day route 208). I've collected the series for you here.

May 8, 1864: The Battle Opens

For two weeks, portions of the Federal army will occupy the area now known as Stevenson Ridge, then part of a 300-acre farm owned by 40-year-old Francis C. Beverley. The five-person family lived in a house on the south side of the road called Whig Hill. They owned 12 slaves. By the end of the battle, at least 379 Federal soldiers would be buried on the property (and later reinterred in Fredericksburg National Cemetery).[1]

The first action to take place at this site happened early on May 8 when Federal cavalry splashed across the Ny River in an attempt to get behind Confederates who were blocking Brock Road—the northwest approach to the village of Spotsylvania Court House—some three miles to the west.

Brother Against Brother by Robert Spear, brother of Stevenson Ridge co-owner Dan Spear, depicts a clash of cavalry—the very action that opened the fighting on Spotsylvania's eastern front. *Dan and Debbie Spear*

Brigadier General James Wilson, who had underperformed thus far in the spring campaign led a full division of horsemen on the expedition. A single regiment of Confederate cavalry under Brig. Gen. Williams C. Wickham—the 3rd Virginia—tried to slow Wilson's advance. A quick fight broke out on the south bank of the river, but Wilson easily brushed the Confederates aside.

The rest of Wickham's brigade appeared, bolstered by Confederate infantry that shifted into position to intercept Wilson, who realized he was outmatched and well beyond the aid of any reinforcements. He wisely chose to withdraw.

Wickham repositioned his brigade to again guard the Fredericksburg Road. Federals would approach again soon enough. . . .

May 9, 1864: Battle of the Ny

On May 8, three-fourths of the Union army had collided with the Confederate Army of Northern Virginia along Brock Road, where

---

1   Noel Harrison, *Gazetteer of Historic Sites Related to the Fredericksburg and Spotsylvania National Military Park*, vol. 2 (Fredericksburg and Spotsylvania National Military Park, 1989), 115.

Whig Hill, the white building in the middle, as seen from the property that's now Stevenson Ridge. The driveway in the foreground extends from the Fredericksburg Road toward Whig Hill. The driveway provided an important defensive position for Federals during the May 9 "Battle of the Ny." *Fredericksburg and Spotsylvania National Military Park*

Confederates successfully bottlenecked them. The Federal army was so large, though, that a quarter of it had to circle around to the east and come to the battlefield a different way—down Fredericksburg Road.

That portion of the army, the IX Corps, was commanded by the genial but mediocre Maj. Gen. Ambrose Burnside. Burnside sent his first division forward under Brig. Gen. Orlando Willcox with orders to clear the way into the village. Willcox's men splashed across the Ny River—now, and then sometimes, called the Ni River—where Confederate cavalry raised an alarm. The previous day, the single brigade of cavalry was the only thing blocking the road, but by May 9, four North Carolina regiments under Brig. Gen. Robert D. Johnston moved into the area to block the road. Initially under the command of Robert Rodes, Johnstons' men would fall under the command of Cadmus Wilcox by day's end by dint of proximity.

Thus, it would be Willcox versus Wilcox for control of the back door into Spotsylvania Court House.

Federals deployed across the property that is now Stevenson Ridge and advanced. Confederates checked them at almost every opportunity,

Willcox vs. Wilcox: The May 9 Battle of the Ny ended with Federals under the command of Orlando (left) vs. Confederates under the command of Cadmus (right). Orlando's extra "l" apparently made the difference, as Federals successfully secured a lodgement along the Fredericksburg Road. *Library of Congress/Library of Congress*

although much of the fighting was back and forth. At one point, nearly the entire Federal line collapsed, but a rally by the 50th Pennsylvania put the Federals back into the fight, eventually capturing all their lost ground and putting Federals within easy striking distance of Spotsylvania. "Thus this division gained a foothold nearer Spotsylvania Court-House than any other part of the line," a Pennsylvanian proudly declared.[2]

By early afternoon, Burnside was content to consolidate his position rather than risk further fighting. He was far from the rest of the Federal army and , if he got into trouble, would have a tough time getting reinforcements. His "play-it-safe" attitude may have seemed prudent at the time, but a more aggressive commander could have used the far superior Federal numbers to force the Confederates back before they had time to consolidate their own position. As it was, Burnside's delay allowed Confederates to dig in and more reinforcements shift into the area.

Burnside would instead try to make a strong push tomorrow.

2   Report of Lt. Col. Byron M. Cutcheon. *O.R.* 36, Pt. I, 968.

May 10, 1864: The Death of Thomas Greely Stevenson

May 10 is the anniversary of the death of Brig. Gen. Thomas Greely Stevenson, the Union officer for whom Stevenson Ridge is named. "Stevenson was arguably Burnside's ablest division commander," historian Gordon Rhea has said.[3] Burnside, who had served with Stevenson for long stretches during the war, said upon hearing the news: "I am pained beyond measure to hear of the death of General Stevenson."[4]

Stevenson, recently promoted to command of the IX Corps's First Division, took a bullet midmorning, "a rifle ball piercing his head, while he was surrounded by his staff, cheerful and confident up to the moment he was struck."[5]

Confederates had "inflicted an irreparable loss" one soldier from Stevenson's home state lamented. "A sagacious, cool, and dauntless soldier, he was an inspiring leader of men, and a gentleman of the noblest stamp."[6]

"Of all losses of gallant men, whom Massachusetts has been called upon to mourn in this war, no one has caused a greater or more general sorrow than that of General Thomas G. Stevenson," wrote *The Boston Post* when reporting news of the general's death. Here, Stevenson looks like a pugilistic leprechaun. *Chris Mackowski's collection*

3   Gordon Rhea, *The Battles for Spotsylvania Court House and the Road to Yellow Tavern, May 7-12, 1864* (Baton Rouge: LSU Press, 1997), 182.

4   Burnside to Wilcox, 10 May 1864, *O.R.* 36, Pt. 2, 613.

5   *Gen. Stevenson.* (Cambridge, MA: Welch, Bigelow, Co., 1864). Available for perusal online at https://archive.org/details/genstevenson00camb. Some accounts put Stevenson's death as late as noon. One account says "dinner time," referring to, I assume, "lunch time" in the antiquated way.

6   Charles Folsom Walcott, *History of the Twenty-First Regiment, Massachusetts Volunteers,* (Boston: Houghton, Mifflin and Company, 1882), 320.

A woodcut in the May 28, 1864, edition of *Frank Leslie's Illustrated Newspaper*, based on a sketch by Joseph Becker, depicted fighting along the Fredericksburg Road on May 10. Whig Hill is in the distance on the left-hand page; Stevenson Ridge is on the right-hand page where the puffs of gunpowder smoke are near the fold. The larger puffs of smoke indicate fighting by Hancock's corps on the far side of the battlefield. *Library of Congress*

May 11, 1864: "Sad but Heroic Hearts"

On May 11, 1864, a pall of disappointment and discouragement sat over what is now Stevenson Ridge.

First, Stevenson's death on the previous day had knocked the wind out of the IX Corps's sails. Then, a late-afternoon push into Spotsylvania Court House ended in an inexplicable withdrawal. The corps had made gains that put the army as close to the village as it would ever get during the two-week battle, but army commander Ulysses S. Grant got cold feet. He thought the IX Corps too exposed and vulnerable and so ordered it back to its previous, more secure position, erasing the day's gains. Then he sent them *back* to their forward positions before Confederates could react, perhaps realizing a mistake.

Such swings in fortune hurt morale. Then it started to rain on May 11, making the mood of the men even worse. "[T]he drenched earth and dripping trees made our positions anything but a comfortable one," a Maine soldier wrote.[7]

Burnside spent the latter part of the day and into the dripping night preparing for a dawn assault against a portion of the Confederate line known as the Mule Shoe.

"With anxious hearts the men stood around their camp-fires in the pitiless storm," one Federal soldier wrote, "speculating as to the chances of

---

7   Henry C. Houston, *The Thirty-Second Maine Regiment of Infantry Volunteers: An Historical Sketch* (Portland, ME: Press of Southworth Brothers, 1903), 121.

the morrow, and with sad but heroic hearts wondering if they should survive the terrible carnage which they knew well was before them."[8]

Dawn will bring renewed fighting, some of the most up-close and personal—and terrible—of the war.

May 12, 1864: The Mule Shoe and Heth's Salient

May 12 would see some of the worst fighting of the Overland Campaign—many would say even of the entire war.

The Federals launched an attack against the tip of a horse-shoe shaped portion of the Confederate line that has since become known as the Mule Shoe Salient. For 22 consecutive hours, the armies were locked in combat, much of it hand-to-hand, in the pouring rain. In some places, water filled the trenches up to the men's knees, and the mud sucked down the wounded and suffocated or drowned them.

In support of the assault, Burnside's IX Corps was to attack the eastern base of the salient. Thus, the area now known as Stevenson Ridge became a staging area on May 11 for troops preparing to go into the May 12 fight. "[W]e formed into line of battle and moved forward a little to the right of the road running toward the court house," a Pennsylvanian said.[9] Then, just as dawn began to lighten the sky, they went into the fight.

Initially repulsed, Burnside's men fell back—not quite all the way to Stevenson Ridge—and then regrouped for a second assault. Tangled in the thickets and woods, the men lost much of their unit-level cohesiveness and instead began fighting in small groups and as individuals. Men called this type of fighting "bushwhacking."

In the afternoon of May 12, both army commanders tried to relieve pressure at the Mule Shoe by launching attacks on the eastern front at a place called Heth's Salient, named for Confederate Maj. Gen. Henry Heth, who commanded the men ensconced in that part of the line. Neither

---

8   Leander W. Cogswell, *A History of the Eleventh New Hampshire Regiment Volunteer Infantry in the Rebellion War, 1861-1865* (Concord, NH: Republican Press Association, 1891), 363.

9   Ephraim E. Myers, "Three Years' and Five Months' Experience of an Orange Recruit," *History of the Forty-Fifth Regiment, Pennsylvania Veteran Volunteer Infantry, 1861-1865*, Allen D. Albert, ed. (Williamsport, PA: Grit Publishing Company, 1912), 287.

knew the other was launching an attack, although both happened almost simultaneously. Confederates got the jump on the Federals and crushed their left flank, leading to yet another retreat.

Overshadowed by the fighting at the Mule Shoe, the fighting on Burnside's front was nonetheless severe for many of the men engaged, some calling it some of the toughest fighting they'd ever engaged in.

And the battle of Spotsylvania Court House was not yet over.

May 13, 1864: All Quiet on the Eastern Front

The morning of May 13 saw carnage across the Spotsylvania battlefield unlike anything the armies had before seen.

Once the fighting at the Mule Shoe wound down and Lee had settled into his new fall-back position, Union forces took stock of their situation. The cries and moans of the injured drifted across the muddy landscape and through the devastated forests. Otherwise, fighting quieted all along the line.

During the previous day's fighting, Burnside's men had shifted westward for their assaults on the Mule Shoe and Heth's Salient. That left some of their original works near the Fredericksburg Road thinly occupied.

Grant decided to shift the bulk of his army toward Burnside's former position astride the Fredericksburg Road. He could not get at Lee along the Brock Road or in the center at the Mule Shoe, so perhaps an opportunity existed against the Confederate right. After all, he reasoned, the Confederates had to be weak somewhere.

He cut orders for his V Corps, occupying a position along the Brock Road called Laurel Hill/Spindle Field, to shift eastward to the Fredericksburg Road. In doing so, the V Corps would disengage from its current position, slide behind the VI Corps and then the II Corps, then cross behind the IX Corps and into the IX Corps's original trenches. The IX Corps, meanwhile, would consolidate its position.

Once the V Corps finished its move, the VI Corps would then disengage from its position and follow the V Corps eastward, eventually extending the line farther east and south. There, Grant saw an opportunity to capture a piece of high ground occupied by Confederates, known as Myer's Hill. Possession of Myer's Hill would protect the new Federal left flank and allow the Federal army to threaten Lee's position—and perhaps even get into Lee's rear.

Grant set his army in motion with an eye toward a dawn attack on May 14. Assault hadn't allowed him to break Lee's line, but perhaps maneuver would.

May 14, 1864: Myer's Hill

On May 14, 1864, Grant planned to throw his V and VI Corps against the Confederate left flank in an early morning attack. Mother Nature worked against him. As his men tried to shift into their new positions, the rain that had started on May 11 continued to drench them. "The weather having been very wet the roads were almost impassable and rendered the march both disagreeable and toilsome," wrote Col Alfred Pearson of the 150th Pennsylvania.[10] A member of the 39th Massachusetts said, "The mud was dreadful, the night dark, we forded streams up to our knees, and the mud all the time was over our shoes."[11]

V Corps commander Maj. Gen. Gouverneur K. Warren, who took up his headquarters at Whig Hill—directly across Route 208 from today's Stevenson Ridge—tried in his official report to put as positive a spin on the movement as possible:

> At 4:00 a.m. I was at the appointed place with about 1,000 men, and all that could be done was assault the enemy's cavalry on a commanding position on our left, which we did and took. It required the whole day to get my command up and together again. A brigade of the Sixth Corps was sent to hold the hill, which we had taken, but the enemy drove it off. After that, I had it retaken with Ayres' brigade.[12]

The "commanding position" the action centered around was called Myer's Hill. Had Federals been able to get into position there in time, they would have had open access to the Confederate flank and rear because Gen. Robert E. Lee, slow to recognize the threat, did not adequately respond.

Following Warren's initial capture of the hill, the VI Corps brigade of newly promoted Brig. Gen. Emory Upton occupied the position, and Army

---

10   *O.R.* 36, Pt.1, 558.

11   Alfred S. Roe, *The Thirty-Ninth Regiment Massachusetts Volunteers, 1862, 1865* (Worcester, MA: Regimental Veteran Association, 1914), 99.

12   *O.R.* 36I, Pt. 1, 542.

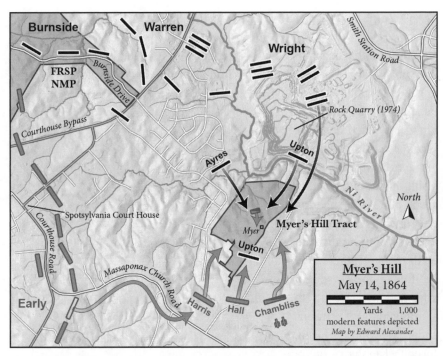

MYER'S HILL—In 2018, the Central Virginia Battlefields Trust began work to preserve the core of the Myer's Hill battlefield, including the site of the Myer homestead. In the years since, CVBT has worked to preserve other portions of the hill, including remaining earthworks. This map is adapted from their original fund-raising map and includes new land added in 2021. *Central Virginia Battlefields Trust (cvbt.org)*

of the Potomac commander Maj. Gen. George Gordon Meade rode to the hilltop to inspect the situation. When Confederates launched a counterattack, they nearly captured Meade, who narrowly escaped by jumping the Ny River. His dander up by the near-capture, Meade sent elements of the V and VI Corps to re-take the hill. (In 2018, the Central Virginia Battlefields Trust launched an effort to preserve Myer's Hill. You can make a donation to help preserve the land at www.cvbt.org).

Myer's Hill wasn't Warren's only excitement on May 14, though. "During the day," he reported, "my pickets were withdrawn, and the enemy's cavalry got into our hospitals before the wounded were gotten off, but they did no damage. They were unable to capture any of our trains."[13]

13   Ibid.

May 15, 1864: Lull on the Eastern Front

The rain that began on May 11 continued without letup for days. By May 15, Spotsylvania was well-sodden. Grant continued to probe for an opening to get at Lee, but with the Federal cavalry away on a raid toward Richmond, Grant was left without his eyes and ears. As a result, his infantry had to grope blindly, hampering effective movement, made even more difficult by the foul weather.

With the Fredericksburg Road under their control, Federals brought in a constant stream of supplies and reinforcements along a shorter and more secure route than the one they had been drawing on from Culpeper. Here, troops cross the Ny River on their way to the front. Stevenson Ridge is on the ascending slope to the right of the road. *Harper's Weekly*

Lee, too, sought information. He sent a division of troops under Maj. Gen. Joseph Kershaw on a "reconnaissance in force" along the Brock Road front to find the Federal right flank. Kershaw's troops ran into Maj. Gen. David Bell Birney's II Corps division, which made up the new right of the Federal army. After a tense engagement, Kershaw's men withdrew, but not before learning valuable information about the Federal position.

Lee also sent a cavalry force under Col. Thomas Rosser to collect information. Rosser's men tried to circle behind the Federal army, aiming first down the Catharpin Road toward the old Chancellorsville battlefield. Along the way, they routed a regiment of Ohio cavalrymen, who sought the protection of the Federal wagon train in the army's rear. Rosser's men pursued, only to run into a deployment of United States Colored Troops (U.S.C.T.). For the first time, U.S.C.T. forces engaged with elements of the Army of Northern Virginia. This time, Rosser's men were routed—an embarrassment so deep that Rosser refused to mention it in his report for the day.

Meanwhile, along Fredericksburg Road, the Union V Corps spent the day settling into their new position, initially laid out and fortified by the IX Corps. While no major fighting occurred, the property now known as

Stevenson Ridge saw a lot of activity as V Corps forces re-fortified and troops along the front line skirmished with their Confederate counterparts.

May 16, 1864: In the Pits

"All day in pits," wrote an officer with the 95th New York infantry on May 14, referring to his men's time in the earthworks. On May 15, he wrote the same: "All day in pits." On May 16, he wrote the same again: "All day in pits."[14]

The pits, indeed. The rain that had begun on May 11 continued through the 16th, continuing to dampen activity along the Fredericksburg Road.

"Spent the day getting affairs in order," V Corps commander Gouverneur K. Warren wrote on the 15th. "In the evening General Burnside threatened with an attack. My troops under arms to attack as a diversion, if needed."[15] The

V Corps engineer Nathaniel Michler inspected the IX Corps earthworks after Warren's men inherited them. He wasn't unimpressed enough that he urged army headquarters to get the IX Corps a new engineer. *Emerging Civil War*

attack amounted to nothing, though. "Rained heavily in the afternoon," Warren noted.

The soggy conditions and dour mood continued through the 16th. "Remained mostly quiet in lines, getting up stores and supplies, and awaiting developments," Warren wrote.[16]

Quiet for Warren, perhaps, but not necessarily for the men in the

14   Ibid., 632.

15   Ibid., 542.

16   Ibid.

trenches, who were, said Brig. Gen. Romeyn Ayres, "exposed to shell fire and sharpshooters" the entire time.[17] "While here there was continuous firing on the skirmish line," added Lt. Col. John E. Cooke of the 76th New York, "but no distinct engagement."[18]

Officers had troubles, too. "About these times it was a serious question with officers as to how they and their horses could exist without rations—cause, mud," said Col. William S. Tilton of the 22nd Massachusetts.[19]

Overall, though, the men of the V Corps welcomed the opportunity to catch their breath. "These operations were most exhaustive to the energies of the men," wrote Lt. Col. Rufus Dawes, commander of the 6th Wisconsin Volunteers, referring to the army's time thus far in Spotsylvania, "and perhaps most trying to their morale of anything in the experience of the oldest in service, but the hardships were always ready to put forth their best efforts in the most perilous undertaking."[20]

On May 17th, the sun would finally make an appearance. Things at Spotsylvania would begin to liven up once more.

May 17, 1864: The Weather Finally Breaks

"We have had five days' almost constant rain without any prospect yet of its clearing up," Grant told Washington on May 16. "The roads have now become so impassable that ambulances with wounded can no longer run between here and Fredericksburg. All offensive operations necessarily cease until we can have twenty-four hours of dry weather."[21]

During the waiting game, the army nonetheless found ways to stay busy. "[T]he army was employed in constant reconnoitering and skirmishing, developing the enemy's position and learning the ground," said Army of the Potomac commander Maj. Gen. George Gordon Meade.[22]

Despite the weather, Grant remained optimistic, and he felt his army

17   Ibid., 554.

18   Ibid., 630.

19   Ibid., 562.

20   Ibid., 620-1.

21   Ibid., 1, 5.

22   Ibid., 192.

did, too. "The army is in the best of spirits and feel greatest confidence in ultimate success," he attested.[23]

On May 17, the break in the weather he'd hoped for finally came. He couldn't immediately set his army into motion because the roads still needed time to dry, but he himself got to work on his next plan. Since the fight at the Mule Shoe on May 12-13, he had been extending his own line leftward, to the east and south. As he did, Lee somehow continued to match him. Yet Grant reasoned that Lee had to be weak *somewhere*.

Perhaps, he mused, Lee had been pulling from the Brock Road front—just as Grant had been doing—in order to extend his line on the Fredericksburg Road front. If that was so, then it might be worth striking a blow at Lee's weakened left flank.

Grant ordered the II and VI Corps to ready themselves for a move back toward the area the army had assaulted on May 12. He planned to once more send the two corps toward the old Mule Shoe—now gone—and assault the Confederate left.

"Whole army moved to the right in the night," observed V Corps commander Warren, ordered to hold tight along the Fredericksburg Road. His corps "took up lines and intrenched so that we could hold our position alone, and allow the rest of the army to be used elsewhere."[24]

The May 18 assault, planned to be every bit as massive as the May 12 assault, would launch at dawn.

May 18, 1864: Grant's Next Attack

At daylight on May 18, Warren ordered a cannonade all along his line. Twenty-six guns came to bear in a thundering roar.

The "whole army had moved off to our right to make an assault on the enemy," he wrote; he opened the artillery bombardment in support of the assault.[25] It was also intended to discourage Confederates from making a counter-attack of their own along his line, which was now stretched thin to cover the works abandoned by the VI Corps when they moved into position for the assault.

---

23   Ibid., 1, 5.

24   Ibid., 542.

25   Ibid., 542.

To Warren's right, Burnside filled the gap between the V Corps and the rest of the army taking part in the attack. Burnside was attacking, too, once more making a push against the Confederate line at Heth's Salient where the Federals had come to grief on the afternoon of May 12.

In essence, that left Warren to cover the line across the Fredericksburg Road—with his support logistics occupying the property now known as Stevenson Ridge—and southeast to the Massaponax Church Road. Grant had originally wanted to attack there, but a reconnaissance by the VI Corps on May 16 found the Confederate defenses too strong. Thus, Grant had opted to attack to the north, across the same plain his army had advanced across on May 12 in its attack against the Mule Shoe.

Warren's bombardment did not go unanswered. "This occasioned a brisk artillery duel between myself and Hill's corps," Warren said.[26]

V Corps artillerist Col. Charles Wainwright said the Confederates countered with twenty pieces of their own. "The engagement was brisk for near three-quarters of an hour, and the practice on both sides was very accurate," he said.[27]

Meanwhile, Grant's main attack bogged down quickly. "Our forces found the enemy prepared and strongly posted on the right," Warren reported, "and made no serious attack."

In the end, Warren said, "Our army moved back to where it was the day before." In support of their return, Warren's artillery kept up fire "at intervals during the day without any express object," Wainwright said, "and with no perceptible result, except the silencing of the enemy's guns."

Grant realized he had exhausted his options at Spotsylvania. Every time he moved, Lee—with the benefit of interior lines—seemed to effectively counter. However, Grant had transportation advantages of his own: he controlled many of the roads out of Spotsylvania, including the important Massaponax Church Road to the southeast of the Fredericksburg Road. That route would allow him to repeat the maneuver that took the Federal army out of the Wilderness two weeks earlier: they could go around Lee's right and once more move south toward Richmond in the hope of drawing Lee out.

Grant cut the orders to begin a move, but before he could execute it, Lee would oblige Grant's wishes and come out from behind his works for battle.

---

26   Ibid.

27   Ibid., 644.

"One thing is certain of this campaign so far," wrote Dr. Daniel Holt of the 121st New York, "and that is that more blood has been shed, more lives lost, and more human suffering endured than ever before in a season." *Library of Congress*

May 19, 1864: The Battle of Harris Farm

The main action on Spotsylvania's eastern front had opened on May 9 during the battle of the Ny River. Ten days later, in a fight that brought the battle full circle, the last major action of the battle also happened on the eastern front—or, more accurately, in the rear, rather than the front.

Robert E. Lee, discontent to remain on the defensive, looked for some way to strike a blow at Grant.

Following the failed attack on May 18 against the Confederate left, the Union VI Corps withdrew back to its original position southeast of the Fredericksburg Road. Lee sent his own Second Corps in a pursuit of sorts. Just as the VI Corps moved in a clockwise arc to get back into its position, the Second Corps moved in a parallel, wider arc. The Confederates' objective: strike into Grant's rear and disrupt the Federal supply line, communications, transportation, and other logistics.

At about 4:00 p.m., Second Corps commander Richard Ewell's men accomplished their goal. After a brief encounter with several Federal units posted on the west side of the Fredericksburg Road, the Confederates reached the road itself. Their breakthrough occurred about a mile to the northeast of modern Stevenson Ridge, on the north side of the Ny River at a place known today as Harris Farm.

When the Confederates got to the road, though, they found more than they had bargained for—not only wagons full of supplies but regiments full of reinforcements. Grant, whose army had been diminished by more than two weeks of constant fighting, had ordered more troops down from the defenses of Washington, D.C. The first regiments, fresh and large, had begun arriving on the battlefield just the day before, with more of them literally marching down the very road Ewell's men tried to cut.

A four-hour fight ensued, with the Confederates getting the worst of it because of the sheer weight of Federal numbers. "The brigade took position in a wood, and although unprotected by any kind of works, and without the assistance of artillery, several [Confederate] attacks made with all the energy of desperation were repulsed," said a member of the 15th New York Heavy Artillery.[28]

As the green Federals held their ground, more seasoned reinforcements came to their aid from the V Corps, which had been straddling the Fredericksburg Road near Stevenson Ridge. Only darkness saved the Confederates, allowing them to slip away. "[T]he resistance proved too much for him," the New Yorker said.

Grant had already made the decision to pull out of Spotsylvania, with a planned departure on the night of May 19. The Confederate attack at Harris Farm delayed Grant's departure while he waited for any other signs of Confederate aggression.

None came.

And so, Grant ordered his army to begin preparations for the departure originally set for May 19. On the evening of May 20—after a 24-hour delay—the Union army would begin to pull out of Spotsylvania Court House and move around Lee's right flank once more, just as they'd done in the Wilderness.

28   Ibid., 609.

Photographer Timothy O'Sullivan began documenting Spotsylvania Court House in the immediate aftermath of the battle of Harris Farm, including the collection of dead Confederates (see previous page). Here, he shows V Corps camps on the Beverly property, with Federal cavalry milling in the distance. Today's Stevenson Ridge is in the upper-left of the photo. *Library of Congress*

May 20, 1864: The Armies Withdraw from Spotsylvania

Think of the village of Spotsylvania Court House as sitting at the center of a clock. Brock Road, where the armies first clashed on the morning of May 8, sits at roughly 10 o'clock. The Mule Shoe, scene of the horrific hand-to-hand battle on May 12, sits at roughly 12 o'clock (you can decide if that's noon or midnight!). The Fredericksburg Road, where Burnside showed up on May 9, runs into the village at about 2 o'clock. By May 15, Grant had shifted the entire Union line all the way down to the Massaponax Road, which runs into the village at about 4 o'clock.

From Grant's perspective, however, the road ran *out* of the village, to the southeast. That gave Grant a clear path to get around Robert E. Lee's right flank—just as he had done at the Wilderness—and begin moving once more toward Richmond.

Grant didn't much care about Richmond, but he knew Lee would have to come out from behind his defenses and stop Grant from capturing the Confederate capital. That, in turn, would give Grant the chance to crush Lee in open combat using superior Federal numbers.

Grant executed his move on the evening of May 20, sending his II

Corps as bait toward Bowling Green. Corps commander Maj. Gen. Winfield Scott Hancock had the authority to go all the way to the North Anna River, cross it, and capture the Confederate rail junction at Hanover Station. With any luck, Lee would see the lone corps and make a move to pounce on it in its isolation—and then Grant would pounce on Lee when he did.

At Massaponax Church, Grant (standing behind a pew) leans over George Meade's shoulder (seated) to consult on and map out plans—the perfect metaphor for the campaign. *Library of Congress*

As the armies shifted away from Spotsylvania, they left in their wake a blighted landscape. Confederates suffered between 10,000-12,000 casualties, while their opponents had incurred nearly 18,000. Since the start of the campaign, Federal casualties had topped 36,000.

Coupled with the absence of practically the entire Federal cavalry corps—more than 10,000 troopers—and the soldiers required to guard the ever-lengthening supply train, Grant's army would be down to almost 68,000 men by the time it reached the banks of the North Anna River on May 23. Lee, meanwhile, would see a small uptick in his strength thanks to reinforcements from the Shenandoah Valley and Richmond, bringing his tally up to around 53,000. It would be the closest, numerically, the two armies would ever be during the entire 1864 Overland Campaign.

But what happened along the North Anna River is a story for another time.

Harris Farm:
The 1st Massachusetts Heavy Artillery's Baptism of Fire

by Terry Rensel

Point of Interest #8 on the map on pg. xiv.

Originally published as a blog post at Emerging Civil War on May 19, 2021

On May 18, 1864 Lt. Gen. Ulysses S. Grant had decided to move around Gen. Robert E. Lee's right once again in another flanking maneuver in the Overland Campaign. That night the Union's Army of the Potomac started shifting away from Spotsylvania Court House.

Private Joseph W. Gardner of Company K, 1st Massachusetts Heavy Artillery, described May 19, 1864 as "beautiful almost beyond description . . . . The stillness and splendor of all nature was to me ominous, and the thought struck me forcibly that any change in the surroundings and situation could not be for the better, but must be for the worse."[1]

At the same time, Lee sent Lt. Gen. Richard Ewell and his Second Corps of the Army of Northern Virginia to perform a reconnaissance-in-force to find the Union army's right, not knowing that the Union VI Corps

---

1   Alfred Seelye Roe and Charles Nott, *History of the First Regiment of Heavy Artillery Massachusetts Volunteers: Formerly the Fourteenth Regiment of Infantry 1861-1865,* (Worcester & Boston: The Regimental Association, 1917), 153.

had already repositioned itself in preparation for Grant's planned movement towards the North Anna River.

Ewell's corps had seen hard service so far during the Overland Campaign. After the fighting in the Wilderness and at the Bloody Angle, it was down to around 6,000 men; those who remained were hardened veterans to a man but not in the best of fighting condition.

As Ewell began moving around the right of the Army of the Potomac, he began to encounter problems. Due to recent heavy rains, his artillery was not able to ford the Ny River and had to turn back.

When Ewell's two divisions were within three-quarters of a mile of the Fredericksburg Road, they discovered skirmishers from the Fourth Division of the Federal II Corps. This Union division, comprised of heavy artillery units converted to infantry, had no previous battle experience; they had previously manned the heavy fortifications around Washington, D.C. Brig. Gen. Stephen Ramseur's brigade attacked these "green" regiments in the late afternoon, striking the 4th New York Heavy Artillery. The 1st Massachusetts Heavy Artillery, followed by the 2nd New York Heavy Artillery and the 1st Maine Heavy Artillery, rushed to support.

Ramseur's brigade attacked three times, twice in conjunction with Pegram's brigade (commanded by Col. John Hoffman), and each time was driven back. The next day Ramseur wrote to his wife that "We had a terrible fight yesterday eve'ng. & last night. My Brig. behaved splendidly & lost severely."[2]

It wasn't until early August that Ramseur had a chance to submit his report about both the battles of the Wilderness and Spotsylvania Court House. Of the action at Harris Farm he wrote, "[A]fter the enemy discovered our movement, and when further delay, as I thought, would cause disaster, I offered to attack with my brigade. I advanced and drove the enemy rapidly and with severe loss until my flanks were both partially enveloped." Of the battle's waning actions he says, "Several attacks of the enemy were repulsed, and we were able to hold our position until night, when we quietly and

---

2   Stephen Ramseur, *The Bravest of the Brave: The Correspondence of Stephen Dodson Ramseur*, George G., Kundahl, ed. (Chapel Hill, NC: The University of North Carolina Press, 2010), 222.

safely withdrew to our original lines."[3]

The battle of Harris Farm continued until dark when Ewell withdrew to his previous position.

The casualties for Ewell's entire corps are estimated to be approximately 900, while the 1st Massachusetts Heavy Artillery alone suffered 394 casualties, almost 25% of their strength. "[T]he ground was strewn with dead and wounded, and it was a sad sight that greeted us with the dawn of the

The Harris Farm battlefield has turned into yet another housing development, but the monument of the 1st Massachusetts Heavy Artillery still stands sentinel among the houses. *Terry Rensel*

next day . . ." wrote Cpl. J. W. Whipple, Company L. "Many a brave fellow we laid away that day."[4]

On May 19, 1901, the 37th anniversary of the battle, surviving members of the 1st Massachusetts Heavies placed a monument on the ground that they held during the battle, a small knoll near the Harris farmhouse.

That small piece of the Harris Farm battlefield has since been preserved by the Central Virginia Battlefields Trust and is a Civil War Trails site. You can now look down between the rows of trees that frame the site, and on a nice spring or summer day, you can see the splendor of nature and feel the stillness that Joseph Gardner felt that day in 1864, just before the whirlwind of battle exploded around him.

3   Ibid., 225-226.

4   Roe and Nott, 158.

"On the Heights": The Field Hospital at Brompton, May 1864

by Ryan Quint

Originally published as a blog post on Emerging Civil War on May 24, 2021

The wagons rolling into the town of Fredericksburg in May 1864 never seemed to stop. Mary Caldwell, a resident, wrote in her diary, "The road near the fair grounds seems to be literally covered."[1] The wagons were filled with broken and bloodied bodies, debris of the successive battles of the Wilderness and Spotsylvania Court House. For almost two weeks, nearly 20,000 wounded soldiers were brought to Fredericksburg for medical treatment and evacuation from the battlefield.

It can be easy sometimes, in the tumult of the Overland Campaign and its never-ending combat and its ever-elongating list of casualties, to forget about those left behind each time the armies went from one battlefield to renew the fighting somewhere else: the Wilderness to Spotsylvania; Spotsylvania to North Anna; North Anna to Totopotomoy; Totopotomoy to Cold Harbor. To give attention to the wounded, this article will examine the medical care provided in Fredericksburg, using one hospital as a case study. That hospital was at Brompton, the Marye family home atop the heights that bore their name.

---

1   "'It Does Appear as if Our Soldiers Were Made Altogether of Patriotism': The Civil War Diary of Mary Gray Caldwell, Part 1", transcribed and edited by Russell P. Smith, *Fredericksburg History & Biography,* (Vol. 11, 2012,) 79.

On May 8, the Army of the Potomac's commander, Maj. Gen. George Meade, issued an order that "The wounded of the army will be immediately transported to Fredericksburg, and there put in hospital."[2] By the next morning, a long wagon train dropped off the first 3,000 wounded soldiers, who were soon housed in all the nearby "churches, warehouses, and convenient dwelling-houses," as one surgeon reported.[3] More would come in the days to follow—so many that the Army of the Potomac ordered wagons formerly carrying officers' personal baggage to be emptied and turned into makeshift ambulances.[4]

As the wounded arrived, the army's medical personnel tried as best as they could to process them. "Every effort was made to systematize as rapidly as possible," wrote Surgeon Edward Dalton, overseeing all the field hospitals in the city. Wounded belonging to the same corps were to remain together, and "from the medical officers present of each corps one was selected as surgeon in charge," Dalton further explained.[5]

Furthermore, not only were the wounded of the same corps supposed to be together, but the army hoped to house soldiers belonging to the same division. This practice was not always followed, but it nonetheless gives a good indication of where soldiers belonging to the same division ended up in Fredericksburg. The IXth Corps, for example, had almost 2,200 wounded soldiers brought to Fredericksburg, and from there the injured were segregated up by their membership in each of the three divisions.[6]

Brompton's importance as a hospital comes to the forefront through this process. Sitting atop Marye's Heights, Brompton was one of the largest buildings available for wounded patients. It had been shot through by musketry and artillery fire during both battles of Fredericksburg in December 1862 and May 1863, but nonetheless remained sturdy enough to house patients. The Marye family had departed Fredericksburg, leaving their home abandoned. Soon enough, it was chosen as a hospital for the 2nd Division,

---

2   *Official Records of the Union and Confederate Armies in the War of the Rebellion*, Ser. 1, Vol. 36, pt. 2, 527. (Hereafter *O.R.*, followed by Vol. and pt. All in Series 1.)

3   *O.R.*, 36, pt. 1, 234.

4   Ibid., 227.

5   Ibid., 270.

6   Ibid., 236.

The Marye Family home, Brompton, seen during its time as a hospital in 1864. *Library of Congress*

IX Corps. James Noyes, assistant surgeon of the 6th New Hampshire, was put in charge of the medical care there. According to a report filed by the IX Corps, the hospital "On the Heights" had 500 patients during the army's stay at Fredericksburg.[7]

To care for the thousands of wounded flooding into Fredericksburg, the army could only spare 50 surgeons, doctors, and attendants, because of the continued combat at Spotsylvania. Outnumbered and overwhelmed, the army's medical personnel had help on the way. Traveling south from Washington came hundreds of relief workers from organizations like the U.S. Sanitary Commission and the U.S. Christian Commission. They brought many of their own supplies and arrived in Fredericksburg eager to help. Shocked by the sights and sounds of the city, these volunteers nonetheless fanned out and began to assist in whatever way they could. William Reed, one of those volunteers, was sent to Brompton, and his writings offer some of the best descriptions of Brompton as a hospital. "Hours prolonged into days, and days into months of suffering," Reed wrote.[8]

The wounded kept coming until "[n]o available space was left unoccupied," Reed recalled. "They lay as close as they could be placed, the contaminated air growing worse every hour." In an ironic twist, the holes blasted open by artillery fire during the battles of Fredericksburg "assisted

---

7   Noel G. Harrison, *Fredericksburg Civil War Sites: December 1862-April 1865, Volume 2* (Lynchburg: H.E. Howard, 1995), 144; William H. Reed, *Hospital Life in the Army of the Potomac* (Boston: William V. Spencer, 1866), 21; "List, 1862, of Hospitals in Fredericksburg, by an unknown author," Virginia Museum of History & Culture (VMHC). Though the title of the document per the VMHC has "1862" in the title, this is an error. "1864" is written at the top of the document itself, and the hospital references are clearly to "1864", not "1862".

8   Reed, 23.

somewhat in ventilation" and provided fresh air to the patients.[9]

One of the wounded at Brompton was Henry Lancaster of the 31st Maine Infantry. Shot on May 12 at Spotsylvania, he dictated to his wife, "I am here wounded in the right thigh and there is a chance of my [losing] my leg." Lancaster had the writer add that he would "write myself but cannot sit up but have to lie on my back all the time." After receiving the letter, Lancaster's wife, Elsada, wrote back, "if I could be with you to night to attend to your wants you may hav good cair," and, she added in the margins, "you will come home." It was not to be, however. Lancaster "died at 12 o'clock midnight Tuesday May 17," and it fell to William Reed of the Sanitary Commission to write Elsada. "I sat down by his side and held his hand & talked with him a long time about you and his dear children," Reed told her. Before he died, Lancaster gave Reed some papers and a ring, which Reed passed on. Reed finished his letter to the new widow by saying, "The writer of this note belongs for the time to the Sanitary Commission. We do all we can for the noble men who lay down their lives & feel that we cannot do too much for them."[10] Lancaster was eventually buried in the Fredericksburg National Cemetery.

Besides the written records of the IX Corps or William Reed, the best available evidence of Brompton's time as a hospital comes from the images of numerous interested photographers who climbed Marye's Heights in late May. They included James Gardner and a cameraman working for Mathew Brady. As the rainy days of early May turned to sunshine, the weather was ideal for the photographers' work. It was perfect for the patients, too, and Reed wrote that they moved the wounded "out of the stifling rooms to the lawn." The photographers found them on the lawns and soon immortalized them with their cameras.[11]

One of the most famous photographs of the entire war, in fact, was taken during Brompton's service as a hospital. In the image, a dozen or so patients rest under an oak tree, while doctors and attendants look on. In the center, lying on a stretcher, is a soldier with his foot amputated. It at once humanizes

9   Reed, 26.

10   Letters of Henry Lancaster, 31st Maine, in Bound Volume 355, Fredericksburg & Spotsylvania National Military Park.

11   Reed, 30; William A. Frassanito, *Grant and Lee: The Virginia Campaigns 1864-1865* (New York: Charles Scribner's Sons, 1983), 71-77.

Wounded soldiers at Brompton in May 1864. *Library of Congress*

the wounded and those who sought to care for them.

Although the hospitals overflowed with patients and the doctors were over-worked, the Army of the Potomac's medical triage system ultimately succeeded. Having been designated as the evacuation point for wounded on May 8, Fredericksburg's time hosting the wounded lasted just shy of 20 days. The medical personnel at Fredericksburg, though understaffed, nonetheless proved their skill and determination. The wounded were stabilized and sent north to continue their travels to more permanent hospitals in Washington, Baltimore, and Philadelphia. "The removal of the wounded went on with great rapidity," the army's medical director wrote, "and by the 27th of May all had been sent off."[12] Nineteen days and 20,000 wounded—all sent through Fredericksburg. It is a testament to the herculean efforts not just by the army's personnel, but by the Sanitary and Christian Commission volunteers, as well.

Brompton was left bloodied and even further torn up by its use as a hospital, but the building remained standing.[13] The oak tree that offered shade on a sunny day in May 1864 still stands, too, gnarled by age but telling its tales even today. The field hospital at Brompton showed simultaneously the best and worst in humanity; the holes made by cannon balls and bricks chipped by musketry proved the devastation of war, but those who answered the call for help in the chaotic days of early May 1864 told of even greater deeds: that wherever there was destruction and bloodshed, there would be those working to put it right.

12   *O.R.*, Vol. 36, pt. 1, 236.

13   Brompton is now property of the University of Mary Washington. It is not open to the public.

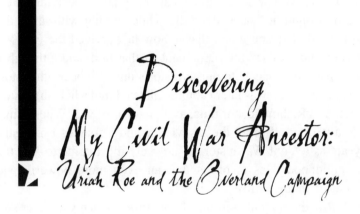

Discovering My Civil War Ancestor: Uriah Roe and the Overland Campaign

by Dan Welch

Based on the blog series "Discovering Your Civil War Past,"
which appeared on Emerging Civil War December 2015–July 2016

It's a common remark many 19th-century historians receive. For those of us in the public history field, even more so. From the battlefields themselves, to public presentations at Civil War round tables, or even manning visitor centers and information stands at historic sites, when the American Civil War is involved, we often hear the following, "I had an ancestor in the Civil War." Having those familial connections most certainly makes those bonds to our past even stronger. Oftentimes as we ask questions to learn more about their ancestor's wartime experiences, usually the responses are, "I'm not sure," or, "I don't know." If there is an answer, oftentimes it is historically inaccurate. Family lore and traditions, in my experience, have placed every single person's Civil War ancestor at the battle of Gettysburg. But, don't worry if this scenario describes yourself. Even many of us historians, public or academic, usually have the same answers as our own research rarely takes us into our own genealogy.

I was much the same way. I had grown up around the holiday extended family dinner table hearing countless stories of one of my Civil War ancestor's war service. The stories told an amazing tale. Receiving a Forest Gump kind of wound at Chancellorsville while serving with an artillery battery, he missed Gettysburg and that is how he survived the war. We'd even visit Gettysburg to see the monument of that unit, and although not at that battle, pay our respects to our ancestor's unit. I'd hear other stories about this same man who was later captured and endured a hellish existence at Libby Prison in Richmond, Virginia, as a prisoner of war. When I finally sat down to avail myself of all the knowledge and resources I had gained over the years as a Civil War historian, not only did I come to find these fascinating childhood tales incorrect, but an even more powerful story previously untold to my family.

Uriah H. Roe did not enlist in the Union armies when war fever swept through the country in 1861. Only 15 at the time, having been born in August 1846, although he could have snuck his way in, concealing his youthfulness or other such measures, he remained at home. Just six months shy of his eighteenth birthday, in the dead of winter of 1864, Uriah finally enlisted in the army. It was February 15, 1864.

Perhaps concerned that his innocent-looking blue eyes, dark hair, fair complexion, and short 5' 6"stature still presented the appearance of a boy too young for service, he inflated his age to nineteen on his enlistment form. Apparently, Uriah had entered the family tradition before heading to the recruitment office. He listed his occupation as a miner, the same as his father on the 1860 Federal census. Later records reveal a personal narrative of confusion. For example, Uriah's Company Descriptive Book lists him as twenty years old at the time of his enlistment, two inches taller at 5'8", and working as a farmer before signing his papers into service. These are not the only occurrences of contradictory biographical information found within his service and pension files housed at the National Archives. At one point the government stopped payment on his pension due to a conflict in his given birth year. He later corrected that issue. Still, the researcher in me yearns for a cup of coffee and several hours of conversation with Uriah to add more clarity to his biographical record.

Regardless of the myriad of answers to the same questions on numerous pieces of governmental and military bureaucracy, nine days later, on February 24, Uriah was officially "Mustered into the service of the United States, in Company 'D', 100th Regiment of Penna Volunteers . . . at New Brighton." He had enlisted for three years of service.

Within weeks, Uriah was sent to join his regiment at Camp Copeland in Pittsburgh. Well over two-thirds of the men of the 100th had just re-upped their service to Pennsylvania and the federal war effort for three more years, and, as a way to sell that offer to the veterans, a furlough had been granted. During the furlough, these veterans had worked hard to recruit and refill their ranks before the coming spring campaigns. Uriah was a byproduct of that recruitment effort. However, he received what many of the hardened veterans of the unit had not in 1861, a $73.00 bounty for his enlistment. Now, as the furlough and recruitment drive came to an end, all were ordered to the camp, veterans and greenhorns alike. Uriah arrived on March 14, 1864. Everyone's stay in Pittsburgh was short lived. On March 23 they boarded a train for Baltimore, Maryland, and by March 25, via steamboat, had arrived in Annapolis. Uriah's transition from civilian to soldier was about to begin.

Upon arrival at Annapolis, the regiment pushed on to their new barracks at Camp Parole outside of the city proper. After a week at the barracks, the men were issued tents and the regiment selected a piece of ground a mile nearer the city. Here they erected a new camp, Camp Burnside, named in honor of their corps commander Ambrose Burnside. It was at Camp Burnside that the raw recruits were drilled endlessly. The veterans of the unit, however, were excused from such labors. As the weeks of drill continued, the regiment was reorganized, and eventually the veterans were brought back to the drill field to be integrated among the new recruits. Ultimately it was their experienced guiding hand that molded these "fresh fish" into part of a solid, veteran fighting force.

Even though recruits worked towards mastering moving from column to line and numerous other commands, by March 31, they had yet to receive their weapons. Through the knowledge of historical hindsight, the fighting at the Wilderness was just a month away. These men still had yet to learn the nine step loading process to fire a musket. Any missed or errored step would either not let the weapon fire or slow the process down significantly. I vividly remember my first time learning this process with my entrance into the field of living history. Getting a percussion cap out of its pouch efficiently and quickly, let alone not dropping it as I worked to get it into its position on the nipple was challenging enough, and I was not doing it under any constraints or combat conditions. To know that Uriah and the other raw recruits would have limited time to receive and train with their weapons before the hellish scene that erupted in the wilderness of central eastern

Virginia just weeks later is a sad reality and frustration that I am sure he and the others felt as well all those years ago.

Other questions filled their minds as well as March turned to April. New recruits like Uriah and hardened veterans were all curious as to where the regiment would be sent as the spring campaign season of 1864 loomed. A part of the IX Corps, the 100th had been reorganized like the rest of Burnside's command. The Roundheads were now a part of the second brigade, first division, of the IX Corps, under the able leadership of Brig. Gen. Thomas G. Stevenson. The Pennsylvanian's brigade commander would be their old regimental commander, Col. Daniel Leasure. Although corps commander Burnside had presented an idea to newly-promoted Lt. Gen. Ulysses S. Grant about an independent campaign in North Carolina, rumors of which swirled around the camp of 100th, Grant had other plans that spring. The men would begin their role in the spring campaign guarding the Orange and Alexandria Railroad as far south as the Rapidan River. They began their assignment during the morning of April 27. Just days later, that assignment came to an end. The IX Corps would join the rest of the Army of the Potomac in its drive through the Wilderness and, with it, battle.

By May 6, Burnside had marched his corps to near Wilderness Tavern and into combat. Some of the units in the corps, such as the 100th, had a march of over thirty miles to get to the front. Just five weeks earlier Uriah was learning his left and right facings with no weapon, and now he had marched a grueling distance and right into combat. I can only imagine his physical condition by the time he arrived into line of battle, exhausted, aching, and thirsty. Yet the thoughts that surely raced through his mind as he was about to see the elephant for the first time are beyond my modern comprehension. Uriah, along with the rest of the 100th and Leasure's brigade were placed along the Brock Road, in support of the army's II Corps. In the thick of the fighting, including a counterassault, the Roundheads sustained thirty-seven casualties. Uriah had seen the elephant, witnessed the horrific scenes of wounded and dead burning in the fires that had sparked during the fight, and the true nature of combat. Just days later, he, along with his comrades and in arms, would be back in at battle at Spotsylvania.

On May 10, 1864, Army of the Potomac commander Maj. Gen. George Gordon Meade ordered the IX Corps to make a "reconnaissance in force" to Spotsylvania Court House. As the corps pushed closer towards their

Burnside's "Advance on Spotsylvania" on May 10 put the Roundheads on the left flank of the entire Union position. According to a short regimental history, the assault "was accomplished with only small loss"—although part of that small loss was Uriah Roe. *Library of Congress*

objective they discovered an enemy line of battle spanning the Court House Road. The Confederate position denied Burnside his final objective, the town itself, just a quarter of a mile beyond. Stopping a half mile from the Confederate line, the second division of the corps set about entrenching their position. Meanwhile, skirmishing and sharpshooting between the lines carried on throughout the remainder of the day. It was during this time that Uriah Roe was wounded. His first battle was just four days earlier and he had been in the Union army less than eighty days.

Initially treated at a field hospital not far behind the line of battle of the corps, Uriah was then sent rearward for further examination and treatment to the much larger general hospitals in Washington, D.C. Upon reaching Douglass General Hospital, the private was admitted on May 16. The examination of his wound revealed a "Compound fracture of phalanges of small finger of R Hand." While at Douglass, an amputation was performed at the second joint of the finger, which later hospital records showed was his index finger, not his small, or pinky, finger. Just eleven days later, Uriah was admitted to another general hospital, this time in Philadelphia. Transported to Summit House General Hospital on May 27, the surgeons there had diagnosed his wound as a "gun shot wound [of the] right first finger," and issued instructions for further treatment of "cold water dressing[s]."

The medical staff at Summit also felt that Uriah "could return to duty July 16-64." My ggg-grandfather, however, extended his recovery via furlough and a trip back to Lawrence County. His hospital card at Summit noted his official return to duty date as August 16. By the time Uriah returned to his unit, much awaited him. First was a bill for $3.00 from the federal government for transporting him back in May to the capital for examination and treatment at Douglass General Hospital. The hits kept coming as Welch family luck and tradition seemed to apply all the way back to Uriah's time as well. He was then further charged "For transportation furnished by Gov't. from Philadelphia hospital, home and return." Three months later, his company muster roll for the months of November and December 1864 revealed that Uriah owed the government even more money as a result of the fallout from being wounded in action. This time the bill was "Due Gov't. $8.14 for equipments carelessly lost during summers campaign."

There were far more important and deeper losses that summer than just equipment, however. The loss of friends and comrades also awaited Uriah upon his return to the unit. Since his wounding on May 10 the 100th had fought at the battles of North Anna, Bethesda Church, Cold Harbor, the beginning of the siege of Petersburg, and the Crater. Each one of these actions had inflicted casualties upon the regiment, yet, there was little time to process these losses. Just days after his return, the Roundheads were back in combat at Weldon Railroad. For Uriah Roe and the men of the 100th Pennsylvania Veteran Volunteer Infantry, the war continued on nearly another year. Over the next nine months, they participated in the actions at Poplar Spring Church, Boydton Road, Picket, Fort Stedman, and the fall of Petersburg. The regiment participated in the Grand Review in Washington, D.C., in May 1865 before being discharged from the army at the end of July in Harrisburg, Pennsylvania. During that time, and only reported decades later on one pension record, he reported a "Slight flesh wound in left hip," with no date or location, and oddly, being "Hit on head at Petersburg VA June 12, 1865" without any context to the what caused the wound or its treatment. Uriah's service also did not come to an end without a curious incident. Despite extensive research, I was unable to determine what happened as he prepared to leave federal service. Buried in only two documents, one in his service record and one in his pension record, the following was reported, "In arrest since July 9, 1865. Charge disobedience of orders." Perhaps I will never know, but knowing the personality of the Welch family line, I have several ideas. None appropriate for publication. But at surface glance, it tells me he was done with active service in the army and was ready to go home. Before he could leave for western Pennsylvania, though, the government was

A LARGE ILLUSTRATED HISTORY

OF THE

100th REGIMENT, P.V.V.

(ROUND HEADS,)

Will be published as soon as we get the pictures and personal incidents necessary to make the book attractive.

Comrades will please send me accounts of personal bravery, special duties performed, incidents of camp, guard or battle, with short biographical sketches, etc., etc.

John H. Stevenson,

No. 100 Fifth Avenue,

PITTSBURG, PA.

Regimental historians compiled a brief history of the Roundheads but they aspired to something more comprehensive. However, like Uriah Roe, many members of the regiment seemed to vanish into the woodwork, and the more comprehensive regimental history went undone. *A Brief History of the One Hundredth Regiment (Roundheads)*

not done dipping into his bounty or his monthly pay. Of the total $140.00 Uriah received as a bounty for his enlistment, by July 1865 he owed the government a total of $160.00, not including a debt to the sutler of an additional $30.50. After nearly eighteen months of service, including being wounded in combat, the almost nineteen-year old traveled back to Lawrence County financially broke and in debt.

My ancestor's postwar life was no easier than his prewar reality. He went back into the coal mines of western Pennsylvania, and, to supplement his income, worked as a laborer for various people. In a written statement in Uriah's pension records, he noted that his seemingly innocuous wound at Spotsylvania plagued his ability to perform these occupations. "Since my discharge I have labored at my occupation as coal miner and have done other kinds of labor," Uriah recalled in September 1881. "But," he continued, "[I] have labored under great disadvantage in doing any kind of manual labor by reason of a bad amputation, leaving the nerve on the end of the stump of my finger exposed very tender." He was not wrong in his assumption of a poorly performed amputation. In 1890, in a subsequent medical examination for the pension bureau, the physician noted in his report "The end of [the] bone of [the] stump is irregular & subcutaneous. The cicatrix is adherent to bone and very tender. Even handling the stump for examination evidently produces pain and trembling of the finger and claimant states 'the pain darts up [the] front of arm.'" At that same physician appointment, the doctor transcribed Uriah's statement in regards to his continued pain from his finger's amputation. It was much the same as he had reported nine years earlier. The "nerves at [the] end of [my] finger or stump are very tender," he told the doctor. It "Interferes with [my] work....[especially] When the end of [the] stump strikes any object considerable pain is produced. A tingling feeling in stump after it has been struck which lasts....and is very annoying." Further, Uriah shared, his stump was "very hard to keep warm in cold weather. Often feels numb." Although he told the doctor that he could still work at that time, he did so "with considerable inconvenience...."

There were happy moments for him, though. He eventually settled down, got married, and started a family. The couple had their first child in 1872. Sadly, the boy, named Walter, died at the age of five. Their next child, Nora, did not survive her first year, and their fourth, Clary, did not either. The Roe's third and fifth children, Elizabeth and William, survived and lived well into adulthood. In fact, during Uriah's future medical ailments it was Elizabeth that took care of him in her home. She passed just two years after her father, but William lived until 1964. Both my father and grandfather spoke during those family holiday get-togethers about William and the stories William shared about his father. Another story for another day.

Over the years, Uriah's prewar and postwar occupations, his wound, and a year of active campaigning in the IX Corps had physically broken down his body. Initially receiving a pension of $2.00 a month in July 1868, as his infirmity increased, so did the financial support he needed to meet his daily necessities and financial commitments. By August 1908, forty years after his initial pension, his monthly disbursement had risen to $12.00. Just four years later, $16.00. In 1916 it had risen to $20.00 a month and by May 1924, Uriah was receiving $72.00 a month from his military service pension. The substantial increase to his monthly disbursement came none too soon. Local physician to Uriah, Dr. W.G. Evans, reported on May 27, 1924 that Uriah "had a[n] areteral hemorrhage May 15, 1924 resulting in

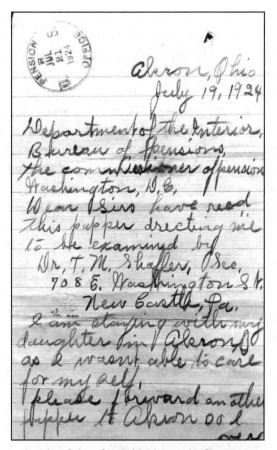

A portion of a letter from Uriah Roe's pension file. *Dan Welch*

paralysis of the right side of the body. Since that time he has required an attendant constantly." Two months later, in July, in Uriah's own hand, he sent a letter to the pension bureau notifying them that all correspondence and payments be forwarded to Akron, Ohio, as he was "staying with my daughter in [A]kron as I wasnt [sic] able to care for myself." Only thirty days later, Uriah was again required by the pension bureau to be medically examined. On August 24, 1924, the examining doctor wrote:

> Unhealthy appearance, stooped, feeble, able to walk with great difficulty with the aide [sic] of a cane. Chest: Emphysematous type. Lungs full of dry and moist rals. Dyspnea upon a light exertion. Heart: The beat is markedly

irregular and the sounds are weak. The muscles of the right side of the body have lost tone and substance. The right leg is very weak and can be used in walking only with great difficulty and for a few steps. Muscles of this leg are flabby and smaller than those of the left. The right arm can be raised but a few inches voluntarily and the grip of the hand is very weak. The skin is bluish and somewhat cold to the touch and although the claimant is right handed the muscles of the right are very soft and smaller than those of the left. On the fifteenth of May of this year, the claimant suffered a stroke of the right side of the body, and for two months was practically helpless. Since then he has recovered to some extent the use of his right arm and right leg, but it is probable that little more improvement will take place. As a result of this disability he requires aid in dressing. He is so feeble that he has to be helped about the house if it be necessary to move more than a few steps. It is unsafe for him to go out unattended.

Uriah's health only continued to decline. It was more than what his daughter could handle on a day-to-day basis. Finally, the family made the tough decision to have Uriah placed at the National Home for Disabled Volunteer Soldiers central branch in Dayton, Ohio. It was incredibly far away, even by train travel, for his two children, his wife having passed years earlier in 1908. It was here, on February 28, 1930 that Uriah passed away at the age of 83, the autopsy noting bronchial asthma as the cause of death.

There is no denying that there is much research to be done on this thread of my family history. The odyssey of researching and discovering just one of my ancestor's military service not only played the mystic chords of memory from over 155 years ago, but also of those moments as a youth just decades ago hearing of those of my familial line that came before. I had to confront the fallacies of family lore and my inadequate knowledge of my own family's participation in the war, despite being a Civil War historian. What I learned was an incredible story of a young man, enticed by a financial bounty, to join the war effort late into its own story. A teenager who in under three months went from civilian life to a soldier, and a casualty of the Overland campaign, a wound and scar he carried for the rest of his life. I had discovered my own Civil War past.

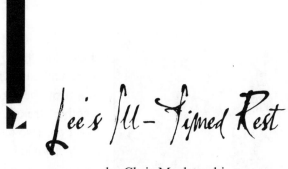

Lee's Ill-Timed Rest

by Chris Mackowski

*Originally published as part of a series of blog posts
at Emerging Civil War between May 20-23, 2014*

Historians often say that one of Gen. Robert E. Lee's greatest talents as a commander was his ability to read his opponents' minds and divine their intentions. I call it "Lee's superpower." While evidence supports that assessment through 1863, Lt. Gen. Ulysses S. Grant's appearance in the spring of 1864 threw Lee's record into disarray. Grant befuddled Lee time and time again. On several occasions during the Overland Campaign, Lee misread Grant's intentions—most notably on May 11 when Grant was preparing to assault the Mule Shoe Salient. Lee mistakenly believed that Grant was trying to slip around the Confederate position as he had done in the Wilderness.

On May 23 at the North Anna River, Lee again misread Grant—with potentially catastrophic results.

Lee began abandoning his line at Spotsylvania in the early morning hours of May 21 and made a beeline for the North Anna River, twenty-six miles to the south. The narrow river had steep banks and made a strong natural position for defense, which Lee had eyed since at least November 1862.

By midday on May 22, Lee's men safely settled in on the south bank, although the march left them exhausted. Rather than direct them to create a strong defensive position, Lee let his infantry rest. Having won the race to the river, he did not believe Grant would be foolhardy enough to follow. Once Lee had secured the Telegraph Road and denied Grant the strategic

By the time the Army of Northern Virginia reached North Anna, Robert E. Lee was too sick to ride his horse, Traveler (above), and had to ride in a carriage. *Library of Congress*

objective of Hanover Junction, there was no apparent reason for Grant to rush headlong into another strongly fortified position. Two hard weeks at Spotsylvania had, Lee assumed, taught Grant that difficult lesson.

Instead, Lee believed Grant would look to once more sidle left and south, pushing east toward the Pamunkey River. Major General Winfield S. Hancock and his II Corps had already led the march in that direction, so it would be easy for Grant to shift the whole Federal army that way.

If Grant did so, Lee would have to counter with a fast march east. That's why he wanted to give his men the chance to rest. Even when Federal infantry showed up on May 23 along the Telegraph Road on the north bank of the river, Lee observed their lines and dismissed their appearance as part of a feint.[1] The real attack would come down river, he concluded.

But those Federals were elements of Hancock's II Corps—the very part of the Federal army Lee expected to be crossing to the east. Indeed, Army of the Potomac commander George Meade had wanted to pursue the easternmost crossing in the face of the Confederate position at North Anna, but Grant overruled him. Lee's army was the objective, Grant had told Meade before the campaign opened: "Where Lee goes, there you will go also."[2]

On the afternoon of May 23, when Federals pushed forward along Telegraph Road at Chesterfield Bridge, and further west at Jericho Mills against Lt. Gen. A. P. Hill's Third Corps, Confederates were ill prepared for what came at them.

---

1   George Michael Neese, *Three Years in the Confederate Horse Artillery* (New York: Neale Publishing Co., 1911), 275.

2   Ulysses S. Grant to George Gordon Meade, 9 April 1864, *O.R.* 33, 828.

Colonel John Henagan's South Carolinians, ensconced in a redoubt next to the bridge on the north side of the river, put up a stout defense but were eventually driven back after a fight one Federal described as "one of the most savage fires of shell and bullets I had ever experienced."

At Jericho Mills to the west, Hill pieced together a credible defense until a gap in the line lead to total collapse. The incident led to the only documented instance when Lee invoked the lost Stonewall Jackson: "General Hill, why did you let those people cross here? Why didn't you throw your whole force on them and drive them back as Jackson would have done?"[3] The rebuke must have surely rankled Hill, whose relationship with the late Stonewall had been extremely rocky.

Assessing the situation that evening, Lee saw an opportunity to turn his near defeat to his advantage, and the elegant trap he then set remains the most memorable part of the North Anna phase of the campaign. What remains forgotten is how close Lee came—once again—to catastrophe because had once again misjudged Grant.

---

3   "The Maneuvers on the North Anna River," *Confederate Military History*, vol. III, edited by Clement A. Evans (Atlanta: Confederate Publishing Company, 1899), 460.

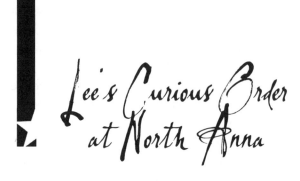

Lee's Curious Order at North Anna

by Chris Mackowski

Originally published as a blog post at Emerging Civil War on March 17, 2015

Reading primary sources is an especially fun part of researching a book. Not only is it interesting to read other people's mail, but as a one-time radio newscaster, I'm always on the lookout for great "soundbites"—those lines or pieces of descriptions that really jump out as colorful or insightful or unique. Another cool part of the experience is finding a puzzle piece that doesn't seem to quite jibe with everything else.

Such was the case as I worked on *Strike Them a Blow: Battle Along the North Anna River*.

Robert E. Lee's army had reached the river early on May 22, 1864, but Lee didn't expect Ulysses S. Grant's army to attack him there. Yet Grant did, on May 23, catching Lee totally by surprise and unprepared.

Lee reacted well under pressure, though, re-configuring his lines into one of the best defensive positions of the war: an inverted "V" that hinged on high ground above Ox Ford. One leg of the "V" extended southwest, manned by Lt. Gen. A. P. Hill's Third Corps; the other leg extended southeast, manned by Maj. Gen. Richard H. Anderson's First Corps. Lieutenant General Richard Ewell's Second Corps extended the line eastward and then refused back on itself to protect the flank.

The formation was elegant. It encouraged Grant's army to advance on two fronts, on either side of the "V," which acted as a wedge, thus separating one wing from the from the other. The isolated wings would have to traverse six miles and cross the North Anna twice in order to support each other—leaving each vulnerable to attack in the meantime.

The apex of the "V" at Ox Ford served as the keystone. Anderson's leg of the "V" made up the center of the entire Confederate line. Hill and Ewell were both anchored to it. In fact, with Maj. Gen. Winfield Scott Hancock's Federal II Corps advancing across Anderson's front, Anderson and Ewell could pin Hancock in place—and then Ewell could swing out of his trenches, pivoting on his junction with Anderson, and crush Hancock between the two corps like jaws snapping shut. This was what Lee had in mind when he later said, "We must strike a blow."

With that in mind, I stumbled across an interesting dispatch. On the night of May 23, as Lee's army reconfigured its entire position into its "V" shape, Lee sent a curious dispatch to Anderson. Stamped 11:30 p.m. and sent by adjutant Col. Walter Taylor, it read:

Major General Anderson:

The general commanding directs that you have the wagons of your corps packed and everything in readiness by daybreak tomorrow to move in any direction.[1]

If Anderson was to serve as the centerpiece for the other wings to attach to, why would Lee want Anderson to be ready to move? Doing so would uncover Hill's right flank and Ewell's left. It would have hobbled the entire Confederate position.

The inverted "V" gave Lee the advantage of interior lines, and the Virginia Central Railroad spanned one flank of the position to the other, giving Lee the easy and quick ability to shuffle reinforcements. However, Lee already held Maj. Gen. John Breckinridge's and Maj. Gen. George Pickett's divisions in reserve for just such a purpose. Anderson would not have been the logical choice for any such redeployment, even as a backup.

---

1   Lee to Anderson, 23 May 1863, *The Wartime Papers of Robert E. Lee*, Clifford Dowdey, ed. (Boston: Da Capo, 1961), 749.

So what did Lee have in mind with this dispatch?

The existing literature doesn't shed much light on the quest. Gordon Rhea and Mike Miller, both of whom have written excellent histories of the battle, both omit this dispatch from their accounts. I admit that I did, too. It just doesn't seem to fit what we know unless I make some assumptions—but in this case, there just isn't enough to go on.

Some pieces of documentary evidence are easy to evaluate and, when appropriate, ignore. One of my favorite examples comes from George M. Neese, a Confederate artillerist who watched Lee on the morning of May 23 as the Federal cavalry first showed up on the north bank of the river. "A single glance from the old warrior's eye, like a flash of genius, instantly penetrated and fathomed the depths of the enemy's design . . ."

Richard "Dick" Anderson was a safe choice to replace James Longstreet in command of the Confederate First Corps after Longstreet's wounding in the Wilderness. While he performed credibly if not brilliantly, one is left to wonder how the battle of North Anna might have played out had Lee's much more experienced and trusted "Old Warhorse," Longstreet, still been with the army. *Emerging Civil War*

Neese wrote in *Three Years in the Confederate Horse Artillery*.[2]

Written in 1911, the author's hindsight has all the hallmarks of embellishment. Lee declared at the time—which Neese recounts as part of the same episode—that the cavalry action he was witnessing was only a feint. Whoops!

An official dispatch from the army commander written on the field in the crucible of the moment is a little harder to simply overlook than is a memoirist's 45-year-old fantasy. What did Lee intend? As ingenious as the inverted "V" turned out to be, was there even more to it than history

---

2   George Michael Neese, *Three Years in the Confederate Horse Artillery* (New York: Neale Publishing Co., 1911), 275.

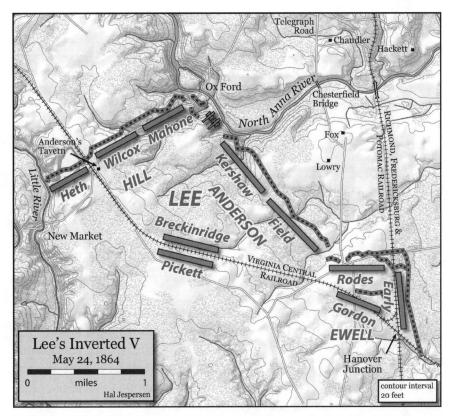

LEE'S INVERTED V *(Confederate position only)*—The commanding ground overlooking Ox Ford gave the Army of Northern Virginia an ideal anchor spot from which to build a strong defensive line that would force the advancing wings of the Federal army farther away from each other. The Little River protected the left flank; a large swamp protected the right. The Virginia Central Railroad, originally Lee's intended line of defense, instead served as an interior axis for shifting possible reinforcements to any threatened part of the line.

has realized? Or had Lee intended a movement that might have ended in catastrophe had he not been too ill to execute? Or perhaps, by 11:30 on the night of May 23, was Lee in his illness starting to second-guess himself? Was he feeling cautious? Pessimistic? Was he just getting confused (and, if so, why didn't Taylor straighten him out)?

It is a thought-provoking puzzle and I don't have an answer, but I thought I would share. Maybe *you* have some ideas. . . .

Lee's Inverted-V Salient

by Chris Mackowski

*Originally published as a blog post at Emerging Civil War
on May 23, 2014*

The Confederate position at the North Anna River in May 1864 has usually been characterized as an inverted "V" *(see map, previous page),* but another way to view it is as a giant salient—a portion of the line that juts out from the main line. Viewed in that light, echoes of the salient at Spotsylvania begin to reverberate. Salients are inherently weak positions, as the Mule Shoe had demonstrated on May 12, 1864.

Converging fire from the exterior of a salient concentrates inward against defenders, whereas the firepower of the defenders diverges outward—it fans out—making it weaker over distance. Also, if an attacker breaks through the line anywhere along the salient, he is then in the rear of the defender's entire position, making it almost immediately untenable.

Gen. Robert E. Lee's salient at North Anna differed from the Mule Shoe in several significant ways, though. The tip of the Mule Shoe pointed toward open fields and, beyond, to a forest that allowed the Federals to mask their approach. The tip of the position at North Anna, in contrast, rested on high banks overlooking Ox Ford. Therefore, the approaches toward the tip of the position could not be so easily assailed.

In addition, the western face of Lee's salient at Spotsylvania did not run along particularly strong ground, and the Union line came within only a couple hundred yards of it—and much of the no man's land in between provided good topography for cover (which Col. Emory Upton exploited for his May 10 attack, for instance). At North Anna, the Confederates dominated a ridge that overlooked open fields with clear views.

The eastern face of Lee's position at North Anna, meanwhile, could be assailed only after the Federals crossed the river farther east, where they could be easily observed, and then would have to face enfilading fire from Maj. Gen. Richard Anderson's corps, which held the eastern side of the position.

At Spotsylvania, when Lee wanted to take advantage of his interior lines for reinforcement, he had to bring his troops along indirect roads and through thick forest. At North Anna, the open, straight bed of the Virginia Central Railroad offered an easy, convenient method for shifting troops if he needed to.

When Lee pulled the wings of his army back into this inverted-"V" formation, he created the illusion that he was withdrawing. He then counted on Grant's aggressiveness to cross the river in pursuit: Maj. Gen. Gouverneur K. Warren's V Corps was already south of the river at Jericho Mills, with Maj. Gen. Horatio Wright's VI Corps in support, and Maj. Gen. Winfield S. Hancock's II Corps seemed poised to cross at Chesterfield Bridge to the east. Maj. Gen. Ambrose Burnside and his semi-independent IX Corps, in the middle, would try at Ox Ford but find himself unable to cross in the face of Lee's strong position there. Thus Grant's army would be divided in two, with two river crossings and six miles of road to march over in order for those wings to support each other.

Lee hadn't expected to fight at North Anna, and as at Spotsylvania he found himself having to adapt to the topography on the fly. When he and his commanders discussed their situation on the evening May 23, they realized that luck was with them this time. The salient that resulted proved to be the strongest Confederate position yet—unlike the Mule Shoe, which had proven to be their most vulnerable.

"We Must Strike Them a Blow!": Robert E. Lee at the North Anna

by Rob Orrison

Originally published on Emerging Civil War
as a three-part series on May 24, 2015

Much is written about Confederate General Robert E. Lee's health throughout the Civil War. Possible heart attacks, strokes, and fatigue began to take a toll on Lee's health as the war progressed. Most physicians agree today that Lee suffered a heart attack in spring/summer of 1863 and that his death in 1870 was due to intermittent rest angina. But it was a common soldier's disease that put Lee in bed at the crucial moment of the Overland Campaign.

The battles of the Wilderness and Spotsylvania saw massive casualties on both sides—casualties the Confederates could ill afford. But the biggest problem for Lee was his loss of generals during those campaigns. The most impactful, of course, was the wounding of Lt. Gen. James Longstreet. Longstreet's replacement, Maj. Gen. Richard Anderson, was still largely untested; outside his ability to successfully win the race to Spotsylvania from the Wilderness, Anderson had little experience and had not earned Lee's full confidence.

Lee had also begun to lose confidence in Lt. Gen. Richard Ewell, who became unreliable at Spotsylvania, first at the Mule Shoe on May 12 and then at Harris Farm on May 19. Lee's other corps commander, Lt. Gen. A.P. Hill, suffered from chronic illnesses that stemmed from his West Point days and became frail and weak—so much so that Hill missed Spotsylvania. Moving forward, Lee had to rely on unproven commanders new to corps leadership. It required more of his time, and he had to change his usual style of dictating broad orders to his commanders. He had to take on matters that he originally delegated to others. As a result, Lee could not afford to be in ill health—but as his army marched southward to the North Anna River, that is exactly what happened.

In April of 1864, Lee wrote his son Col. G. W. Custis Lee that his health was declining from the rigors of the various campaigns and from the weight put on his shoulders by the hope of the Confederacy. Lee told Custis that he was "less competent for duty than ever."[1] The upcoming campaign against Grant required all the fortitude the Confederate commander could muster. From May 5 until May 22, Lee barely slept. As his staff officer Lt. Col. Walter Taylor noted, Lee worked most nights till midnight and woke up at 3 a.m. This was not a healthy regimen for a man already weakened.

By May 24, Lee was stricken with what historian Douglas Southall Freeman called "a sharp intestinal ailment."[2] Lee was so ill that when he met with Hill to go over the previous day's events at Jericho Mills, the army commander rode in a buggy. After Lee heard of Hill's mismanagement of the Third Corps in the face of an opportunity to defeat the Federal V Corps, Lee lashed out at him: "General Hill, why did you let those people cross there? Why didn't you throw your whole force on them and drive them back as Jackson would have done?"[3]

A few days before, Lee had admonished Maj. Gen. Jubal Early over his

---

1   Robert E. Lee to George Washington Custis Lee, 9 April 1864, *The Wartime Papers of Robert E. Lee*, Edited by Clifford Dowdey and Louis H. Manarin, (New York: Da Capo Press, 61), 695-6.

2   Douglas Southall Freeman, *R.E. Lee: A Biography*, Vol. 3 (New York: Charles Scribner's Sons, 1935), 356.

3   "The Maneuvers on the North Anna River," *Confederate Military History*, vol. III, edited by Clement A. Evans (Atlanta: Confederate Publishing Company, 1899), 460.

failure to have his men prepare defenses. "General Lee is much troubled and not well," Early reportedly said afterward.[4]

Lee's health was impacting his demeanor and frame of mind, and his frustration with his commanders, the campaign, and his own health began to impact his conduct.

*   *   *

The Confederate line along the North Anna was one of the strongest the Army of Northern Virginia held during the war. Laid out by engineers, the line was an inverted "V" positioned along the heights of the river. The line was designed to encourage Grant to cross his various wings across the river and to separate them. Lee told Dr. Gwathmey of his line: "If I can get one more pull at him, I will defeat him."[5]

Unfortunately, not only would Lee be struck down with illness but so was his veteran corps commander, Lt. Gen. Richard Ewell. Ewell had suffered various ailments since his wounding at Second Manassas, but that night Ewell passed on his command duties to Early. Early was a good officer and had served brief stints as temporary commander of the Second Corps during the Mine Run campaign and Third Corps at Spotsylvania.

The trap Lee set for Grant was only effective if Grant obliged. In a twist of fate, Grant did just that. Reports from the front indicated to Grant that Lee and his army were in full retreat southward. Most of Grant's corps commanders confirmed as much, and Grant ordered his II and IX corps across the North Anna at two separate crossings, Chesterfield Bridge and Ox Ford; meanwhile, his V and VI corps were already on the far side of the river at Jericho Mills (the incident Lee had scolded Hill for).

The II Corps crossed the river without incident and advanced toward the awaiting Confederates. However, the IX Corps could not advance because Confederate artillery dominated the crossing point. That meant the II Corps'

---

4   George Booth, *Personal Reminiscences of a Maryland Soldier in the War Between the States* (Press of Fleet, McGinley, 1898), 110-111.

5   John Esten Cooke, *A Life of Gen. Robert E. Lee*. http://www.gutenberg.org/cache/epub/10692/pg10692.html.

movement on the left was independent of the V and VI Corps advancing on the right, without being connected by the IX Corps.

Lee's plan was to hold the Federal V Corps with a small contingent of his forces behind earthworks while the bulk of his army attacked the isolated II Corps, aimed at pinning it against the North Anna River. The plan was a rare chance for the Confederate commander to use his aggressive tactics in a defensive position—and Grant gave him the great opportunity.

But as the moment arrived for Lee to attack, his intestinal ailment became severe and he was bedridden in his tent. Without Jackson, Longstreet, or a healthy Ewell or Hill, Lee was prone to indecision. Who could he trust this most important action to? What subordinate could carry out one of the most important counterstrokes of the war? Lee's staff member Lt. Col. Charles Venable wrote that Lee was "prostrated by sickness," and that he called out from his cot, "We must strike them a blow, we must never let them pass us again, we must strike them a blow!"[6]

The coordination of such an attack, however, required the commanding general to be in the front and in control, not supine in his tent. As Venable wrote, the "Lee confined to his tent was not the Lee on the battlefield."[7]

That night, as time slipped by for the Army of Northern Virginia to attack the II Corps, Lee's demeanor worsened. Because of his dysentery, his immobility, his lack of sleep, his frustration with his commanders, and now the missed opportunity, he began to take his frustration out on his staff around him. After a tense moment in Lee's tent, Venable said to cavalry staff officer H. B. McClellan, "I have just told the old man that he is not fit to command this army and that he had better send for Beauregard."[8] Even Lee's trusted advisors saw that he was at a breaking point.

Due to the inaction of Lee and his lieutenants, Grant was able to extract his two wings from the trap Lee had laid for them, and soon the entire Army of the Potomac was safely on the north bank of the North Anna. After the war, Grant wrote in his memoirs that at North Anna "six miles separating

6   Charles Venable, "Campaign from the Wilderness to Petersburg," *Southern Historical Society Papers*, vol. 14, 535.

7   Ibid.

8   Ibid.

the two wings guarded by but a single division. To get from one wing to the other the river would have to be crossed twice. Lee could reinforce any part of his line from all points of it in a very short march. . . . We were, for the time, practically two armies besieging."[9]

A few days went by, and Lee finally recovered from the "common soldier's ailment"—dysentery was something many men in both armies suffered through, and Lee had been no different.

Though Lee recovered, he was always dealing with the stress and pressure of the constant campaigning in 1864. Instead of holding the initiative, he was forced to respond to Grant's maneuvers. In the back of his mind, Lee knew that unless he could do something to check Grant's army, he would be forced backwards against Richmond. Grant was losing battles but winning the campaign—and Lee knew it.

Historians have argued that even if Lee was physically well, the Confederate attack may have punished Hancock severely but would not have destroyed the Army of the Potomac. Obviously Grant proved that high casualties did not dictate his conduct of the campaign. And as the future demonstrated, even the losses at Cold Harbor did not break Grant's path to Richmond or Lee's army.

On the other hand, if Hancock's entire corps had been severely damaged, how would this have played out politically? Large numbers of casualties spread out among corps may have provoked a different response from the public than the virtual annihilation of an entire Federal corps.

We will never know what might have been if Lee were in good health at North Anna or if James Longstreet were present. His present corps commanders were not up to the task and no longer held Lee's confidence. This was Lee's best chance to thwart the Army of the Potomac's offensive through central Virginia. Lee was prophetic in his comments to Jubal Early when he'd said, "We must destroy this Army of Grant's before he gets to the James River. If he gets there it will become a siege, and then it will be a mere question of time."[10]

9   Ulysses S. Grant, *Ulysses S. Grant: Memoirs and Selected Letters* (New York: Library of America, 1990), 567.

10   William Jones, *Personal Reminiscences, Anecdotes, and Letters of Gen. Robert E. Lee* (New York: Appleton and Company, 1874), 40.

These Men I Feel I Know, a Little, at Ox Ford

by Chris Mackowski

Originally published as a blog post at Emerging Civil War on May 24, 2019

To the west, the sounds of industry clank and crunch through the forest. The insistent warning of a backing-up truck beep-beep-beeps in discordant competition. The gravel pit, nestled up to the edge of North Anna Battlefield Park, does not rest today on the anniversary of the battle.

Aside from those audible reminders, there is also the gravel path crunching beneath my footsteps to remind me that I am not far from civilization, although it otherwise might seem so as I make the trek out to Ox Ford. One of the things I love most about this battlefield is the immersive green in all its shades and hues.

To my left run earthworks built by Brig. Gen. Nathaniel Harris's Mississippians, part of Maj. Gen. William "Little Billy" Mahone's division. After 155 years, they remain formidable. On the afternoon of May 24, 1864, the heavens opened on these men as they repulsed an ill-advised assault by Brig. Gen. James H. Ledlie's brigade of the Federal IX Corps. Ledlie, drunk and against orders, felt the need to prove something—what, we don't really know unless it was history's disapproving judgment condemning his own lack of judgment and talent.

Any men deserved better, but I have come to know these men in particular a little better over the last few years. Their brigade had served under division commander Brig. Gen. Thomas G. Stevenson when Stevenson was killed at Spotsylvania on May 10. The four Massachusetts regiments of the brigade—the 35th, 56th, 57th, and 59th—came mostly from Worcester and from the Reedville neighborhood of Boston. They had been posted along the driveway to Whig Hill, the Beverley plantation house directly across modern Route 208 from today's Stevenson Ridge, where I serve as historian-in-residence. Meanwhile, the brigade's two regiments of U.S. Regulars—the 4th and 10th—had been, during the battle at Spotsylvania, detached to the right flank of the corps, stretching from the northern edge of Stevenson Ridge through Ny River swampland to connect with the Union II Corps.

The proximity of these men to me, in geography and in history, has made me sympathetic to them.

For years, their story has hung in the upstairs hallway of my home. In 2008, when my writing partner Kris White got married, he gave to me a copy of Donna Neary's painting *Even to Hell Itself,* which depicts the attack of the 57th Massachusetts against the extreme right of Lt. Gen. A.P. Hill's line held by the Mississippians. Kris knew of my love of the North Anna battlefield, and Neary's was the only painting that showed any action related to the battle. It's a gift I treasure.[1]

As the assault started, reported John Anderson of the 57th Massachusetts, "The brigade was finally launched out like a thunderbolt from the dark, threatening clouds from which the rain was just beginning to descend."[2]

Neary's painting picks up the story shortly thereafter. In it, the regiment's commander, Lt. Col. Charles Chandler, tries to rally his men. Beside him, a corporal wheels around from the impact of a bullet. Lightning tears the sky. Rain, Confederate gray, blots the sky. The far end of the Mississippians' line blends into the raging weather itself. In a few moments, Chandler himself will be struck down, mortally wounded and "the gallant charge," wrote Anderson, would be "turned into a complete rout"—although at this moment of courage, captured on canvas, Chandler has no way of knowing that yet.

There's nothing to say things would have worked out differently for

---

1   Visit Donna's website and order a print of her wonderful painting for yourself: https://donnaneary.com/works/307582/even-to-hell-itself.

2   John Anderson, *The Fifty-seventh Regiment of Massachusetts Volunteers in the War of the Rebellion* (Boston: E. B. Stillings & Co., 1896), 101. Anderson's account of the North Anna, which comprises chapter six, is outstanding. It's available free online: https://archive.org/details/fiftyseventhregi00ander.

these Massachusetts men had Stevenson lived except that his death at the division level opened a vacancy that led to the command shuffle that placed Ledlie in charge of the first brigade. Stevenson, said the 57th's Anderson, "was esteemed very highly by all who knew him as possessing those brave and sterling

The author stands in front of Donna Neary's painting *Even To Hell Itself* at Hanover County's North Anna Battlefield Park. *Chris Mackowski*

qualities which can be relied upon in the performance of duty."

Ledlie, meanwhile, possessed "artificial courage . . . the quantity of which seemed to be sufficient to sustain him through this or any other trying ordeal, but the quality was not of the enduring kind. . . . [T]here was no knowing how long it would stay or when it would be there again."

The descriptions of the two men could not paint more different portraits of their respective leadership attributes.

Such ponderings are ultimately useless because there is no changing what happened, but they are nonetheless inevitable when tied to people you hae come to know through reading and research and shared geography. Empathy is often a historian's greatest tool for understanding, but today, wondering about these poor men in the pouring rain following orders from a drunk buffoon, it just makes me feel bad.

Knowing that Ledlie will send them to calamity in the Crater at Petersburg two and a half months after doing wrong by them at the North Anna makes me feel even worse.

A copy of Neary's painting greets visitors to Hanover County's North Anna Battlefield Park. Beside it stands the park's only monument, honoring "all the valiant men who lost their lives on the battlefield of the North Anna." The trail that leads from there to the ford— made possible by the very gravel company whose work churns onward in the distance—connects memory to history to geography. It is a good path to walk.

Exploring Totopotomoy

by Chris Mackowski
(with a cameo by Phill Greenwalt)

Originally published as a blog post at Emerging Civil War
on May 31, 2014

The first time I visit the Totopotomoy Creek Battlefield at Rural Plains, it's an unseasonably mild day in late winter. I'm taking pictures for the upcoming Emerging Civil War Series book *No Turning Back*, so I can't stay long because I have the entire Overland Campaign to photograph. But I plan to come back for more pictures once things have greened up just a tad, and I'll set aside a couple hours to explore.

When I do, it's unseasonably bitter—low teens. The daffodils look like bright yellow popsicles. Someone froze tiny bits of the sun solid and popped them onto green sticks and stuck them in the ground. That sounds a lot more quaint than I want it to for being as damn cold as it is.

"Totopotomoy" has eluded me for years, and I've decided that the cold temps are the battlefield's way of exacting its revenge on me.

When I say it has eluded me, I mean that on almost all levels. I've not been able to spell its name for the life of me—which, as a writer, makes it a bigger issue than it might be for most people. As a Civil War author who spends a lot of time on the Overland Campaign, it's even more of a problem. It makes me long for something easier to spell, like "Chickamauga."

I've never been able to pronounce "Totopotomoy," either. Working at Spotsylvania, I often refer to Totopotomoy as one of the next steps in the Overland Campaign—yet it's always proven to be a tongue-twister.

"Top-o-pop-o-mee." No, that's not right. "Top-on-top-o-mee?" No, too Irish. "Tot-o-pop-o-mee?" No, no, no.

Say it with me slow: "Tot-o-POT-o-mee." Never mind that the last syllable is spelled "MOY"—it's pronounced "mee."

It doesn't help that a state historical sign along the roadside also refers to "Totopotomoi," a chief of the Pamunkey tribe. Totopotomoi was a British ally killed at the battle of Bloody Run in 1656—one of the bloodiest Native American battles in

The first signs of spring show up on a cold day in Totopotomoy. *Chris Mackowski*

Virginia history, or so I find out later when I do a little research.

It's one of three layers of history—and the earliest one—overlaid atop this property. The second, more recent is its Revolution-era history. Rural Plains, the home that sits on the grounds, belonged to the family of Sarah Shelton. In 1754, Sarah married Virginia politician Patrick Henry in the home's front parlor. The man who later said "Give me liberty or give me death" was happy to tie himself down.

Then there's the most recent layer: the site's Civil War history, which rolled in on May 29, 1864. Francis Barlow's II Corps division occupied this ground. During the three-day contest along the creek, Federals lost just under a thousand men.

Like the pronunciation of the creek, Totopotomoy's Civil War history has eluded me—and I'm not the only one. People are generally so anxious to get to the big ugly fight at Cold Harbor that they skip right over Totopotomoy, which is only a couple of miles away and a couple of days

Lt. Robert Robertson of the 93rd New York was wounded at Totopotomoy. His journal serves as the basis for much of the Park Service's interpretation along the hiking trail. *National Park Service*

earlier. I often cite the North Anna River as the forgotten stage of the Overland Campaign, but if I'm honest, Totopotomoy Creek gets the shaft even worse.

That is, it would get the shaft if the public even knew about it—but generally they don't. It's more like oblivious ignorance than willful neglect. The larger narrative of the Overland Campaign goes: Wilderness—>Spotsylvania Court House—>North Anna River —>Cold Harbor. Totopotomoy Creek, which should be shoe-horned in between North Anna and Cold Harbor, eludes almost everyone.

Richmond National Battlefield preserves 124 acres of the original 1,000 acres of Rural Plains, offering a fairly representative perspective of the Federal position at Totopotomoy. I come here on this most frigid of days to walk the ground with my buddy Phill Greenwalt. Phill and Dan Davis have just finished work on their book *Hurricane from the Heavens: The Battle of Cold Harbor* (which has since been released and is now available). Editing Dan's and Phill's book has given me an excellent understanding of events at Totopotomoy Creek and how those essentially dovetailed first with the battle around Bethesda Church and then down toward the Cold Harbor crossroads.

Phill and I walk the trail, both of us pretending that we're not as cold as we really are. The sun is out, and the day is daffodil-bright—but damn, it's cold.

The trail, a two-mile loop with six stops, leads us past the Shelton House and some dilapidated outbuildings before curling around past some Federal earthworks. The area along the path is wild, but a patch around the earthworks has been cleared so that the neatly-trimmed humps of dirt stand out starkly. In this area, parts of the Union II Corps hunkered down after lead elements encountered "a strong force of the enemy . . . behind [e]ntrenchments of a formidable character."

The path continues on past an old family cemetery. Headstones jut at impossible angles out of the earth, like the nubs of crooked old teeth.

Farther down, past a pair of freshly tilled fields, the path runs into the woods and across a cleared right-of-way for massive powerlines. The last time I saw power towers this large, they were strung around Tokyo to keep Godzilla out.

The Park Service's path

The long bridge over Totopotomoy Creek itself speaks to its swampy nature. When the stream is high, it creates a wide bottomland with several deep channels. *Chris Mackowski*

terminates at the north bank of Totopotomoy Creek itself, but a wooden footbridge crosses the waterway. The creek itself doesn't seem too wide or deep, but spring rains haven't swollen it yet, either. What makes it particularly unappealing as a geographic barrier, though, is that the creek meanders through a wide, marshy bottomland. Stagnant pools, muddy ground, clumpy marsh grass, and finger-thin tributaries make the terrain a mire. Crossing must have been an ugly business.

And then to try and scale the steep bank on the south side in order to assail the Confederate position? No, thank you. Yet Federal soldiers did—or tried to, anyway. Their gritty determination to do their duty never ceases to amaze me.

Today, a path on the south side of the stream switchbacks up that steep hill. It's not Park Service property, but it's been set aside through preservation efforts—a sturdy enough partnership that the wooden bridge connects the NPS trail to the private trail so that the foot tour can continue. Phill and I decide to push straight up the hill as the Federal soldiers might have tried to do rather than take the path (which we follow on the way back down a little while later).

With Lee's men posted along the top of this ridge in a well-fortified position, it's no wonder Grant looked for a way to once more out-flank Confederates. "A few hours were all that were necessary to render a position so strong by breastworks that the opposite party was unable to carry it," wrote one II Corps officer, "and when the enemy had occupied a position . . . ahead of us . . . it was useless to attempt to take it."[1]

I think one reason Totopotomoy Creek tends to get overlooked, then, is because Grant didn't stay here long. Initial assaults met grief, so he said, "Uh-uh." He left men here long enough to tie down the Confederates as he looked for a way around, and once he found one, his men were out of here, snaking further to the left and south.

The Confederate works along the top of the ridge are still in good shape, although they're not so well preserved as others I've seen on the campaign trail. The topography speaks for itself, though. Looking downhill in the direction the Federals had to assault from, I think, "Damn."

Like earthworks everywhere, I have a tough time taking their photos—which is particularly aggravating because that's why I'm here. I give it a shot, as does Phill, but mostly I just marvel at how fortunate it is that this position has been preserved. A housing development abuts it just a dozen yards away or so.

The walk back to Rural Plains is pleasant. The sun has come out, and it's pretending to warm us. Now that we're eyeball-deep in conversation about the war, though, Phill and I don't mind the cold. We're talking about our next book projects. Like Grant, we've come to Totopotomoy Creek, found it imposing, and we're already plotting our next steps for moving on.

But I don't feel as though this ground eludes me any more. Nor has the fighting here. This place, I've come to realize, is a gem. I can't wait for warmer weather—or for the house itself to be open—so I can come back to spend even more time.

In the meantime, I'll work on my spelling and pronunciation.

---

1   Quoted in Daniel T. Davis and Phillip Greenwalt, *Hurricane From the Heavens: The Battle of Cold Harbor* (El Dorado Hills, CA: Savas Beatie, 2014), 33.

"Great Food Service":
The Union Cavalry Holds Cold Harbor, June 1, 1864

by Daniel T. Davis

*Originally published as a blog post at Emerging Civil War
on June 1, 2017*

After taking command of the Army of the Potomac's cavalry corps in April 1864, Maj. Gen. Philip Sheridan was determined to expand the duties of his troopers. Traditionally, the primary role of cavalry was that of scouting, screening and intelligence gathering. But throughout 1863, beginning at Kelly's Ford and Brandy Station, the role of the blue horsemen had transitioned into one of a mounted strike force. Sheridan hoped to build on this hard-earned reputation. His horsemen, he believed, "ought to be kept concentrated to fight the enemy's cavalry."[1]

Sheridan's ambition, however, often came to the detriment of the operational objectives. The Union cavalry failed to secure the main route to Spotsylvania Court House following the battle of the Wilderness. While they managed to mortally wound Confederate cavalry commander Jeb Stuart at the battle of Yellow Tavern on May 11, the following day, on May 12, in a bid to threaten the Outer Defenses of Richmond, Sheridan became ensnared and nearly cut off outside the Confederate capital. Quick and

---

1   Philip Sheridan, *Personal Memoirs of P. H. Sheridan*, Vol. 1 (New York: Charles Webster & Co., 1881), 354.

Federal cavalry cluster around Old Church, a congregation that dates back to 1679, although the building in the photo only dates back to 1853. *Library of Congress*

determined action by subordinates George Custer and Alfred Gibbs opened the way to safety and saved the corps. Sheridan's mistakes continued for on the evening of May 31, 1864, he prepared to abandon a road junction critical to the Potomac army.

In the aftermath of the battle of Haw's Shop, Sheridan withdrew to the vicinity of Old Church with Brig. Gen. Alfred Torbert's division. Brigadier General David Gregg's division was ordered to patrol the crossings along the Pamunkey while Brig. Gen. James Wilson's division remained north of the river. On May 30, Confederate cavalry under Matthew C. Butler and Martin Gary attacked Torbert south of Old Church along Matadequin Creek. Torbert eventually pushed the enemy horsemen back to a crossroads known as Old Cold Harbor.

The next morning, his dander up, Sheridan dispatched Torbert to capture the intersection. Torbert ran into Maj. Gen. Fitzhugh Lee's division, which had relieved Butler and Gary. Supporting Lee was a brigade of Maj. Gen. Robert Hoke's division, recently arrived from Bermuda Hundred, under Brig. Gen. Thomas Clingman. Despite Clingman's added weight, Torbert was able to capture Cold Harbor.

Sheridan, however, remained uneasy after encountering gray infantry. "I felt convinced that the enemy would attempt to regain the place," he admitted. Isolated with only Torbert's three brigades, Sheridan decided to abandon Cold Harbor and notified his superiors.

Unfortunately—and nearly calamitous to the Federals—Sheridan did not fully appreciate the importance of the junction. One road led directly to the Confederate capital of Richmond, another to the Union supply depot at White House Landing. When Lt. Gen. Ulysses S. Grant and Maj. Gen. George Meade received Sheridan's message at army headquarters, they immediately sent a courier galloping off to direct Sheridan to return to Cold Harbor and hold it until reinforcements arrived. Sheridan received the message late that night and reoccupied Cold Harbor under the cover of darkness. To support the cavalry, Grant and Meade decided to pull Maj. Gen. Horatio Wright's VI Corps from the Union line on Totopotomoy Creek and send it to Cold Harbor.

Federal cavalry held the intersection at Old Cold Harbor, which got its name from Burnett's Inn. The inn thereafter remained behind Union lines. "Our position was anything but satisfactory, and we began to dig for our lives," one Maine trooper later wrote of the cavalry's initial posting there. *Library of Congress*

Robert E. Lee was also troubled by Sheridan's presence at Cold Harbor. Late on the afternoon of May 31, he decided to shift Maj. Gen. Richard Anderson's First Corps to the area to reinforce Hoke.

Shortly after daylight on June 1, Maj. Gen. Joseph Kershaw's division from Anderson's corps approached Cold Harbor where Sheridan waited. Torbert had positioned Brig. Gen. Wesley Merritt's brigade on the right, Brig. Gen. George A. Custer held the left. Colonel Thomas Devin backstopped Custer.

Leading Kershaw's advance was his old brigade, under the command of Col. Lawrence Keitt. "As soon as the line was formed the order of advance was given, with never so much as a skirmish line in front," wrote a member of the 3rd South Carolina. "Keitt led his men like a knight of old—mounted upon his superb iron gray . . . across a large old field the brigade swept towards a densely timbered piece of oak-land. . . . Colonel Keitt was a fine target for the sharpshooters, and fell before the troops reached the timber."[2]

Behind makeshift barricades, the Union cavalry unleashed a "furious"

---

2   David Augustus Dickert, *History of Kershaw's Brigade* (Newberry, SC: Elbert H. Aull Company, 1899), 24.

volley recalled Maj. James Kidd of the 6th Michigan in Custer's brigade. Like Keitt, Custer also made a conspicuous target, riding up and down the line observing the engagement. On Custer's right, a member of the 1st New

York Dragoons in Merritt's brigade wrote "that those brave Confederates . . . were literally piled in heaps from the effects from our destructive fire."[3]

"The woods took fire from exploding shells," wrote one of the regiment's officers, "and the shrieks of the rebel wounded were first heightened, then stifled by the flames."[4]

"Two severe charges were made," Merritt wrote in his official report, "but each time they were repulsed with considerable loss. The First New York Dragoons and Second Cavalry did great good service in this fight."[5]

Around 10 a.m., Wright's infantry arrived to relieve Sheridan's troopers. Although Cold Harbor was secure, Sheridan's lack of foresight nearly cost the intersection to the Confederates. Its loss to the Confederates would have opened the road to Grant's and

While Confederate cavalry ended on the losing side of most of the encounters leading up to Cold Harbor, Jeb Stuart's replacement, Wade Hampton, ultimately benefitted from the experience. His abilities as a commander continued to grow. A little over a week after Cold Harbor, Hampton would defeat Sheridan at the battle of Trevilian Station, and Hampton would continue to perform exceptionally through the remainder of the war. *Library of Congress*

Meade's supply base and effectively cut off further Union movement to the southeast. But for the second time in two days, Sheridan's troopers had bested enemy infantry. His transformation of the corps was proving successful and would continue in the weeks and months ahead.

---

3   James Riley Bowen, *Regimental History of the First New York Dragoons During Three Years of Active Service in the Great Civil War* (published by author, 1900), 182.

4   Ibid.

5   *O.R.* 36, Pt. 1, 249.

The Union Assaults at Cold Harbor, June 1, 1864

by Daniel T. Davis

Originally published as a blog post at Emerging Civil War on June 1, 2015

All through the night of May 31 and into June 1, 1864, Maj. Gen. Horatio Wright's VI Corps trudged along dusty and choked Virginia byroads. Pulled from the Union right flank, Wright had received orders to relieve Maj. Gen. Philip Sheridan's cavalry at Old Cold Harbor. Nearing the crossroads, Wright's men undoubtedly heard gunfire ahead. Around daybreak that morning, Maj. Gen. Richard Anderson's First Corps of Robert E. Lee's Army of Northern Virginia reinforced Confederates under Maj. Gen. Robert Hoke and attacked Sheridan's cavalrymen in their lines around the junction. Fortunately for the Federals, their line held.

Around 10 a.m., Wright arrived and relieved the tired troopers. Despite the condition of his exhausted men, Wright had orders to attack. Joining in the assault was the newly arrived XVIII Corps and one division from the X Corps under the overall command of Maj. Gen. William "Baldy" Smith. The Union veterans spent the morning deploying into line of battle for the assault.

As the Federal soldiers got into position, many of them caught a glimpse of the Cold Harbor tavern and surrounding countryside. "Of all the wastes I have seen, the first sight of Cool Arbor was the most dreary," wrote Col. Theodore Lyman, a Union staff officer. "Fancy a baking sun to begin with

Edwin Forbes sketched the VI Corps in action at Cold Harbor on June 1, 1864. *Library of Congress*

. . . wretched house . . . open plain, trampled fetlock deep into fine, white dust...on the sides and in the distance . . . were pine woods. . . . [I]t was Sahara intensified and was called Cool Arbor!"[1]

It took most of the day, some eight hours, for Wright and Smith to deploy. Not until 6 p.m. did Wright, in overall command, gave the order to move forward. Although both Wright and Smith shared responsibility for the assault, the most unique aspect of the attack occurred in the left center of the Union line near the Cold Harbor Road.

The main characteristic that marked the Overland Campaign from a tactical perspective was the evolution of field works by the Army of Northern Virginia. Beginning at Spotsylvania, without a natural defensive position to utilize, the Confederates began constructing earthworks. As the armies moved from Spotsylvania to the North Anna and finally to Cold Harbor, the

---

1   George R. Agassiz ed. *With Grant and Meade From the Wilderness to Appomattox by Colonel Theodore Lyman* (Lincoln, University of Nebraska Press 1994), 140.

soldiers from both sides refined their craft and, by early June, the trenches resembled small, fortified cities.

To compensate and adapt to this change, a V Corps colonel from New York named Emory Upton had spearheaded a revolutionary idea. At Spotsylvania, Upton launched an assault utilizing a column formation of four successive lines, each containing three regiments, ordering his men not to fire until they reached the Confederate trenches. The Union army implemented this tactic on a grander scale against the Mule Shoe Salient on May 12 and six days later on "Lee's Last Line." For the Union assault on the evening of June 1, Upton (now a Brigadier General) planned a similar assault.

Upton formed his brigade by stacking his regiments one upon the other. The 2nd Connecticut Heavy Artillery, divided by battalions, formed the first line; the 5th Maine, 95th and 96th Pennsylvania and elements of the 121st New York formed the second line. Upton probably planned for the lines to move forward in concert; however, the 2d Connecticut would bear the brunt of the assault while the second line awaited the outcome. If the "Heavies" were successful, the second line would move up and exploit the breach in the enemy works. Should the first line meet heavy resistance, individual regiments from the second line would move forward to their support in the hopes that the weight of the additional regiments would eventually crack the enemy position.

"The front line started on a running charge toward the breastworks, obliquing to the right where the breastworks were on a little eminence in the edge of a pine woods," remembered a soldier in the 121st New York watching from the distance:

> As soon as the heavies began to charge, the Rebel works were bordered with a fringe of smoke from the muskets and the men began to fall very fast, and many wounded began going to the rear. A little in front of the works there was a hollow, and as the column went into this it seemed to pause and the rear lines closed up. The Rebel fire was very effective and it seemed to us from where we stood that our poor fellows would all get shot. The ground over which they had passed was covered with men. We could see them fall in all shapes. Some would fall forward as if they had caught their feet and tripped and fell. Others would fall backward. Others would stagger about a few paces before they dropped . . . our men could not get up to their works . . . because the trees had been cut and so piled together that in places men could not get through. In some places, gaps or lanes had

been left in the slashings, and it was in these places that our men reached the works. After a determined and desperate attempt to take them they lay down in front of them and General Upton took a portion of the command to the right where the works had been carried, and moving down to the left, drove the Rebels out of the works in front of which our men had been repulsed . . . here . . . an incessant fire was kept up . . . until after midnight.[2]

"The Second Connecticut . . . moved to the assault in beautiful order crossing an open field, it entered a pine-wood, passed down a gentle declivity and up a slight ascent," Upton recalled.

Here the charge was checked. For seventy feet in front of the works the trees had been felled, interlocking with each other, and barring all further advance. Two paths, several yards apart, and wide enough for four men to march abreast, led through the obstructions. Up these, to the foot of the works, the brave men rushed, but were swept away by a converging fire, unable to carry the [e]ntrenchments. I directed the men to lie down, and not to return fire. Opposite the right of the regiment, the works were carried . . . the regiment was then marched to the point gained, and, moving to the left, captured the point first attacked. In this position, without support on either flank, the Second Connecticut fought, when the enemy fell back to a second line of works.[3]

Darkness ultimately brought an end to the fighting. Despite the limited hours of daylight, Wright and Smith gained ground and captured the first line of enemy earthworks and emboldened Lt. Gen. Ulysses S. Grant. Perhaps another, much larger assault in the coming days would finally crack the Confederate line and open the road to Richmond.

---

2   Isaac O. Best, *History of the 121st New York State Infantry* (Baltimore: Butternut and Blue, 1996) 155-156.

3   United States War Department, *The War of the Rebellion: A Compilation of the Official Records of the Union and Confederate Armies,* 70 vols. in 128 parts (Washington D.C.: Government Printing Office, 1880-1901), Series I, volume 36, part 1, 671.

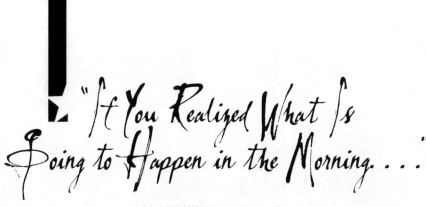

"If You Realized What Is Going to Happen in the Morning...."

by Phillip S. Greenwalt

Originally published as a blog post at Emerging Civil War on June 2, 2014

As June 1, 1864, turned into the history books, both sides reevaluated the current dispositions of their respective forces—and both leaders, Grant and Lee, sidled troops to the now very critical Virginia crossroads of Cold Harbor.

"What are your views about to-morrow?" George Meade, the nominal head of the Union Army of the Potomac, wrote on the night of June 1 in a dispatch to Grant.

During that day, action had raged back and forth around Cold Harbor. On the Confederate side, Robert Hoke's division, which had been reassigned to the Army of Northern Virginia in late May, along with elements of Richard Anderson's First Corps, had tried their best to not only stem the Union advance but recapture the important crossroads.[1]

Grant wanted to continue the offensive, but wanted to wait until more men could be shuttled down to the Union left flank. When Confederate lookouts spotted movements of Union forces shifting from the Confederate

---

1   Louis J. Baltz III, *The Battle of Cold Harbor, May 27 – June 13, 1864* (Lynchburg, VA: H.E. Howard, 1994), 117.

Confederates continued to strengthen their lines throughout June 2, 1864, in anticipation of renewed Federal assaults. *Library of Congress*

left to the right, Lee had to respond in turn. He chose for the assignment another division of recently arrived reinforcements.

Under the command of a one-time vice president, the troops serving under John C. Breckinridge had come east after defeating a Union force at the battle of New Market. Yet, Breckinridge's forces would have a difficult night of marching ahead of them, compounded by the fact that their guide was not all that familiar with the road network behind the Confederate lines.

Two more Confederate divisions would also be detached from the Confederate left and marched behind the lines to reach the Confederate right flank: Cadmus Wilcox's and William Mahone's Third Corps divisions would continue the Confederate build-up and finally anchor the right flank on the Chickahominy River.

Yet, Lee was cagey and was not just going to react to Grant's movement of troops. While three divisions sidled to the right, the now-extreme left flank of the Confederate army, occupied mostly by the Second Corps, moved forward with the remaining Third Corps division under Harry Heth and drove into Ambrose Burnside's Union IX Corps.

Remembered by participants as "a heavy discharge of shot and shell" and "heavy fighting," Early's attack initially drove elements of the IX Corps "from their entrenchments," but the advanced sputtered and then was driven back when the Union V Corps lent a hand. Once again, Bethesda Church was the scene of intense fighting.[2]

Meanwhile, other Confederates used the lull in fighting along most of the rest of the line to continue digging, making their earthworks even stronger. An exchange between soldiers in the 4th Alabama highlighted the importance of these earthworks for the fighting that both sides knew was coming on the morrow:

Sergeant Murphy stopped to chat with a lieutenant that had completed his work on the his portion of the entrenchments: "My goodness, Lieutenant, you can certainly beat any of us at it [digging of trenches]."[3]

"Yes, and if you realized what is going to happen in the morning you would be at it yourself," the young junior officer replied.[4]

"What is going to happen in the morning. . . ."

That was the question—more pondered than asked—by thousands of restless souls, from army commanders to the lowliest private, on the night of June 2.[5]

---

2   Ibid., 125.

3   Coles, R.T., *From Huntsville to Appomattox, R.T. Coles's History of 4th Regiment, Alabama Volunteer Infantry, C.S.A., Army of Northern Virginia*, edited by Jeffrey D. Stocker (University of Tennessee Press: Knoxville, TN, 1996), 174.

4   Ibid.

5   Information for the general movements described above came from the following two sources: Gordon, C. Rhea, *Cold Harbor: Grant and Lee, May 26 – June 3, 1864* (LSU Press: Baton Rouge, 2007) and Daniel T. Davis & Phillip S. Greenwalt, *Hurricane From the Heavens: The Battle of Cold Harbor, May 26 – June 5, 1864* (Savas Beatie, LLC: El Dorado Hills, CA, 2014).

Fighting on the Same Ground: The 10th New York Infantry at Gaines's Mill and Cold Harbor

by Edward Alexander

Originally published as a blog post at Emerging Civil War on June 27, 2021

Civil War soldiers occasionally found themselves fighting on the same battlefield multiple times. However, veteran members of the 10th New York Infantry had a distinction of attacking the exact spot they had defended two years before. Both battles included two of the war's more notable assaults, and the New Yorkers' experience illustrated how the war had changed over those two years.

The 10th New York Infantry mustered immediately into service in late April and early May 1861. New York City and Brooklyn companies composed the regiment, which took its nickname "National Zouaves" from the color uniforms the soldiers wore. The regiment sailed straight for Hampton Roads and disembarked at Camp Hamilton. They saw limited service at Big Bethel before settling into camp for the remainder of the year. After a brief expedition during the capture of Norfolk, the 10th New York joined the Army of the Potomac in early June 1862. The regiment, then under the command of Col. John E. Bendix, reported to Gouverneur Warren's brigade in Fitz John Porter's V Corps. They paired with another

Zouave regiment, the 5th New York Infantry, but by that point the Tenth had rotated a more practical fatigue uniform in with their fancy outfits.

George McClellan's advance of the Army of the Potomac toward Richmond isolated Porter's corps on the north side of the Chickahominy River. The 10th New York did not fight at Beaver Dam Creek during the first Confederate attack of the Seven Days' Battles. However, the next morning, June 27, the regiment's 575 officers and men took their place near the right of Porter's rear-guard line on a ridge between Boatswain Creek and the Chickahominy River. There they awaited another Confederate attack. "The ground, generally open in front, was bounded on the side of the Confederate approach by a wood with dense and tangled undergrowth, and traversed by the sluggish stream which formed the bed of the ravine on the left," recalled Sergeant Charles W. Cowtan.[1]

The first Confederate charges at the battle of Gaines's Mill occurred in the early afternoon. Warren's brigade, still composed of just the two New York Zouave regiments, moved down into the wooded Boatswain Creek valley and repulsed spirited charges by Maxcy Gregg's South Carolinians and Lawrence Branch's North Carolinians. Sergeant Cowtan afterward wrote in his regimental history:

> The contest in these woods was fierce for a time, each company of our regiment coming in for its full share in the action. It was the first battle for us, and the manner in which the wings of the regiment were doubled and lapped over each other, with utter impossibility of keeping the line intact, in consequence of its peculiar formation and the converging fire of both musketry and artillery, was a novelty to those who had often imagined the command in battle dressed as if on parade.[2]

With the arrival of reinforcements, Warren took advantage of a brief lull to pull his men back to their original position to support an artillery battery. They remained in reserve as additional Confederate attacks on both flanks began overwhelming Porter's position. Warren once again rushed his two regiments

---

1   Charles W. Cowtan, *Services of the Tenth New York Volunteers (National Zouaves,) in the War of the Rebellion* (New York, NY: Charles H. Ludwig, 1882), 90.

2   Ibid., 92.

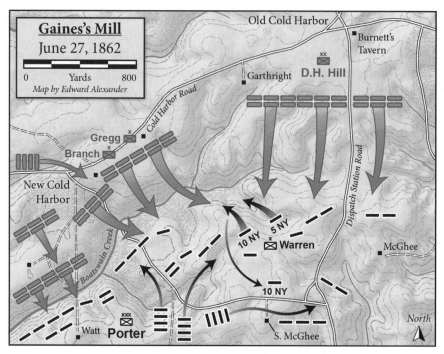

GAINES'S MILL—The 5th and 10th New York felt the brunt of Confederate attacks from both their twelve o'clock and their ten o'clock. The 10th fell back to a piece of high ground near the McGhee house.

forward, but the ferocity of the attacks compelled the Union high command to abandon the position north of the Chickahominy. The 10th New York suffered eight men killed and two mortally wounded, over forty wounded, and an additional seventy missing in the one day of fighting. They remained in reserve through the rest of McClellan's withdrawal to the James River.

Later that year the regiment saw hard combat at Second Bull Run and Fredericksburg. In between those two battles the 10th New York transferred from the V to the II Corps. The majority of the regiment had signed up for two years of service, so in the spring of 1863 those with remaining time consolidated under Col. George F. Hopper into a battalion of four companies. Spared a large role at Chancellorsville and Gettysburg, this smaller force saw its numbers boosted with new recruits. The following year, it fought again at the Wilderness and Spotsylvania. The transfer to the II Corps meant that when Ulysses S. Grant ordered Winfield Hancock's corps to Cold Harbor in early June, the 10th New York found themselves facing the position they had previously held at Gaines's Mill, albeit from a different angle.

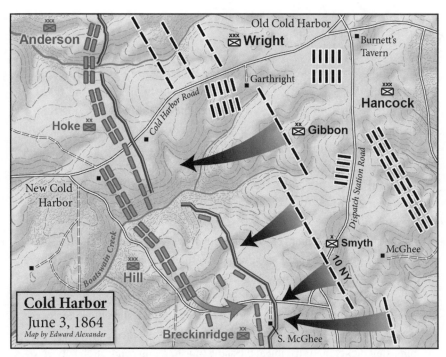

COLD HARBOR—The battlefield at Cold Harbor was reoriented ninety degrees counter-clockwise compared to the fight at Gaines's Mill the year before. The 10th New York found itself attacking the very ground near the McGhee house the regiment had held in the earlier fight.

Grant intended for Hancock to attack on June 2, but the exhausting march to get into place prevented the swift fulfillment of those orders. As the II Corps marched from the far right to far left end of the Union line, the 10th New York passed well to the rear behind their former comrades in the V Corps who maintained a position near Bethesda Church. As the II Corps reached its assigned position south of Burnett's Tavern at the Old Cold Harbor crossroads, the 10th New York recognized the familiar landscape. Cowtan, now a company adjutant, afterward noted:

> The tavern by the roadside, and the antiquated well hard by, recalled fast
> trooping memories to the minds of those who had braved the Seven Days
> battles and the campaigns following, and who were now enabled to again
> look upon some of the scenes of their earlier military experience. Many
> members of the regiment, sanguine in their expectation of a speedy close
> of the struggle, then but just begun, had since that time given up their lives
> for the cause they deemed just. Such thoughts were hardly calculated to

brighten the minds of our soldiers, already overtaxed by want of rest, and they were glad to recall their senses to present surroundings.[3]

Undaunted by the delayed march and attack, Grant expected Hancock, alongside the VI and XVIII Corps, to charge westward from the Old Cold Harbor crossroads into a heavily entrenched Confederate position the following morning. Colonel Hopper's soldiers recognized a house where they had supported the V Corps artillery in 1862 as an objective of their assault. The infamous attack on June 3, 1864, proved highly costly and unsuccessful across the entire front. Cowtan vividly described the 10th New York's experience:

At the appointed moment our brigade advanced with its full front, passing its vidette posts and entering the woods without a sound being emitted by the men. A scattering volley from the enemy's pickets was followed by a discharge of artillery from their lines—the shot sweeping and crashing amid the trees and the shrapnel doing execution in all directions. Silence was now useless and our line swept forward with a cheer, capturing the opposing pickets and striving at the same time to retain connection between the regiments—broken by the swampy ground and natural obstructions, which caused portions of the line a considerable detour.

The brigade swung along on its forward course, regardless of the missiles of death which decimated the ranks, until the woods were cleared by the Tenth and the enemy's intrenchments broke into full and unobstructed view across an open space completely swept by cannon and musketry. The fire at this instant was murderous—the men of the brigade falling as thick as forest leaves.

Our little battalion made a brave attempt to breast the storm, but it threatened inevitable death to all, and the scattered regiments at this point of the line threw themselves flat on the earth for protection. No troops followed us, and it would have been a sheer impossibility to have crossed

3   Ibid., 280.

the open ground which intervened and captured the intrenchments with our thin and straggling line.[4]

Whereas the Confederate attack at Gaines's Mill attacks in 1862 spanned all afternoon and into the evening, the Union charge went to ground just after it began that 1864 morning. The veteran soldiers did not budge for the remainder of the day. The construction of field fortifications altered the tactics of the assault as well as the willingness of the men to make those attacks. Strategic goals also mattered. While Robert E. Lee needed to drive the Army of the Potomac away from Richmond in 1862 and personally desired to achieve a decisive tactical victory, even at high cost to the Army of Northern Virginia, Grant disengaged from lost battles and stalemates to position his armies to continue the campaign's strategic vision.

Thus, in addition to being a neat trivia piece as what appears to be the only Army of the Potomac infantry regiment fighting at the same place in those two famous battles, the 10th New York's experience on the same ground at both Gaines's Mill and Cold Harbor demonstrated the evolving nature of Civil War strategy and combat.

4   Ibid., 281-282.

The Myths of Cold Harbor

by Robert "Bert" Dunkerly

Originally published as a blog post at Emerging Civil War
on June 3, 2021

Certain battles have numerous myths and misconceptions attached to them. Perhaps one of the most myth-shrouded battles is the June 1864 Cold Harbor engagement near Richmond. Part of the Overland Campaign, it was at the tail end of Grant's grueling drive across central Virginia.

Many readers likely know that one of the most persistent myths of Cold Harbor is the estimate of 6,000 (or whatever high number you insert here) Union killed and wounded in just 30 minutes on June 3. Total Federal losses for the entire day were about 3,500, including the morning attack and later fighting. That's fewer men than fell in the Union attack at Fredericksburg or in Pickett's Charge at Gettysburg.[1]

To many of us, Cold Harbor seems like a nameless, senseless battle, lacking maneuver and without key landmarks. Gettysburg has its Wheatfield, Peach Orchard, and High Water Mark. Antietam has the Cornfield and the Sunken Road. Shiloh has the Hornets' Nest and Bloody Pond. What does Cold Harbor have?

In fact, in the first few days, there was open-field fighting and maneuver at Cold Harbor. And there were landmarks on the battlefield named by

---

1 Gordon C. Rhea, *Cold Harbor* (Baton Rouge: Louisiana State University Press, 2002), 359-62; Daniel T. Davis and Phillip S. Greenwalt, *Hurricane From the Heavens* (El Dorado Hills, CA: Savas-Beatie, 2014), 97.

the soldiers: Bloody Run, the Allison Farm, the Crossroads, Fletcher's Redoubt, and more. This battle simply has not been studied in the same detail as many others, nor has it been as well preserved, thus the lack of familiarity with these landmarks.

Another misconception is that the entire affair was a lopsided Union defeat. In the end, it was. But for the first few days it was touch and go, and in fact, when one dissects the fighting, it was not such a neat, clean, and easy Confederate victory. On May 31, Union cavalry wrestled the vital Cold Harbor crossroads from Confederate troopers. Then on June 1, a Confederate infantry counterattack failed miserably. That evening Union troops arrived and successfully

In his memoirs, Grant wrote, "I have always regretted that the last assault at Cold Harbor was ever made. . . . No advantage whatever was gained to compensate for the heavy loss we sustained." Because he wrote little else about the battle compared to other topics in his memoirs, his statement seemed to settle the matter—spawning decades of misconceptions. *Emerging Civil War*

drove their adversaries back. That makes three Confederate failures within two days, with significant numbers of prisoners taken. No wonder Grant wanted to escalate the battle here.[2]

Once the main battle began, a Confederate counterattack on June 3 led by Floridians failed disastrously, as did smaller attacks against Union troops on June 6 and 7. By then, both sides had dug in. One Union observer wrote of the June 6 attack against Fletcher's Redoubt that, "beyond making a great noise resulted in very little damage."[3]

2   Davis and Greenwalt, 64-5.

3   Jacob Roemer, *Reminiscences of the War of the Rebellion 1861-1865* (Flushing, NY, 1897), 214-16; Samuel A. Beddall, *Diary* (United States Army Military History Institute, Carlisle, PA).

So why do we look at Cold Harbor as a Union disaster? These Confederate missteps were overshadowed by the scope and scale of the Union failed assaults. Yet we should not forget that they occurred. While most of the Army of Northern Virginia saw Cold Harbor as a victory, for a select few units it was frustrating and deadly.

This brings up another point: to truly appreciate Cold Harbor, we must recognize that it was more than the events of June 1 and 3—much more. The battle lasted from May 31 to June 12—two weeks. Name another engagement that lasted that long, with the armies in constant contact. Perhaps that is why the one- or two-day battles are easier to study; they are easier to grasp.

Those who study the Civil War recognize that Cold Harbor showcased the inefficient system of replacing troops in the Union army. A number of heavy artillery regiments had joined the Army of the Potomac recently and fought their first battle here. Converted to infantry and marching and fighting in the field for the first time, they often suffered terribly. Examples include the 330 men lost by the 2nd Connecticut Heavy Artillery and the more than 500 lost by the 8th New York Heavy Artillery.

Yet the Confederates were bringing in rookies, too, and they suffered just as badly. Both armies needed fresh manpower by late May, and just as the Union was stripping its garrisons in Washington and Baltimore, the Confederacy was doing the same thing.[4] New troops joined the Army of Northern Virginia from Florida and South Carolina.

In the days preceding Cold Harbor, South Carolina cavalry suffered terribly at Haw's Shop and Matadequin Creek, giving ground both times. The 20th South Carolina infantry, larger than the rest of its parent brigade under Col. Lawrence Keitt, failed in their June 1 attack. Florida troops suffered terribly in their failed counterattack on June 3. Again, the magnitude of the Union losses overshadow these shortcomings.

It's not only the troops we tend to focus on. We often compare generalship in the two armies. Certainly, Grant and Meade had to deal with a cautious Ambrose Burnside and prickly Gouverneur Warren as corps commanders. But let's not forget that Lee's corps leadership was suffering by the summer

---

4   Augustus D. Dickert, *History of Kershaw's Brigade* (Dayton, OH: Morningside Bookshop, 1988), 369; Francis P. Fleming, *Memoir of Captain C. Seton Fleming of the Second Florida Infantry, CSA* (Stonewall House, 1985), 85-87.

of 1864. James Longstreet, his most experienced and trusted commander, was badly wounded in the Wilderness and was out recuperating. In his place was Richard Anderson, who continually came up short. Jubal Early led the Second Corps and was not aggressive enough at times. A. P. Hill commanded the Third Corps, also with mixed results. All three failed to cooperate at crucial times, such as June 1, 5, and 6 when the Confederates were launching attacks. And Jeb Stuart, the cavalry commander, was dead. Lee was desperate for good leadership and wasn't getting it.[5]

A monument to the 2nd Connecticut Heavy Artillery is one of the few on the Cold Harbor battlefield. The regiment suffered heavy losses during the June 1 assaults. *Emerging Civil War*

Studies and popular memory of Cold Harbor also tend to portray the Union troops with a sense of doom prior to the big June 3 attack—that the charge would be a failure and they were resigned to go forward and face annihilation. In fact, in the hundreds of letters, diaries, and accounts this author has studied, hardly any mention the coming attack as foreboding. Afterwards, the frustration and sense of despair jump off the pages, but not in the accounts that were written before the attack. Too much have modern authors projected a sense of impending doom onto the troops.

Finally, Cold Harbor was not simply a trench warfare engagement, with one side charging senselessly and the other blazing away from cover.

5   Gordon C. Rhea, *On To Petersburg* (Baton Rouge: Louisiana State University Press, 2002), 94-96.

Both sides tried innovation. Union troops attempted different attacking formations. They brought in mortars to shell the interior of Confederate works. They responded by digging out holes behind the trails of their cannon to elevate them, turning them into mortars, to return fire from behind Union trenches. The men of the 148th Pennsylvania began a tunnel, which they planned to pack with explosives to blow a hole in the Confederate lines. Does that sound familiar? The July 30 Crater explosion and attack almost happened here. But the army pulled out before it was completed.[6]

Rather than simply a senseless bloodbath, Cold Harbor was a two-week long, intense, and complicated engagement with maneuver and innovation on both sides. Although not as well preserved as many other battlefield sites, groups like the Richmond Battlefields Association and American Battlefield Trust are working to change that. Both have saved more land in recent years and, along with Richmond National Battlefield Park, have expanded what is available to the visiting public.

---

6   *Official Records of the War of the Rebellion*, Vol. 36, Part 1 (Washington, D.C.: War Department, 1895), 1002; Rhea, *On To Petersburg*, 70.

Brigade Command Bled

by Phillip S. Greenwalt

On May 5, 1864, the Confederate Army of Northern Virginia precipitated the Overland Campaign by stopping the Federal Army of the Potomac in the Wilderness west of Fredericksburg, Virginia. What ensued was two days of bloodletting that developed into an extended death dance southward through Virginia that ended with the Confederates besieged around Richmond and Petersburg.

In that six-week time period, from the banks of the Rappahannock River to the Army of the Potomac's James River crossing, the casualties mounted on both sides at a terrific rate. The officer corps, especially in the southern army, was not immune. The loss at the brigade level was significant. While any life lost in war is tragic, the experience, caliber, and leadership highlighted by four brigadier generals below show the magnitude of loss that Lee's army suffered and would struggle mightily to replace.

Much is made of the severe wounding of Lt. Gen. James Longstreet, in charge of the First Corps, on May 6 during a successful counterattack near the Brock Road in the Wilderness. Riding alongside Longstreet was 29-year-old South Carolinian, Micah Jenkins. Born on Edisto Island, South Carolina, on December 1, 1835, Jenkins graduated first in his 1854 class at the South Carolina Military Academy, now known as the Citadel. He organized and operated his own military school, King's Mountain Military School, until the Civil War broke out in 1861. He recruited a company for the 5th South Carolina, was then elected its colonel, and was promoted to brigadier general on July 22, 1862. Shortly thereafter, at Second Manassas the "boy general" received wounds to the shoulder and chest. He was back

Micah Jenkins had the duel benefits of relentless ambition and the support of his corps commander, James Longstreet, who saw Jenkins as a kind of protegé.
Fredericksburg and Spotsylvania National Military Park

before the end of the year to continue in command of a brigade under Maj. Gen. George Pickett but saw no action during the battle of Fredericksburg in December 1862. He served during the Suffolk Campaign with James Longstreet in Pickett's division but then had his brigade retained around Richmond, Virginia when Pickett's division was summoned back to the Army of Northern Virgina, and so missed the bloodletting at Gettysburg. His brigade was then incorporated into Maj. Gen. John B. Hood's Division by the time Longstreet's First Corps went west to fight with the Army of Tennessee.

Jenkins became embroiled in a command dispute later in 1863 with Brig. Gen. Evander Law when their division commander, Hood, was elevated to corps command. Although Law had commanded the division in the past, Jenkins's commission to general was three months senior to Law's, and Jenkins had the support of Longstreet. The situation was resolved in early 1864 when Brig. Gen. Charles Field was assigned the division command and, senior to both already, he was also given a major general's commission.

On May 6, 1864, Jenkins's South Carolinian brigade had been part of the successful flank assault that had smashed the Union lines near the Brock Road. During the forward movement that followed, the brigadier general was hit in the forehead by the same friendly fire that knocked out Longstreet. He was paralyzed on one side of his body but lifted his nonparalyzed hand to his head and continued to talk incoherently in his delirium, although he never regained full consciousness after his mortal wounding. He expired five hours after being struck. His body was sent back to South Carolina and laid to rest in Magnolia Cemetery in Charleston.

On May 12, South Carolinian Brig. Gen. Abner Monroe Perrin was killed while leading a counterattack at the Bloody Angle during the battle of Spotsylvania Court House. Before riding into the combat, he remarked, "I shall come out of this fight a live major general or a dead brigadier." He was struck by seven enemy rounds.

Perrin, a pre-war lawyer and veteran of the Mexican American War, enlisted in the 14th South Carolina Infantry at the start of hostilities as a captain. His regiment was brigaded under fellow Gamecock Brig. Gen.Maxcy Gregg and became part of Maj. Gen. Ambrose Powell Hill's "Light Division" in the Army of Northern Virginia. Gregg was mortally wounded at Fredericksburg on December 13 and replaced by Brig.

Abner Perrin, killed at Spotsylvania, was buried in the Fredericksburg city cemetery. *Fredericksburg and Spotsylvania National Military Park*

Gen. Samuel McGowan, who in turn was wounded at Chancellorsville on May 3, 1863. Perrin commanded the brigade at Gettysburg with the rank of colonel. Under the Third Corps division led by Maj. Gen. William Pender, Perrin's command played a role in the July 1 fighting that captured Seminary Ridge for the Confederates. When the army returned to Virginia and McGowan recovered from his wound, Perrin was transferred to command a brigade of Alabamans previously led by Brig. Gen. Cadmus Wilcox in the Third Corps. He also received his brigadier general rank with a promotion date of September 10, 1863.

Perrin continued to prove his capability as a brigade commander during the opening battle of the 1864 campaign, in the fighting in the Wilderness. When subsequently called upon to stem the breakout of the Union soldiers through the Confederate defenses at Spotsylvania on May 12, the veteran of many fields answered the call with alacrity. He also fulfilled, tragically, the first part of his statement above, dying a brigadier.

That same day, North Carolinian Brig. Gen. Junius Daniel, whom

One contemporary said of Tar Heel Junius Daniel: "He was decidedly the best general officer from our state." *Fredericksburg and Spotsylvania National Military Park*

a fellow officer from the Tarheel State, Bryan Grimes, remembered as "decidedly the best general officer from our state," was shot in the abdomen, a mortal wounding. He would succumb to it the very next day. Hailing from a family with political ties, his father was attorney general for North Carolina and a congressman, while his mother could trace her family lineage back to William Randolph, one of the most prominent early Virginians. He had a stellar early education and was appointed to West Point by the sitting president in 1846, James K. Polk. He graduated 33rd out of 42 cadets in the graduating class of 1852. During his subsequent assignment in the United States Army, he temporarily served under Richard Ewell, with whom he would later cross paths during the Civil War, and saw action against the Apaches in 1855. He resigned in 1858 and joined his father in Louisiana to start the life of a genteel planter. Two years later, he married Ellen Long.

With the outbreak of the Civil War, Daniel was initially chosen as colonel of the 4th and later 14th North Carolina Infantry, and after that unit's disbanding he had a few options, both in cavalry and infantry command. He chose to take the colonelcy of the 45th North Carolina infantry. Although sent to Virginia, Daniel, the 45th North Carolina, and the rest of the brigade saw limited action, but Daniel did gain his brigadier's stars on September 1, 1862—the fourth officer from Halifax County, North Carolina, to reach that rank.

Daniel and his North Carolinians, one of the larger regiments in the Army of Northern Virginia, became part of its Second Corps post-Chancellorsville and fought heroically during the battle of Gettysburg, suffering the most casualties of any Southern brigade on July 1. Daniel's brigade leadership continued to impress Robert E. Lee and, unbeknownst to Daniel, in the spring of 1864 Lee had brought his name forward for promotion to a major generalship—although the promotion was not approved.

At Spotsylvania Court House, Daniel's command was in the right place at the right time and called upon to counterattack after the Army of the Potomac's II Corps had broken through the Mule Shoe. Daniel's men aggressively charged, but Daniel was mortally wounded and died the next day.

Another Confederate brigadier survived two fights in the same area where Daniel fell, only to fall himself

George Doles made it out of Spotsylvania, but he left his mark behind: the position his men defended is still called "Doles's Salient." *Fredericksburg and Spotsylvania National Military Park*

a few weeks later: 34-year-old Georgian George P. Doles. During a May 10 attack on his trench line—which would be remembered as "Doles's Salient"—Doles had faked being wounded by falling to the ground. He avoided capture and was there to help orchestrate the counterattack when Confederate forces pushed out the blue-clad attackers. He also survived the larger breakthrough at the Mule Shoe on May 12.

Doles had been in a prewar militia unit in his hometown of Milledgeville, Georgia which became the nucleus of Company H of the 4th Georgia Infantry. By May 1861, Doles had been elected colonel before being wounded at Malvern Hill on July 1, 1862. He was back in time for the Antietam campaign, where he assumed temporary duty when his brigade commander, Roswell Ripley, was wounded near the Mumma Farm on September 17. He officially received the brigade and a brigadier general's star on November 1, 1862. His brigade went through some changes in

January 1863 when the composition was changed to an all-Georgia brigade. He would retain command of his band of Georgians until June 2, 1864. While inspecting his lines at Bethesda Church, Doles was shot through the breast by a sharpshooter, which killed him instantly.

Three of the four brigadiers would go back to their native states for their final resting spots: Jenkins to South Carolina, Daniel to North Carolina, and Doles to Georgia. Perrin's remains still rest in downtown Fredericksburg, Virginia, at the Confederate Cemetery, just a dozen miles from the battlefield where he fell.

These four men are just a snapshot of the losses of brigade-level officers the Army of Northern Virginia suffered during the Overland Campaign. Looking at just the three major engagements—Wilderness, Spotsylvania Court House, and Cold Harbor—the Confederates had eight brigade commanders killed, three mortally wounded, one captured, one too ill to continue in command, and nineteen wounded. Furthermore, nine of the wounded officers either never returned to command, did not return until the Siege of Petersburg, or were transferred to other theaters of operations, further depleting the army of experienced commanders.

That's a total of thirty-two casualties. Totaling the number of brigade commands, which at Wilderness and Spotsylvania was thirty-four and at Cold Harbor, with the addition of Maj. Gen. John C. Breckinridge's reinforcements, expanded to forty-seven, there were 115 command openings at the infantry brigade level, meaning a casualty rate among brigadiers of slightly under 28 percent. (As an aside, none of Breckinridge's officers fell at Cold Harbor.)

Rounding down a bit, that means that one out of every four brigade commanders in the Army of Northern Virginia became casualties in that approximate six-week span of the Overland Campaign.

Quite accurately, brigade command bled.

The Last Days of Cold Harbor: A Reassessment

by Nathan Provost

Originally published as "Lee's Last Great Field Victory: A Reassessment of Cold Harbor" at Emerging Civil War on June 3, 2020

On June 3, 1864, Federal soldiers waited anxiously to assault the seven-mile-long Confederate line near Mechanicsville, Virginia. The largest engagement of the battle of Cold Harbor was about to take place. Lieutenant General Ulysses S. Grant ordered Maj. Gen. George G. Meade, commander of the Army of the Potomac, to coordinate a successful offensive against what he thought was a weakened Confederate army.

Unfortunately, the II, XVIII, and IX Corps attacked at different places at differing times. Only the II Corps managed to briefly break through Confederate lines on the left while the VI Corps marched a few paces and stopped before the trenches, not even making an attempt to break Confederate lines.

The assault failed by noon.

Federal losses for June 3 amounted to 6,000 killed, wounded, and missing. Conversely, the Army of Northern Virginia lost 1,500 and scored a tactical victory over their Federal foe. The Confederates once again drove off Federal forces at little to no cost.

The Army of the Potomac did not achieve a single objective that morning.

Meade's efforts at coordination were a disaster. Despite the initial failures on the front, he did not suspend his order. Around noon, Grant personally rode to each corps commander to assess the situation. He found that no further progress could be made and issued the following order to Meade: "Hold our most advanced positions and strengthen them. Reconnaissances should be made in front of every Corps and advances made to advantageous positions by regular approaches."[1]

Grant wanted to fight by using siege tactics rather than sanguinary assaults. The Confederate line was not broken, so their Federal opponents now entrenched themselves in place.

Grant stated, "I have always regretted that the last assault at Cold Harbor was ever made. . . . At Cold Harbor no advantage whatever was gained to compensate for the heavy loss we sustained."[2] He recognized the extreme loss of life, and the subsequent memory of Cold Harbor reflects deeply on that cost. Nonetheless, the casualties did not force Grant to retreat; there would be no great Confederate victory. General Grant once again overcame adversity and began planning one of the greatest operations of the war the following day.

He began by shooting off a new message to Maj. Gen. Henry W. Halleck for a new plan of action:

> I will continue to hold substantially the ground now occupied by the Army of the Potomac, taking advantage of any favorable circumstance that may present itself, until the cavalry can be sent west to destroy the Virginia Central Railroad from about Beaver Dam for some 25 or 30 miles west. When this is effected, I will move the army to the south side of James River, either by crossing the Chickahominy and marching near to City Point, or by going to the mouth of the Chickahominy on the north side and crossing there. To provide for this last and most probable contingency six or more ferry-boats of the largest size ought to be immediately provided.

1   Earl Hess, *Trench Warfare under Grant and Lee: Field Fortifications in the Overland Campaign* (Chapel Hill: The University of North Carolina Press, 2007), 162.

2   Ulysses S. Grant, *Personal Memoirs of U.S. Grant* (New York: The Library of America, 1990), 588.

Once on the south side of James River I can cut off all sources of supply to the enemy, except what is furnished by the canal.[3]

Grant used common sense to pierce a thick fog of war. Maneuver was his best option; meanwhile, Gen. Robert E. Lee's army was pinned in place. Grant understood the significance of Petersburg as a supply center. However, this plan also now created new issues and left the Army of the Potomac vulnerable to an assault by the Army of Northern Virginia.

Brigadier General Adam Badeau served on Ulysses Grant's staff throughout the Overland Campaign and wrote *A Military History of Ulysses S. Grant*. He recounts the Army of the Potomac's disengagement from Cold Harbor and its maneuver across the James River, "It transcended in difficulty and danger any that he had attempted during the campaign."[4] While Grant looked for ways to disengage from Cold Harbor, Lee looked for new openings in Grant's lines as Confederate probes continued from June 4-7.

Even though the Federals remained firmly entrenched in front of their enemy, there was still concern that the IX Corps was too far from the main force on June 4. Grant recommended to Meade that he should contract the Federal line from the right flank so Maj. Gen. Ambrose Burnside of the IX Corps would not be separated from the rest of the Army of the Potomac.[5]

Skirmishing took place between the entrenched armies the rest of the day. A few probing attempts by the Confederates that night forced the Federals to stay vigilant. Intelligence was brought to Lee suggesting Grant would move south across the Chickahominy.[6]

On June 5, Lee found an opening in the Federal line when Maj. Gen. Gouverneur Warren's V Corps left the Army of the Potomac's flank vulnerable as he maneuvered his men out from the trenches. Lee authorized both Maj. Gen. Jubal Early and newly promoted Lt. Gen. Richard Anderson

---

3   U.S. War Department, *The War of Rebellion: A Compilation of the Official Records of the Union and Confederate Armies* (Washington DC: Government Printing Press, 1884), 30.

4   Gordon Rhea, *On to Petersburg: Grant and Lee* (Baton Rouge: Louisiana State Press, 2017), 183.

5   Ibid., 46.

6   Ibid., 60.

to coordinate a probing attempt against his flank. However, neither Early nor Anderson managed to coordinate their assault with the other.[7]

More good news came to Grant and Meade on June 6. Maj. Gen. David Hunter, commander of the Army of the Shenandoah, found success in the Shenandoah Valley at the battle of Piedmont.[8] These events caused Lee great concern because it meant he needed to send men back to the Valley under Maj. Gen. John Breckinridge even as Grant's massive force still stood in front of the Army of Northern Virginia.

Lee attempted to probe Federal lines on June 7, but the effort proved just as insignificant as the one the previous day. Early and Anderson failed to inflict any type of damage on General Burnside's IX Corps. Some rifle pits were taken, but the Federal line held.[9]

On that same day, after two tense days of prolonged negotiations, Grant and Lee agreed to a ceasefire in order for Federals to collect their dead. Both men had genuine concerns, but their delays only caused more suffering.[10] Skirmishing continued to take place after the ceasefire, but Grant quietly continued the Federal withdrawal from the battlefield.

On June 11-12, Lee's cavalry decisively beat Maj. Gen. Philip Sheridan at Trevilian Station. However, the engagement left Lee without any force to reconnoiter the Army of the Potomac's movements at the very time the Federals began to move past Lee's forces. On the night of June 11, Grant successfully disengaged from Cold Harbor without any detection by the Army of Northern Virginia.[11]

Lee faced a dire situation by June 12. Hunter was moving in on his supply lines in the Valley, and Lee did not know the location of the Army of the Potomac. Lee's best option was to send Early to the Shenandoah Valley in order to prevent Hunter from taking Lynchburg, but the detachment of Early's force on June 13 only weakened his army further. In the meantime, all Lee could do was wait until he knew the location of the Federal forces.

---

7   Ibid., 92.

8   Ibid., 81.

9   Ibid., 110.

10   Gordon Rhea, "On a House Divided," Author's Voice, 9:00, YouTube.

11   Rhea, *On to Petersburg*, 196.

Confederate artillerist Brig. Gen. Edward Porter Alexander, reflecting on the results of Cold Harbor well after the war, gave credit to the Federals for this final act: "Grant had devised a piece of strategy all his own, which seems to me the most brilliant stroke in all Federal campaigns in the entire war."[12]

This success came at a high price to the Army of the Potomac—although not any higher than that extracted by the battles of the Wilderness or Spotsylvania Courthouse. However, casualties seem to define the battle of Cold Harbor, even though the numbers vary between different sources: Federal casualties range from 12,000-14,000 while Confederate casualties range from 1,500-6,000 soldiers.

In *Cold Harbor: Grant and Lee,* historian Gordon Rhea calculates that "Totopotomoy Creek and Cold Harbor (up until June 3) had cost Lee about 6,000 soldiers, slightly less than ten percent of his army."[13] However, even these numbers do not take into account the 2,287 casualties sustained by the army during the events of June 4-12.[14] Therefore, the total Confederate casualties amount to 8,287 (13%) while Federal casualties amount to around 13,000 (12%) between May 28 to June 12.[15] The casualty figures are comparable in the percentages of men lost by each side.

General Grant's innovative tactic of "Continuous Contact" took a devastating toll on both armies, but Grant continued to fill his ranks with raw recruits. Historian Alfred Young III spent the last decade researching Confederate casualties during the Overland Campaign. In his book *Lee's Army During the Overland Campaign: A Numerical Study*, he concludes, "By the close of the Battle of Cold Harbor in mid-June 1864, it is apparent that the condition of the (Confederate) army was changing. Fractures started forming in the standards of success and unit pride." His evidence relies heavily on the number of Rebel desertions within this new command structure.[16]

It is equally important to interpret how the Federal soldiers viewed the

---

12   Ibid., 188.

13   Gordon Rhea, *Cold Harbor: Grant and Lee* (Baton Rouge: Louisiana State Press, 2002), 393.

14   Alfred Young, *Lee's Army During the Overland Campaign: A Numerical Study* (Baton Rouge: Louisiana State Press, 2013), 240.

15   Young, 2.

16   Ibid., 224.

In one of the most iconic images from the Civil War, photographer John Reekie, working for Alexander Gardner, captured burial parties collecting the dead at Cold Harbor. *Library of Congress*

results of the battle. Meade wrote home to his wife after the assault on June 3. "The battle ended without any decided results," he told her, "we repulsing all attacks of the enemy and they doing the same." Another Federal private wrote home, "We have faith to believe we will enter Richmond soon. . . . The entire army have unlimited confidence in Gen. Grant, and do not doubt the triumphant results of the campaign." Meade's aide, Maj. James Biddle, had a more jaded view of events. "The rebel army fight desperately and have contested heroically every inch of ground," he wrote. "They have fallen back because they have been outflanked, but in no case has it been a disorderly retreat with our army on their heels."[17]

All the military actions and operations that took place between June 4 and June 12 are essential to understanding how Grant successfully maneuvered an army of 100,000 out of an ongoing battle. The events of

17   Ibid., 387.

June 3 further caused a change in tactics and operations, but it did not inflict lasting damage on the morale of Federal soldiers, with many still confident in victory. Lee and a few other Confederate officers recognized the danger they faced as the Army of the Potomac disengaged.

The results of Cold Harbor are more mixed if all the events from June 4-12 are taken into account. Grant once again used common sense after the uncoordinated assault on June 3. Unlike Lee after Gettysburg, Grant held the initiative and found no need to retreat as his men entrenched in front of Confederate lines. Meade and other Federal soldiers recognized this as another setback, just like the Wilderness, Spotsylvania, and North Anna, but not a decisive defeat.

J. F.C . Fuller, a British military historian and military theorist, analyzed the generalship of both Ulysses Grant and Robert E. Lee in the early 20th century. He states that Cold Harbor was "a battle which in the history of the Civil War has been given the prominence it does not deserve. It was not a great battle or a decisive one, Lee's losses were slight and Grant's not excessive."[18]

Even the northern press recognized the final result of June 3. As an example, *The Detroit Press* described the outcome thus: "no decisive result was achieved."[19] The reporters did not believe Cold Harbor meant defeat for the Army of the Potomac. By June 4, Grant determined it futile to try and destroy Lee's entrenched army, but he adjusted his objective by targeting the Army of Northern Virginia's supply center at Petersburg. Lee, meanwhile, continued to probe for openings between June 4-7 even as Grant continued to contract his line. Lee failed to find an opening.

Neither Grant nor Lee achieved a major objective after the assault on June 3, but Grant was closer to his overall goal by eliminating Lee's offensive capabilities. The public remembers how General Lee inflicted a significant loss to the Federal juggernaut on June 3, but memory omits how, on June 12, General Grant left Lee blind on the battlefield of Cold Harbor.

---

18   J. F. C. Fuller, *Grant and Lee: A Study in Personality and Generalship* (Bloomington: Indiana University Press, 1982), 220.

19   "FROM GRANT'S ARMY: The Second Battle of Cold Harbor A SHARP AND BLOODY CONFLICT," *Detroit Free Press* (Detroit, Michigan), 9 June 1864.

The Battle of Petersburg

by Sean Michael Chick

Points of Interest #1, #2, and #3 on the map on pg. xv.

*Originally published at Emerging Civil War June 14-18, 2021,
as a five-part series*

From the Chickahominy to the James: June 4-14, 1864

In the aftermath of Cold Harbor, the armies led by Robert E. Lee and George Meade were at a strategic stalemate fewer than twenty miles from Richmond. The advantage, though, had fallen to the Confederates. Lee still held Richmond, and his army was in overall better shape. Despite some heavy officer losses, Lee's men had high morale and, with some exceptions, his brigades were battered but still cohesive fighting units.

The Army of the Potomac, while not destroyed, had suffered a reverse that was even worse than the infamous charges at Fredericksburg. Their morale had plummeted. John West Haley of the 17th Maine wrote, "We were tired of charging earthworks. Many soldiers expressed freely their scorn of Grant's alleged general ship, which consists of launching men against breastworks. It is well known that one man behind works is as good as three outside the works."[1] Surgeon Daniel M. Holt of the 121st New York wrote, "If losing sixty thousand men is a slight loss, I never want to see a heavy one. We, as a regiment, have almost ceased to exist, and if the next six months prove as

---

1   John West Haley, *Rebel Yell and Yankee Hurrah: The Civil War Journal of a Maine Volunteer* (Camden: Down East Books, 1985), 165.

disastrous to us as the last six weeks have, not a soul will be left to recite the wholesale slaughter which has taken place on the sacred soil of Virginia."[2] Col. Charles S. Wainwright, chief of artillery for the V Corps, sharply criticized the frontal attacks as "a mere shoving forward of a brigade or two now here now there, like a chess-player shoving out his pieces and then drawing them right back."[3] Colonel Joshua Lawrence Chamberlain, who was a little less critical, thought Grant "was like Thor, the hammer, striking blow after blow, intent on his purpose to beat his way through, somewhat reckless of the cost."[4]

Just as bad, a fresh round of bickering took place, mostly between Meade and Maj. Gen. William F. Smith, commander of the XVIII Corps. Maj. Gen. James Wilson, one of the army's cavalry commanders, and

General Meade, the "old snapping turtle," sits (center) surrounded by his staff. *Library of Congress*

Col. John Rawlins, Grant's chief of staff, blamed the poor tactics on Grant's aide Lt. Col. Cyrus Comstock. Although a capable engineer, Comstock had encouraged aggressive assault tactics throughout the 1864 campaign. After Cold Harbor, Rawlins worked to limit Comstock's influence on Grant.

In the aftermath of Cold Harbor, Grant's advisers offered him several plans. Comstock proposed taking the army on a large swing to destroy Lee's railroad network. Meade preferred to pin Lee at Cold Harbor and let Maj. Gen. Philip Sheridan's cavalry raid the rear. Henry Halleck suggested that Grant position himself north of Richmond in order to protect the approaches to Washington and invest Richmond through an attritional campaign.

Not wishing to settle for a siege, Grant wanted to take Petersburg. The

---

2   Daniel Holt, *A Surgeon's Civil War* (Ohio: Kent State University Press, 2000), 205.

3   Charles Wainwright, *A Diary of Battle* (New York: Harcourt, Brace and the World, 1962), 381.

4   Ernest B. Furgurson, *Not War but Murder: Cold Harbor 1864* (New York: Alfred A. Knopf, 2000), 254.

OPPOSITE: Crossing the James—Effective cavalry screening allowed Grant to move to the James River and cross without interference from Confederates. Once across, he moved on Petersburg before Robert E. Lee realized it, and even once Lee heard the news, he was slow to believe it. *Library of Congress*

city was a key Southern railroad hub and manufacturing center. Its fall would mean the fall of Richmond and, in turn, the reelection of Abraham Lincoln, who for his part was in a tough political situation. The proposed Thirteenth Amendment, which would abolish slavery, was now in danger of being scuttled, while Lincoln angered the Radicals by rejecting the Wade-Davis Bill, which would enact a relatively stern Reconstruction plan on the defeated South. On May 31, some Radical Republicans met in Cleveland, Ohio, and nominated former general John C. Fremont for president. Maj. Gen. Benjamin Butler, himself a War Democrat turned Radical, declared, "This country has more vitality than any other on earth if it can stand this sort of administration for another four years."[5]

Lincoln needed a victory, and in early June he could hardly look elsewhere. In the west, the Confederates had scored victories at New Hope Church and Pickett's Mill in the Atlanta campaign, as well as a cavalry victory at Brice's Crossroads. A minor and much-publicized victory at Dallas, Georgia, gave Lincoln's allies some hope, but for now the Union war effort had stalled.

To take Petersburg, Grant decided to swing Meade's army across the James River. It would take hard marching and fighting to seize Petersburg, but Grant seemed unsure if he could take Petersburg by storm. "This is likely to prove a very tedious job I have on hand but I feel very confident of ultimate success," he wrote on June 6.[6] This uncertainty would have a detrimental effect upon the coming campaign as it unfolded.

Grant's developing plans were influenced by good news from the Shenandoah Valley. On June 5, Maj. Gen. David Hunter smashed a Confederate force at Piedmont and was ravaging the area. The South was in an uproar and Lee had to do something. Now confident that his lines would hold, Lee felt free to send forces into the Shenandoah Valley. He dispatched Lt. Gen. Jubal Early

5   Benjamin F. Butler, *Private and Official Correspondence of Gen. Benjamin F. Butler* Vol. IV (Norwood, MA: The Plimpton Press, 1917), 337.

6   Ulysses S. Grant, *The Papers of Ulysses S. Grant,* Vol. XI, (Carbondale: Southern Illinois University Press, 1967), 25.

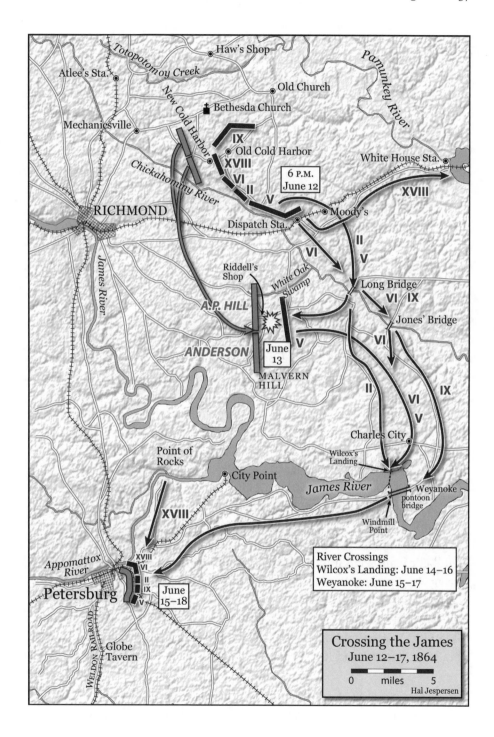

Haw's Shop

Atlee's Sta.

Totopotomoy Creek

Pamunkey River

Old Church

✝ Bethesda Church

Mechanicsville

New Cold Harbor

IX

Old Cold Harbor

White House Sta.

Chickahominy River

XVIII

VI

II

6 P.M.
June 12

V

RICHMOND

Dispatch Sta.

Moody's

XVIII

James River

Riddell's
Shop

VI

II

V

White Oak Swamp

Long Bridge

VI   IX

A. P. HILL

Jones' Bridge

ANDERSON

June
13

V

VI

MALVERN
HILL

II

VI

IX

V

Charles City

Point of
Rocks

City Point

Wilcox's
Landing

James River

Weyanoke
pontoon
bridge

Windmill
Point

XVIII

River Crossings
Wilcox's Landing: June 14–16
Weyanoke: June 15–17

Appomattox River

XVIII
VI

II

IX

June
15–18

V

Petersburg

WELDON RAILROAD

Globe
Tavern

Crossing the James
June 12–17, 1864

0   miles   5

Hal Jespersen

with 10,000 men to defeat Hunter and, if possible, threaten Washington D. C., similar to the strategy he encouraged from Stonewall Jackson in the spring of 1862. Early's assignment to the Shenandoah was threatened when Sheridan was sent on a massive raid. It culminated in the battle of Trevilian Station on June 11. Although both sides claimed victory, Sheridan was prevented from joining Hunter, and Early made his way to the Valley. The battle would also deprive both Lee and Grant of most of their cavalry, with major repercussions for the fighting ahead.

On June 7, Grant sent Col. Horace Porter of his staff and Comstock to choose a site for the crossing of the James River and to meet with Butler. They discussed Grant's river crossing, but not Grant's plans for Petersburg. After the meeting, Butler decided to seize Petersburg, likely guessing that Grant intended the same thing. He sent a force under Maj. Gen. Quincy Gillmore after the latter had insisted that his seniority required this, but Gillmore failed in his June 9 attack. All the battle achieved was to cause Gen. P.G.T. Beauregard, the commander south of the James River, to send more men to Petersburg. However, Beauregard kept most of his men at Bermuda Hundred, facing the X Corps.

For the march on Petersburg, Grant had Smith's XVIII Corps return to Bermuda Hundred. The rest of the army would shift to the James River, where engineers would build a massive pontoon bridge. Grant informed Butler that Petersburg was the goal but informed neither Smith nor Meade. Smith did not know until June 14 when he met with Butler, and the day was spent preparing to attack on June 15.

On June 12-13, the Army of the Potomac moved across the Chickahominy River, which ran along the south of Cold Harbor. The withdrawal was mostly successful. Lee's men detected nothing. Yet there was one major delay. The Long Bridge across the Chickahominy was gone. The area was contested by Rebel cavalry, and it took hours to defeat them and build a new bridge. During the fighting, Wilson ran afoul of Maj. Gen. Gouverneur Kemble Warren, the touchy commander of the V Corps. "Tell general Wilson if he can't lay that bridge to get out of the way with his damned cavalry and I'll lay it!" Warren told one messenger.[7] Wilson refused to shake Warren's hand later that day and told Grant, "Send for Parker the Indian chief, and

---

7   James H. Wilson, *Under the Old Flag* (New York: D. Appleton and Co., 1912), 399.

Crossing the James River constituted one of the most impressive—and least appreciated—feats of the Army of the Potomac during the entire war. *Library of Congress*

after giving him a tomahawk, a scalping knife and the worst whiskey the Commissary Department can supply, send him out with orders to bring the scalps of major generals."[8] When Grant asked who should be scalped, Wilson described Warren's behavior in detail.

On June 13, the armies fought a fierce skirmish at Riddell's Shop, a crossroads less than twenty miles from Richmond. Meanwhile, the vanguard of the Federal army reached the James River at Wyanoke Neck, although there were no transports ready to move them across. Meanwhile, nearly 500 engineers under Col. James Duane, assisted by Brig. Gen. Godfrey Weitzel of Butler's staff, started the work and, by June 14, they finished an impressive bridge, nearly 2,100 feet long and consisting of 101 pontoon boats.

On June 14, Grant met with Butler and told him to pressure Bermuda Hundred. Smith would move south of the Appomattox River and attack Petersburg. The II Corps would be ferried over and march to Petersburg to support Smith.

The Confederate reaction to Grant's maneuvering was muddled. Before Grant withdrew, Lee actually feared Grant was about to strike again. Brigadier General Martin Gary, commanding cavalry at Riddell's Shop, thought the main Union thrust was in his sector. With Early gone, Lee's options were limited and one error could expose Richmond. With most of his cavalry elsewhere, Lee's horsemen could not penetrate Wilson's screen. Lee decided Grant was moving on Chaffin's Bluff and shifted his men to guard it, covering Riddell's

8   Ibid., 401.

Shop, Malvern Hill, and the New Market Road. Although troop transports were reportedly seen going to Bermuda Hundred, it was confirmed that only the XVIII Corps was on board. In reaction, Lee sent Brig. Gen. Robert Hoke's division to Beauregard, an outfit Beauregard had loaned him weeks before.

On the evening of June 14, Grant and Meade were in a good position to take Petersburg. Lee had failed to detect their position and was instead fixated on the spot Grant had no intention of attacking. Beauregard, while aware of the danger to Petersburg, was at Bermuda Hundred.

Yet the Army of the Potomac had a history of defeats that sprung from movements begun so beautifully. Before the battles of Fredericksburg, Chancellorsville, and the Wilderness, the army had out-maneuvered Lee only to meet defeat in battle. Would this time be different?

Petersburg Day One: Wednesday, June 15, 1864

On June 15, the Army of the Potomac began to cross the James River. It was an emotional moment. Capt. A. M. Judson of the 83rd Pennsylvania likened the army's arrival at the James to Xenophon and his 10,000 Greeks reaching the Black Sea. As the 7th Rhode Island marched past a nearby swamp, a band played "Ain't we glad to get out of the wilderness."[9] Col. Rufus Dawes, commander of the 6th Wisconsin and a hero of Gettysburg, wrote to his wife that "it is very refreshing to get to the beautiful slopes of this broad river."[10] From Abraham Lincoln, Ulysses S. Grant received that morning a simple message: "I begin to see it. You will succeed. God bless you all."[11]

Back at Bermuda Hundred, things were less encouraging. Smith's XVIII Corps was scattered, and he would not be able to strike Petersburg at dawn. The XVIII Corps ran into resistance almost from the moment it crossed the Appomattox River, being delayed by James Dearing's cavalry brigade. At Baylor's Farm, the corps then ran into 850 troopers and two cannon, commanded by Col. Dennis D. Ferebee, which faced off against Brig. Gen. Edward Hinks's division of black soldiers.

9   William P. Hopkins, *The Seventh Rhode Island Volunteers in the Civil War 1862-1865* (Providence: Snow & Farnham, 1903), 90.

10   Rufus R. Dawes, *Service with the Sixth Wisconsin Volunteers* (Marietta: E. R. Alderman & Sons, 1890), 290.

11   Butler, 373.

Hinks's men were green and varied in quality of drill. Ferebee, meanwhile, had a strong position, and marshy woods lay in the middle of the field that Hinks's troops would have to cross. The inexperience of the black troops led to confusion, and the marshy underbrush broke up their lines, while the Rebel fire was disciplined and accurate. Some Union regiments even fired on each other and many broke. Yet the 22nd USCT managed to press ahead and capture a cannon. Losses, though, were lopsided. The Confederates lost one cannon, and the 4th North Carolina Cavalry reported nine casualties, including a wounded Ferebee. Union losses were 300, but the captured cannon made Hinks's men rejoice.

Confederates clearly got the best of the 22nd USCT at Baylor's Farm, but the USCT got an artillery piece. The success of the black troops, although limited, unnerved the Confederates. *Library of Congress*

Back in Petersburg, Brig. Gen. Henry Wise mustered his troops while bells tolled to call out the militia. He brought the city's convalescents to the front. Guards were posted along the roads with orders to arrest any soldier trying to leave the city. In Wise's uneven career, June 15 was his high point. Still, Wise had to cover miles of trenches with 3,000 men, although the defenses, known as the "Dimmock Line," were strong. Beauregard immediately surmised that Smith's advance was a full attack, and he ordered Hoke's division to Petersburg. Wise's only advantage was in artillery. He had some twenty-five cannon, including a few heavy pieces.

Smith was unnerved by the heavy losses at Baylor's Farm. He paused for a time before moving on Petersburg, his men arriving slowly. It was not until 2:00 p.m. that every unit in the XVIII Corps was up and ready for battle. As the Union regiments formed up, William Russell of the 26th Virginia observed that "we had such a small force here it made me tremble to see them."[12]

12   Thomas J. Howe, *The Petersburg Campaign: Wasted Valor, June 15-18, 1864* (Richmond: H. E. Howard, 1988), 31.

OPPOSITE: Battle of Petersburg—Most people who think of Petersburg recall a nine-month siege, but the armies' arrival in the city actually began with an oft-forgotten battle that lasted June 15–18, 1864, which consisted of seven major Federal assaults. Army of Northern Virginia commander Robert E. Lee recognized the danger in Petersburg nearly too late, but effective work by P. G. T. Beauregard combined with ineffective Federal leadership allowed Lee to finally shift troops into place for a stronger defense.

As the lines formed, Brig. Gen. August Kautz's cavalry moved on the Baxter Road. By 5:30 p.m., Kautz's skirmishers were out of bullets and he decided to fall back. Only forty-three men were casualties, although among them was Col. Simon Hoosick Mix, one of Kautz's brigade commanders. Mix's men tried to rescue him, but he told them to save themselves. He apparently once said he prayed to die while leading the 3rd New York Cavalry in a glorious charge. The attack of June 15 was more bungling than glorious, but Mix got the second half of his wish. Without medical care he perished on the field.

While Kautz was wasting time, Smith scouted the ground. This was made difficult because Smith was still recovering from the dysentery he had contracted at Cold Harbor and moved on foot in the heat. After two hours, he surmised that the Dimmock Line was an impressive position, but lightly held. He would attack all along the line and spent the next two hours conferring with his division commanders and planning. Smith decided the first line would advance in a loose formation, a pace apart from each other, to avoid heavy losses. The second line would be arrayed for a heavy assault.

The Union artillery opened just after 6:20 p.m. The barrage was effective in confusing the Confederates and silencing their guns. After roughly twenty minutes, the XVIII Corps advanced. The attacks along the Appomattox River were a limited success, but Jordan's Hill was overrun. Captain N. A. Sturdivant, who commanded the artillery on Jordan's Hill, openly lamented that his men were "captured by a Yankee skirmish line."[13] In total, 227 Rebels, including sixteen officers, capitulated. The flag of the 26th Virginia fell into Union hands along with five artillery pieces.

Even more impressive was Hinks's attack. Christian Fleetwood, a free black businessman in the 4th USCT, boasted that they "swept like a tornado over the works."[14] In two hours of nearly constant fighting, the USCT

13   Thompson S. Millett., *Thirteenth Regiment of New Hampshire Volunteer Infantry in the War of the Rebellion, 1861-1865* (Boston: Houghton, Mifflin and Company, 1888), 390.

14   Edward G. Longacre, *A Regiment of Slaves: The 4th United States Colored Infantry, 1863-1864* (Mechanicsburg, PA: Stackpole Books, 2003), 91.

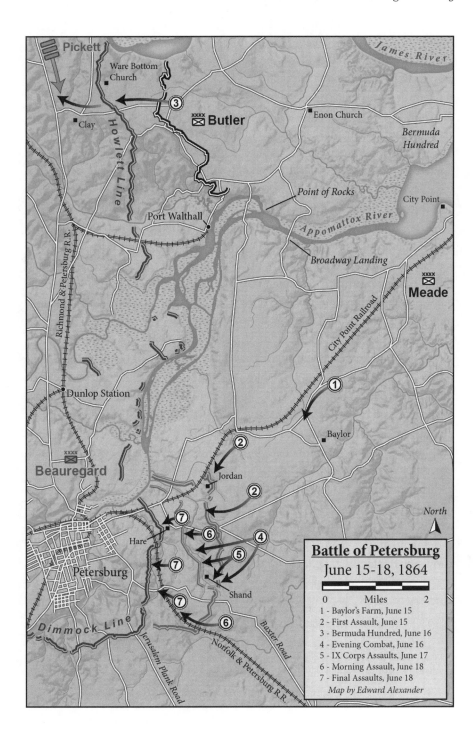

Pickett

Ware Bottom
Church

James River

③

XXXX
⊠ **Butler**

Enon Church

*Bermuda
Hundred*

Clay

Howlett Line

Point of Rocks

City Point

Port Walthall

Appomattox River

Broadway Landing

XXXX
⊠
Meade

Richmond & Petersburg R.R.

City Point Railroad

Dunlop Station

Baylor

①

②

XXXX
⊠
Beauregard

Jordan

②

North

⊿

⑦

Hare

⑥

④

⑤

Battle of Petersburg
June 15-18, 1864

⑦

Petersburg

Shand

⑦

Dimmock Line

⑦

⑥

Baxter Road

Jerusalem Plank Road

Norfolk & Petersburg R.R.

0	Miles	2

1 - Baylor's Farm, June 15
2 - First Assault, June 15
3 - Bermuda Hundred, June 16
4 - Evening Combat, June 16
5 - IX Corps Assaults, June 17
6 - Morning Assault, June 18
7 - Final Assaults, June 18

Map by Edward Alexander

regiments, relatively green before June 15, had carried nearly a mile of enemy trenches. They cheered their victory and yelled "Fort Pillow!"[15] The path to Petersburg was wide open.

Smith, who had been dismissive of the USCT beforehand, praised them highly in his official report and declared that they had "no superiors as soldiers." Smith personally congratulated Hinks, telling him, "This is a stronger position than Missionary Ridge."[16] John Rawlins dropped his opposition to using the USCT in pitched battles. Petersburg was the first time black troops had been actively used in the bloody fields of Virginia, and they had exceeded expectations. Ironically, this triumph came on the same day that the House of Representatives failed to pass the Thirteenth Amendment, which would have abolished slavery in its entirety.[17]

Smith had been successful, but with the sun setting he grew cautious. Smith made no effort to advance into the tangled ravines, hills, and woods that lay before him. He was also sure Robert E. Lee was on the way. Smith likely lost around 1,400 men on June 15, which was no pittance.

Major General Winfield Scott Hancock's II Corps arrived on the field just as Smith's attack began. He should have been there sooner, but Grant failed to inform him that Petersburg was the target, and Hancock waited hours for orders. The maps were so poor that Hancock had to rely on local black guides to find Petersburg. Despite these problems, the II Corps made good time, advancing fourteen miles in a little under five hours. He arrived with the divisions commanded by generals David Birney and Francis Barlow, two proven fighters.

However, the II Corps did not pitch into the battle. The men were in a ragged state. James McDonald of the 5th New Hampshire wrote, "There was a rage amongst us for water; the burning thirst should be satisfied, and many of the men were seized with diarrhea. But military necessity knows no obstacles save those of the enemy. . . . We rested our weary limbs

15   Williams, *A History of the Negro Troops in the War of the Rebellion*, 238.

16   Thomas L. Livermore, "The Failure to Take Petersburg, June 15, 1864." In *Papers of the Military Historical Society of Massachusetts: Petersburg, Chancellorsville, Gettysburg.* (Boston: Military Historical Society of Massachusetts, 1906), 68.

17   Charles A. Dana, *Recollections of the Civil War: With the Leaders at Washington and in the Field in the Sixties* (New York: D. Appleton and Company, 1899), 220.

The failure of Federals to exploit their breakthrough at the Dimmock Line on June 15, 1864, represents one of the great "What Ifs" of the Civil War. *Library of Congress*

within about two miles of the doomed city of Petersburg, having marched something like twenty-one miles."[18]

At the outset, Grant had told Hancock, "If Petersburg is not captured tonight it will be advisable that you and Smith take up a defensive position and maintain it until all the forces are up."[19] These were hardly words meant to inspire an all-out drive on Petersburg.

Smith did not believe a night attack was sound, even with a full moon. Hancock, his superior in rank and now in overall command, agreed with him and wanted to press on in the morning. Despite the urging of Hinks, Smith paused. The II Corps spent the night taking up position at Jordan's Hill, thereby allowing Smith to withdraw some of the XVIII Corps. This, however, meant that the II Corps was no longer in a good position to outflank Beauregard's men. Some soldiers yelled, "Put us into it, Hancock, my boy;

18   "Letter from the 5th New Hampshire Vols." *Irish American Weekly*. July 16, 1864.

19   Grant, 53.

we will end this damned rebellion to-night!"[20] The high command, though, remained unfazed.

Smith possibly thought the battle as all but won. He informed Butler around midnight, "It is impossible for me to go further to-night, but unless I misapprehend the topography, I hold the key to Petersburg."[21] Smith seemed to forget the real lesson of Cold Harbor: if given sufficient time, the Confederates could erect nearly impregnable entrenchments. Butler later wrote, "Smith says . . . he held the key to Petersburg. True, he did; but what is the use of holding the key when you have not the courage to turn it in the lock?"[22]

Meanwhile, Grant and Meade offered a study in contrasts on June 15. In a letter to his wife, Julia, Grant said, "A few days now will enable me to form a judgment of the work before me. It will be hard and may be tedious however. I am in excellent health and feel no doubt about holding the enemy in much greater alarm than I ever felt in my life."[23] While these words were optimistic, they no longer reflected the fighting spirit of his dispatches from Spotsylvania. By contrast, once Meade heard of Smith's success, he stopped his dinner and gave new orders to speed along the march of the V and IX Corps to Petersburg.

Beauregard arrived at Petersburg at 6:00 p.m. and, while inspecting the lines, witnessed the flight of Wise's command. He established headquarters at the Customs House and set about organizing the city's defenses. Losses were about 400 for the day; two regimental commanders had been captured and another was wounded. Wise's brigade was battered but still capable of combat. Meanwhile. Brig. Gen. Johnson Hagood, representing the vanguard of Hoke's division, arrived. The citizens of Petersburg cheered and some wept, declaring, "We are safe now." By morning Beauregard would have around 10,000 men.[24]

---

20   Frank Wilkeson, *Recollections of a Private Soldier in the Army of the Potomac* (New York: G. P. Putnam's Sons, 1887), 160.

21   Butler, 383.

22   Benjamin F. Butler, *Autobiography and Personal Reminiscences of Major-General Benjamin F. Butler* (Boston: A. M. Thayer, 1892), 690.

23   Grant, 53.

24   Thomas, "The Slaughter at Petersburg, June 18, 1864," 224.

But Beauregard needed more. He asked Gen. Braxton Bragg, Jefferson Davis's military advisor, whether he was to hold the Howlett Line at Bermuda Hundred or hold Petersburg, since he could not hold both. Bragg told Beauregard to use his judgment, and at 10:25 p.m. he ordered Maj. Gen. Bushrod Johnson to abandon the Howlett Line.

To the North, Lee remained fixed on protecting Richmond, even when Lt. Gen. A.P. Hill informed him that he only faced a cavalry screen. Lee didn't dare move because Beauregard could only confirm the existence of the XVIII Corps. So, he sent to Beauregard one brigade and four batteries but no more. Lee wrote that night, "Nothing else of importance has occurred to-day."[25]

Although Bragg and Lee were not too worried about Petersburg, J. B. Jones, a clerk in the War Department, did see the situation for what it was. He assumed that Grant was swinging at Petersburg with most of his army and, after the fighting on June 15, he wrote, "The war will be determined, perhaps, by the operations of a day or two; and much anxiety is felt by all."[26]

Petersburg Day Two: Thursday, June 16, 1864

On the night of June 15, Beauregard sent Lee a letter, received at 2:00 a.m., June 13, explaining the situation and asking him to cover the Howlett Line. Unfortunately, the letter failed to convey the desperate character of the situation. Beauregard explained to Lee that Petersburg was under attack, but so far, he could confirm only the presence of the X and XVIII Corps. As of yet, Beauregard's men had not encountered II Corps, so they could not confirm whether the Army of the Potomac was at Petersburg. Lee acted with the information he had and sent Maj. Gen. George E. Pickett's division to cover the Bermuda Hundred lines. Lee also decided to go to Bermuda Hundred and review the situation himself.

Hancock, meanwhile, had at least 20,000 troops near Petersburg. George Meade was expected to arrive shortly to command the components of the Army of the Potomac, but until then, it was Hancock's show. However,

---

25   *Richmond Examiner*, 17 June 1864.

26   J. B. Jones, *A Rebel War Clerk's Diary* Vol. II (Philadelphia: J. B. Lippincott & Company, 1866), 232-33.

the morning of June 16 saw only light fighting. Hancock ordered Maj. Gen. David Birney to stage a reconnaissance in force to find a weak spot in the lines for a future attack. Birney selected Col. Thomas W. Egan's brigade. The attack at first carried a portion of the lines but Beauregard counterattacked. In the fighting, Egan was severely wounded along with his second-in-command, Lt. Col. Augustus Warner. Further assaults were called off while Johnson's division filed into the right flank.

Grant, too, had decided to visit the Petersburg front, leaving City Point around 10:00 a.m. He congratulated Smith for his efforts and was hopeful that victory would be achieved. He ordered Meade

Winfield Scott Hancock (seated) looks rakish with his hat askew, but his seated pose hides the fact that his Gettysburg wound from the summer before was plaguing him. His division commanders surround him: Francis Barlow, David Bell Birney, and John Gibbon. By fall, Hancock would resign corps command because of his injury, Barlow would be out on sick leave, Birney would transfer to corps command in the Army of the James but then die of typhoid fever, and Gibbon— slighted that Andrew Humphreys would get command of the II Corps instead of him—would transfer out of the corps. *Library of Congress*

to carry out an all-out attack, although he also warned Meade to guard his flank.

Meade arrived at Petersburg around 2:00 p.m. He sent Brig. Gen. John G. Barnard and Comstock, on loan from Grant's staff, to scout the ground. They advised that a concentrated attack would meet success. Maj. Gen. Francis Barlow recommended, specifically, a flank attack. In the end, however, Meade decided on a concentrated blow on Beauregard's center with Hancock's II Corps rather than a general assault, as the army had attempted disastrously at Cold Harbor. Barlow's flank attack proposal was sound, but the intense heat meant that Maj. Gen. Ambrose Burnside's IX Corps was arriving in an exhausted condition on Meade's left. Meade conferred with Hancock and Burnside—but not with Smith, probably because the two men detested each other. Meade wanted an attack on Hare House Hill, the woods due south of the hill, and the Shand House, which was straddled by hills, ravines, and streams. It would be a frontal assault against an entrenched position.

On the Confederate side, Lee crossed the James at 9:40 a.m. He knelt in prayer upon reaching the south bank, then set up his headquarters at Drewry's Bluff. Brig. Gen. Eppa Hunton, a brigade commander, observed that on June 16, "Lee was in a furious passion."[27] This was likely because Lee was still uncertain where Meade was located, his cavalry having failed to penetrate Wilson's screen. Beauregard failed to shed any light, either: messages on June 16 varied from dire predictions that Petersburg would fall to a request for men to launch a counterattack. It was a confusing situation.

Meanwhile, Benjamin Butler had noted Johnson's absence and ordered forward his command. They scooped up a haul of prisoners. His men wrecked the Richmond-Petersburg Railroad and tore up telegraph lines. Brigadier General Adelbert Ames's division, recently arrived from Petersburg and transferred from the XVIII to the X Corps, destroyed telegraph wires. Butler asked for reinforcements from Meade. Grant sent two divisions of the VI Corps.

Around noon, Pickett's men engaged Butler's troops. Lieutenant General Richard Anderson, Pickett's superior, notified Lee, who dispatched Maj. Gen. Charles Field's division. In a running battle, Pickett forced Butler back to his old lines. Grant and Butler now became cautious, and Grant ordered Butler to withdraw to the captured Confederate lines at Bermuda Hundred. Butler instead withdrew to his own old lines, leaving only pickets in the captured Rebel works.

Meade made his late-afternoon attack, but losses were heavy as the compact attack columns were shredded by artillery. Some Union troops made it to the Confederate lines but could not storm them. The famous Irish Brigade took particularly heavy losses. Col. James E. McGee, commander of the 69th New York, was wounded. The Irishmen pressed on and pierced the main Rebel lines as some of Wise's Virginians broke. The 17th North Carolina shifted to cover the breech. During the attack Col. Patrick Kelly, the brigade's commander, was shot in the head and died instantly. Kelly had fought

---

27   Eppa Hunton, *Autobiography of Eppa Hunton* (Richmond: William Byrd Press, 1933), 86.

in nearly every major battle in the Eastern Theater since First Bull Run, leading the brigade at Gettysburg. His death caused many to weep, from privates all the way to members of Meade's staff.

Federals enjoyed a numerical superiority but faced formidable defenses—even after capturing portions of those defenses. *Library of Congress*

Edwin B. Houghton of the 17th Maine aptly described the attack as "sublimely awful."[28] Of the seven brigades that actively assaulted, four lost their commanders. Combined with Egan's loss in the morning, Hancock saw nearly half of his brigade commanders fall in one day. Among the junior officers in the II Corps, seven captains and nine lieutenants died. Casualties for the evening attack were estimated to be 2,000 total. Although Meade considered these losses to have "not been great," reporter David Power Conyngham of the *New York Herald* was more accurate when he said, "Thousands of brave men were ruthlessly sacrificed."[29] The casualties were on par with those suffered by the II Corps in its more famous attack at Cold Harbor.

The Union still held a considerable numerical advantage, however, and had captured parts of the Confederate defenses. Beauregard believed there was "much vigor being displayed by the Federals."[30] June 16 had been a Confederate victory, but it gave Meade an excellent point from which to strike the next day.

To counter this, Beauregard ordered numerous night attacks designed both to regain the lost portion of his lines and to add stress and strain to the Union forces. The lost lines were not recovered, but the attacks had the desired effect on Federal morale.

28   Edwin B. Houghton, *The Campaigns of the Seventeenth Maine* (Portland: Short and Loring, 1866), 202.

29   D. P. Conyngham, *The Irish Brigade and Its Campaigns* (New York: William McSorley & Company, 1867), 456.

30   P.G.T. Beauregard, *Battles and Leaders of the Civil War*, Vol. IV, 542.

Meanwhile, Beauregard ordered Col. David Harris, his able chief engineer, to set up a defensive line behind his current position. Harris was assisted in this by Capt. John Postell, an accomplished civil engineer from Georgia. The two men mapped out a line, but it needed to be fortified before the Rebels could withdraw from their current positions. The new line would be constructed by slaves, militia, and men from Stephen Elliott's South Carolina brigade.

Meanwhile, the leading elements of Warren's V Corps arrived on the field. Warren was placed in position by Comstock, who even after Cold Harbor had moved about camp pounding his fist into his palm and yelling "Smash 'em up! Smash 'em up!"[31] Comstock, though, showed caution on June 16 and placed Warren behind the IX Corps.

The morning of June 17 would see roughly 35,000 Union troops confronting no more than 14,000 Confederates holding an exposed line, with some 20,000 more Union troops on the way. Furthermore, Meade had been informed by Capt. Samuel P. Lee, the local naval commander, that thousands of Rebels were at Deep Bottom, just north of the James River. This showed that most of Lee's army was out of position. If the Federals could not gain victory on June 16, they seemed assured to win one the next day.

Petersburg Day Three: Friday, June 17, 1864

George Meade's June 17 battle plan conformed to Francis Barlow's suggestion for hitting the flank. The proposed attack would be carried out by Burnside's IX Corps, namely the divisions led by generals Robert Potter and James H. Ledlie. Potter had a good reputation, but Ledlie was a drunk and a coward. One member of his staff confessed that "He was a good soul, but a very weak man, and no more fit to command a division than half the privates under him."[32]

Burnside ordered Potter to take Hickory Hill, an exposed piece of high ground held by a Tennessee brigade. Ledlie was to follow Potter's attack and exploit any breakthrough. Several ravines cut into the hill and provided cover to any attacking force that could reach them. Barlow had driven out

---

31   Wilson, 445.

32   John Anderson, *The Fifty-Seventh Regiment of Massachusetts Volunteers in the War of the Rebellion* (Boston: E.B. Stillings & Company, 1896), 140.

Potter's division swept forward in long lines against the entrenched Confederate position. *Library of Congress*

the Confederate pickets on June 16, and Potter managed to place his men that night.

At 3:15 a.m. the officers of Potter's division whispered "All ready!"[33] The officers then drew their sabers, the sign for the men to attack. They achieved almost total surprise, bagging 600 prisoners, five flags, and four cannon. Unfortunately, Ledlie did not have his division ready. When they did march out, their advance was broken up by rough terrain. As such, Potter's success was not exploited. As the hours passed, a new Confederate line of entrenchments took shape along the Baxter Road, a turnpike that offered a direct path into Petersburg.

After the disaster at Hickory Hill, P. G. T. Beauregard begged Robert E. Lee for troops. Lee did not act, but Beauregard called in his last reserves, some 2,000 men who were guarding the northern approach to Petersburg.

Meanwhile, Ulysses Grant remained absent from the events at Petersburg. Instead, he was overseeing what might have been the most ridiculous battlefield transfer of the war. He became focused on Benjamin Butler's request for Smith's XVIII Corps to replace Maj. Gen. Horatio Wright's VI Corps at Bermuda Hundred. Wright immediately disliked Butler and refused to cooperate. When Wright would not attack, Butler shot back, "I send you an order to fight; you send me an argument."[34] However, Wright's men agreed with their commander. Brigadier General Emory Upton, one of

---

33   Charles Carleton Coffin, *Four Years of Fighting* (Boston: Ticknor and Fields, 1866), 365.

34   Alfred S. Roe, *The Ninth New York Heavy Artillery* (Worcester, MA: Alfred Seelye Roe, 1899), 109.

Wright's shrewdest and bravest brigade commanders, believed the attack would be "a deliberate murder of our troops" and mockingly referred to such an attack as "a *glorious charge!*"[35]

Robert E. Lee could have pushed on to Petersburg, but he concentrated on Butler and restored the Howlett Line. Beauregard, in the meantime, requested troops in order to launch an attack. Beauregard's erratic messages were possibly products of his tendency for wild mood swings, but they were also possibly born out of frustration. Beauregard might have thought that Lee, with his reputation for audacity, would react well to an attack plan, but apparently, Beauregard's confusing messages seemed to have the opposite effect. Indeed, on June 17, Lee kept A.P. Hill's Corps north of the James River.

Back at Petersburg, Meade became cautious. He feared that Beauregard might strike his flank, likely with Lee's army. Hancock suggested that Meade hit the exposed Confederate right flank. Warren's V Corps was nearby, but per Cyrus Comstock's orders Warren had most of his corps behind the IX Corps.

Around 11:00 a.m., Meade ordered Warren to scout the ground east and south of Baxter Road, but did not encourage Warren to make an all-out attack. Warren's ability to scout the area, though, was compromised because August Kautz's cavalry returned to Butler's command, leaving Warren without mobile eyes and ears and infantry in poor condition. The soldiers of the 118th Pennsylvania were so parched that they drank water from a swamp, disregarding the green scum on the surface. Whenever they stopped, some men dug holes in a frantic search for something to quench their thirst.

As an additional complication, Meade was emotionally erratic throughout the summer of 1864. Sarah Butler, wife of Benjamin Butler, wrote, "I would rather be a toad, and feed upon the vapors of a dungeon, than in Meade's place now. If success attends, the glory is Grant's. . . ."[36] This last line echoed a complaint Meade had made to his own wife earlier in the campaign.

In addition, the failure of June 16 may have dampened his enthusiasm for the attack. He had a penchant to sulk when things did not go his way. Rather than plan an attack, Meade sat down at noon to compose a letter to his wife,

---

35   Peter S. Michie, *The Life and Letters of Emory Upton* (New York: D. Appleton and Company), 117.

36   Butler, *Private and Official Correspondence*, 364-65.

Sarah. He had not written her since June 12, but writing a personal letter in the midst of a major battle during daylight hours was baffling. Tellingly, he admitted that "it looks very much as if we will have to go through a siege of Petersburg before entering on the siege of Richmond. . . . Well, it is all in the cruise, as the sailors say."[37] Meade was already settling for a siege.

Meanwhile, Burnside prepared his IX Corps for another major attack, this time with Brig. Gen. Orlando B. Willcox's lone division, which would be hurtled at an entrenched position. Willcox struck at 2:00 p.m. The men advanced with a cheer but came under a murderous fire. On the left flank, the 2nd Michigan came under heavy fire and marched to the north, gradually throwing the attack into disarray. Nearly 800 fell in only a few minutes. The leftmost companies of the 2nd Michigan suffered 80% casualties. Among the wounded was brigade commander Col. Benjamin C. Christ, who had fought with the IX Corps since its inception. Christ never returned to field command.

Burnside tried again. For the next attack, he chose Ledlie's division. Ledlie, though, was drunk and passed command of the division to Col. Jacob P. Gould of the 59th Massachusetts, a brave and outstanding officer. Gould aligned his men well and they attacked with a shout. One soldier in the 56th Massachusetts recalled, "We charged—and such a charge—the whole line seemed to move on wings. I do not think in all my boyhood days I ever ran so fast."[38]

After two horrific charges and at least one close-range volley from Gould's men, the 23rd South Carolina broke for the rear at around 7:00 p.m. They captured more than 100 troops, a stand of colors, and some artillery. Beauregard would later say that at that moment he feared that "the last hour of the Confederacy had arrived."[39]

Gould's men had a lodgment in Beauregard's lines, but there were no reserves to help them expand it. To add to the dilemma, said William B. Phillips of the 2nd Provisional Pennsylvania Heavy Artillery, "Our ammunition gave

---

37   George Gordon Meade, *Life and Letters*, Vol. II, (New York: Charles Scribner's Sons, 1913), 205.

38   "Camp of 56th (Mass) Reg.," *Quincy* (MA) *Patriot*, 27 August 1864, p. 1, col. 6.

39   Bruce Catton, *A Stillness at Appomattox* (New York: Doubleday and Company, 1953), 196.

out and we held our ground at the point of the bayonet."[40] Nearby Confederate units adjusted their lines and contained the breakthrough but were too weak to wipe it out. Barlow, meanwhile, made an attack to aid Gould. His assault pinned Robert Hoke's division, but his losses were quite heavy.

At 8:00 p.m. Meade ordered Warren to advance. Warren, though, failed to move his men with any vigor, although they were opposed by only light forces. Partially it was due to the rough terrain and Meade's orders, which indicated that Warren should only press ahead if success was certain.

While Warren dithered, the fighting around Gould's lodgment continued. By 10:00 p.m., Beauregard had assembled his reserves and ordered a series of counterattacks. Fighting was hand to hand, and by midnight Gould's lodgment was no more. D. Oscar Brunson of the 23rd South Carolina later recalled it as "the grandest struggle between the North and the South." The fighting lasted for five hours and was recalled by nearly everyone as one of the most desperate contests of the war.

The opportunity to seize Petersburg was now quickly evaporating. Lee at long last ordered a major cavalry probe, which confirmed that Meade's army was south of the James River. Lee shifted A.P. Hill to Chaffin's Bluff, but still did not send any troops to Petersburg. That night, Beauregard sent Lee a message where he made it clear that, without fresh troops, he would have to abandon Petersburg on June 18. Lee ordered Maj. Gen. Joseph Kershaw's veteran division to Petersburg, but there was no urgency in the orders. Kershaw was allowed to rest his men and head out in the morning.

Petersburg Day Four: Saturday, June 18, 1864

Having rested throughout June 17, George Meade's energy returned. He made preparation for a full attack along the entire front on June 18. Yet, the attack would not be easy. The II and IX Corps had already taken heavy losses. Ambrose Burnside advised against an attack while Winfield Hancock was too ill to continue and passed command of the II Corps to David Birney. As such, Meade pinned his hopes on Gouverneur Warren's V Corps to turn Beauregard's right flank.

---

40   "Interesting Letter," *Pittston* (PA) *Gazette* 14 July 1864.

In the Confederate lines, Beauregard was gloomy. He had at most 11,000 men facing roughly 50,000 Federals. His men were exhausted, some having been in constant action since June 15. Beauregard took drastic measures. He sent three members of his staff to personally implore Robert E. Lee to hurry the army to Petersburg.

The first was Col. Alexander Chisolm, who arrived at 1:00 a.m. He was told that Kershaw's division was on the way, although Lee promised to come and inspect the situation in the morning. Lee went to sleep and his staff would not allow the second messenger, Col. Alfred Roman, to awaken him. The last, Maj. Giles B. Cooke, was also told that Lee was asleep, but he refused to leave without first seeing Lee. Lt. Col. Walter H. Taylor, Lee's chief of staff and Cooke's roommate at the Virginia Military Institute, allowed him to converse with Lee. Cooke told Lee that "nothing but God Almighty can save Petersburg."[41]

P. G. T. Beauregard played second fiddle to Robert E. Lee for most of the war despite being one of the Confederacy's first heroes. However, it was Beauregard's diligence, not Lee's, that kept Petersburg in Confederate hands. *Library of Congress*

With this plea, Lee sent nearly the entire Army of Northern Virginia in motion. Given the urgency of the situation, Lee had the men force march at a merciless pace. In total, Lee was coming to Petersburg with around 23,000 confident veterans. Once they arrived, Meade's chances of victory would be greatly diminished.

While Beauregard's messengers pleaded with Lee, the Confederates at Petersburg took desperate action. Fearing his lines would be overwhelmed by a morning attack, Beauregard had his men fall back to the unfinished defensive line. The withdrawal was masterfully executed, in no small part because Harris had the new line staked out with white poles. So successful was the retreat, hardly any Federals noticed it. Yet there was no rest. As soon as the men reached the new lines they pitched in with slaves and militia to finish the defensive line.

At 4:00 a.m., a quick Union artillery barrage preceded a general

41 Howe, 109.

advance. The men soon found the Rebel lines abandoned, with campfires still ablaze. At the site of Jacob Gould's lodgment, the dead were found shot in the head and, in places, piled up. Confederate skirmishers withdrew quickly, warning the rest of their army of the enemy's advance. Johnson Hagood, one of Beauregard's most trusted brigade commanders, reported hearing "vociferous cheering" since Meade's men thought Beauregard had abandoned the city.[42]

Any vague hopes that Beauregard had abandoned Petersburg faded when the II Corps fought a sustained engagement with Rebel skirmishers at around 5:30 a.m. Meade was in a predicament. He did not know the terrain in front of him, and the broken ground had already separated the battle lines. Still, at 5:55 a.m. he ordered the advance to continue. Shortly after Meade issued his new attack orders, William F. Smith left with part of the XVIII Corps without bothering to tell Meade. The remaining elements of the XVIII Corps and a division of the VI Corps were assigned to John Martindale, who declared to Meade, "I will take command, as I believe I am the oldest brigadier-general in the army."[43] His proclamation did not sound encouraging, as Martindale had not done particularly well in the battle, and he mostly gave Meade cautious advice.

The initial Union advance was broken up by rough terrain and only the V Corps came to grips with the Rebels. After covering the longest distance and marching over the most difficult terrain, Warren's men engaged the Rebel right at 7:30 a.m. just as Kershaw's veterans were filing in. James Carson Elliott of the 56th North Carolina was at first dismayed because Kershaw's regiments were depleted, but one hardened veteran proclaimed, "This is a good place; we would like for them to come on ten lines deep, so we won't waste any lead."[44]

Lee arrived at 11:00 a.m. and conferred with Beauregard at the Customs House. Lee commended Beauregard on his choice of defensive terrain. Beauregard then asked Lee if they should attack Meade's left flank.

42   Johnson Hagood, "General P. G. T. Beauregard. His Comprehensive and Aggressive Strategy—Drewry's Bluff and Petersburg," in *Southern Historical Society Papers*, Vol. XIV, (Richmond: Southern Historical Society, 1900), 335.

43   Thomas L. Livermore, *Days and Events* (New York: Houghton Mifflin, 1920), 364.

44   James Carson Elliott, *The Southern Soldier Boy: A Thousand Shots for the Confederacy* (Raleigh: Edwards & Broughton Printing Company, 1907), 24.

The XVIII Corps' morning advance kicked off the last day of the battle of Petersburg. Wary of assaulting fortified positions, many soldiers gave less-than-full effort, which arguably prolonged the war because they would not strike a decisive blow when they had a chance. *Library of Congress*

Beauregard believed the Federals were demoralized while Confederate spirits were riding high. He also noted that they should strike before Meade could fortify. It was a bold proposition, but only two divisions were on hand and both were tired after a hard march. A. P. Hill's Corps would not arrive until late afternoon. Lee decided not to strike.

Meade ordered a renewed set of attacks at noon. The II Corps suffered greatly and made no gains. The attacks of the V and IX Corps were preceded by a grand barrage of some fifty cannon. The IX Corps struck at Poor Creek where the men made it to a nearby railroad cut. The V Corps had two divisions enter the railroad cut, while the other two failed to make contact on Beauregard's right. In general, many units were refusing to go forward, and most officers had little faith that Petersburg would be stormed on June 18.

The failure of each corps to make a full effort frustrated Meade. Only Birney seemed optimistic about penetrating the Confederate lines. When Warren indicated that he feared his flank might come under attack—the very thing Beauregard had proposed to Lee—Meade shot back: "I am greatly astonished at your dispatch. . . . My orders have been explicit and are now repeated, that you will immediately assault the enemy with all your force."[45] Meade issued new orders. Each corps would attack, with no provision given for coordination.

Martindale gained a bit of land at the cost of more than 400 losses. Warren and Burnside made more full-blooded attacks and suffered

45   *O.R.*, XL, Pt. 2, 179.

accordingly. Colonel J. William Hofmann's brigade lost 300 men, and all seven of the unit's regimental commanders were killed or wounded. Rufus Dawes, who led the 6th Wisconsin, wrote, "The suicidal manner in which we are sent against the enemy's entrenchments is discouraging. Our brigade was simply food for powder."[46] Joshua Lawrence Chamberlain, one of the most lionized officers in the Union army, found himself leading a brigade for the first time. He suffered a wound so terrible he was believed to be dead. Grant promoted Chamberlain on the spot to brigadier general in honor of his gallantry at both Gettysburg and Petersburg. Chamberlain, somehow, miraculously survived.

The IX Corps suffered just as much, if not worse than, the V Corps. Burnside's soldiers came within some 125 yards of the Confederate lines before halting and entrenching. Orlando Willcox, whose division had started the battle with about 3,000 men, now counted fewer than 1,500 men in the ranks, one of the highest divisional loss ratios in the entire war. For their efforts, the IX Corps held the most forward position in the army, but it was a dangerous spot. Lt. Amos Buffum of the 36th Massachusetts told his men that he was the last officer in the regiment to avoid death or wounding and noted, "It is the rule for all to be struck; but every rule has an exception."[47] Buffum was then shot dead.

Birney faced something of a near mutiny in the II Corps. The men would not attack. Frank Wilkeson of the 11th New York Artillery concluded the soldiers "were supremely disgusted with the display of military stupidity by our generals."[48] The only regiment that seemed willing to go in was the 1st Maine Heavy Artillery. Brig. Gen. Robert McAllister, a veteran brigade commander, thought "It is a death trap, a brigade can't live in there for five minutes."[49] McAllister, though, could not get the attack halted.

The 1st Maine Heavy Artillery struck so swiftly they overran the Confederate skirmish line. They were then met with a murderous fire. They

46   Rufus R. Dawes, *Service with the Sixth Wisconsin Volunteers* (Marietta: E. R. Alderman & Sons, 1890), 291.

47   Edwin Bearss, and Bryce Suderow. *The Petersburg Campaign: Volume 1: The Eastern Front Battles, June - August 1864.* (El Dorado Hills, CA: Savas Beatie, 2012), 125.

48   Wilkeson, 173.

49   Andrew J. MacIsaac, "Here the Reaper was the Angel of Death: The First Maine Heavy Artillery During the Overland Campaign," 95.

got within fifty yards of the Rebel lines when they finally withdrew, having lost 632 out of 900 men—the worst losses any regiment suffered during the Civil War. A nearby supporting attack lost 200 men.

Meade, after hearing of the fate of the 1st Maine Heavies, ordered the attacks to stop at 6:30 p.m. Oddly enough, Warren then recommended that a night attack be made, but Meade ignored this suggestion. He informed Grant that Petersburg was in Confederate hands. Grant replied, "We will rest the men and use the spade for their protection until a new vein has been struck."[50]

The losses at Petersburg were appalling, coming between 11,000-12,000 for the Union army, with the II and IX Corps suffering the most. While no division or corps commanders had been lost, twelve brigade commanders had been wounded with two other brigade commanders killed, making Petersburg one of the worst battles for Union brigade commanders. The Philadelphia and Irish Brigades were so depleted both were being considered for consolidation. Maj. Gen. Andrew Humphreys, Meade's chief of staff, wrote, "The incessant movements, day and night . . . the constant close contact with the enemy during all that time, the almost daily assaults upon entrenchments having entanglements in front, and defended by artillery and musketry in front and flank, exhausted officers and men."[51] The once-mighty Army of the Potomac was now incapable of sustained hard combat.

Confederate losses are harder to place, being anywhere from 2,900-4,700. However, nearly all were suffered by the divisions led by Robert Hoke and Bushrod Johnson, which each suffered a high percentage of losses, with a few brigades being particularly eviscerated. Regardless of the figures used, Petersburg was the thirteenth-bloodiest engagement of the war, and no battle fought after June 18, 1864, surpassed it in combined losses.

The fall of Petersburg would have meant the fall of Richmond and the reelection of Abraham Lincoln. Instead, Union morale fell, the price of gold shot up, and Lincoln's political rivals, both in the Democratic and Republican parties, were hopeful that he would not be president for much longer. Grant and Meade knew this, and they each tried to break the deadlock at Petersburg. Only a few days after the battle, the II Corps (despite its appalling losses)

---

50   Howe, 135.

51   Andrew A. Humphreys, *The Virginia Campaign of '64 and '65* (New York: Charles Scribner's Sons, 1883), 225.

was sent on a wide flanking movement that ended in an embarrassing defeat at Jerusalem Plank Road. After the late-July disaster at the Crater, Grant and Meade all but gave up on storming Petersburg, instead extending siege lines and working to cut off the railroads that fed Lee's army.

By contrast, when Maj. Gen. William Tecumseh Sherman reached Atlanta, he did so with an intact army in high spirits, bloodied but still capable of quick offensive action. Colonel Theodore Lyman of Meade's staff observed after the defeat, "You cannot strike a full blow with a wounded hand."[52] Sherman did not arrive at Atlanta with a wounded hand. Grant and Meade did at Petersburg.

There were many reasons for the defeat. Beauregard was the Confederacy's second-best independent commander. Only Beauregard and Lee won more battles than they lost. He was a skilled defensive tactician and engineer. Outside of his confusing messages to Lee on June 16 and 17, he made no errors. By contrast, every Union commander, from Grant, Meade, and Butler down to their corps commanders, made grievous errors.

There were, however, deeper factors. In the west, Ulysses Grant had used maneuver to achieve major victories, going after strategic points. He was given a lot of latitude by Lincoln, who was focused on affairs in Virginia. When Grant came east, he had similar ideas, but it was soon made plain to him that Lincoln wanted him to destroy Lee's army. Lincoln did not take into account that, lacking massed cavalry trained for pursuit, it was impossible to destroy a Civil War army unless it was tied to a strategic point such as Vicksburg.

In the aftermath of the defeat at Fredericksburg, Lincoln said, "If the same battle were to be fought over again, every day, through a week or days, with the same relative results, the army under Lee would be wiped out to its last man, the Army of the Potomac would still be a mighty host, the war would be over, the Confederacy gone. . . . No General yet found can face the arithmetic, but the end of the war will be at hand when he shall be discovered."[53] War, though, is not a matter of mere numbers, and men who

---

52   Theodore Lyman, *Meade's Headquarters, 1863-1865* (Boston: Atlantic Monthly Press, 1922), 170.

53   Donald Stoker, *The Grand Design: Strategy and the U.S. Civil War* (Oxford: Oxford University Press, 2010), 218.

face defeat on the scale of Fredericksburg will not be willing to constantly wage such a battle. Grant, however, bowed to Lincoln's wishes and waged an aggressive campaign—one that highlighted Grant's penchant for frontal assaults and his overall detachment from the battlefield.

The ultimate repudiation of Lincoln's ideas on the Virginia war was made by Abner R. Small of the 16th Maine: "We couldn't help thinking how McClellan had got the army almost to Richmond with hardly the loss of a man, while Grant had lost already thousands more than we cared to guess."[54]

Despite the scale, drama, and strategic importance of the battle of Petersburg, it is mostly forgotten. The reasons are many. Battles fought after 1863 tend to get less coverage, both in contemporary histories but even by the veterans themselves. The battle, while a major Confederate victory, only postponed defeat, and it is wrongly considered the first act of the siege of Petersburg, when really it was the last battle of the Overland Campaign.

Yet, there is a more personal reason. Outside of Beauregard, no major figure in the battle looks good. Lee was indecisive, slow to react, and did not perceive the threat to Petersburg until the eleventh hour. Grant was distracted. Meade was erratic and ordered a round of attacks on June 18 that were hopeless. Hancock was arguably at his career nadir, not counting Ream's Station. For anyone hoping to redeem the careers of Butler, Smith, Burnside, and Warren, Petersburg would not aid their case. Only Beauregard comes out ahead, but for many he is still a flamboyant Creole given to gaudy proclamations and strategic plans hashed out in an opium den.

A deeper look at Beauregard, though, shows him to be a shrewd tactician, a capable although not brilliant strategist, and a leader with an uncanny ability to win the trust of his men and subordinates. At Petersburg he won his best battle.

---

54   Abner R. Small, *The Road to Richmond* (New York: Fordham University Press, 2000), 146-47.

A 1st Maine Artilleryman

by Douglas Ullman Jr.

Point of Interest #4 on the map on pg. xv.

*Originally published as a guest post at Emerging Civil War
on September 27, 2019*

James S. Emerson could not have been pleased with his army career.[1] Standing at five feet, six inches, he had been one of the early volunteers, enlisting in the Third Maine Infantry less than two weeks after the firing on Fort Sumter. His regiment fought at the First Battle of Bull Run, but he was absent sick. He took sick again the following summer, just as Robert E. Lee's army prepared to attack the Federals outside of Richmond. Sunstroke incapacitated him, sending him to the rear just before the Seven Days' battles. In August he was sent to a general hospital in Washington, D.C., then to a hospital on Long Island—still suffering from diarrhea, vertigo, and even epilepsy. Following his discharge in December of 1862, one surgeon declared Emerson "two thirds incapacitated" and speculated that it would take one-to-two years for him to fully recover.

Emerson left no record of his wartime experience, so we can never know for certain what happened to him when he returned home. According to one of his parents, Emerson's wife, Lydia, "refused to live with him, and said she never would live with him again, and refused to speak with him when he went to see her." Neither Lydia nor James left a record of this.

---

1   Sources: James S. Emerson Pension File, WC #37846, National Archives Building, Washington, DC; Horace Shaw, *The First Maine Heavy Artillery* (Portland, ME: 1903).

However, on January 5, 1864, Emerson enlisted in the First Maine Heavy Artillery. Was he well enough that the ardor of patriotism that inspired him in 1861 was reinvigorated? Did he re-enlist to win back the affections of his disappointed wife? Or did some other motive induce Emerson to once again put on the uniform of the United States Army?

Like many heavy artillery regiments, the First Maine had occupied the defenses of Washington since the earliest days of its service in 1862. In spite of their artillery designation, these men were also trained to operate as infantry—in fact, the 1st Maine Heavy had originally been recruited as the state's 18th Infantry Regiment. By the late Spring of 1864, the war effort eventually needed them in just that capacity. After more than five months of relative inactivity, Lt. Gen. Ulysses S. Grant called for 10,000 of these troops to join the Army of the Potomac, which had been severely bloodied in its weeks of constant combat with Lee's army. Though they lacked combat experience, the massive size of the heavy artillery regiments—some mustered as many as 1,800 men—would offset their other deficiencies. If Emerson regretted his less-than-active military career, he would soon have the chance to remedy that situation.

Emerson got his reintroduction to combat on May 19, 1864, when the 1st Maine Heavy and several other regiments of "heavies" met Lt. Gen. Richard Ewell's Confederate corps at the Harris Farm, near Spotsylvania. Lieutenant Horace Shaw remembered the "vigorous attack . . . and the stubborn tenacity with which the 'raw troops' as we were called, held on to their ground against Ewell's whole corps and gave the Confederates sudden check and forced them back."

Though often overlooked by historians, the battle of Harris Farm made a big impression on the Mainers, who lost 579 in the action.

Nearly a month passed before Emerson and his comrades saw serious action again. In the interim, the heavy artillery regiments were distributed among the other brigades of the Army of the Potomac. A few took part in the bloody repulse at Cold Harbor on June 3. (By sheer chance, Emerson's brigade was kept out of that assault.) Following the defeat, Grant still determined to make his way south, this time by assaulting Petersburg, just below Richmond. With Petersburg and its vital railroads in Federal hands, Richmond would inevitably fall. However, delays on the Union side had afforded the Confederates ample time to strengthen their defenses and more than enough

On June 18, 1864, the 900 men of the 1st Maine Heavy Artillery charged across an open field of fire and sustained sixty-seven percent casualties: 115 men killed, 489 wounded, and 28 missing. It's the highest casualty rate sustained by any unit in the army during any single action of the entire war. *Chris Mackowski*

opportunity to shift troops to meet the threat.

James Emerson probably knew little of this on June 18, 1864, when the 850 remaining men of the 1st Maine Heavy formed a line of battle along Prince George Courthouse Road. The Confederate line, bristling with *abatis*, loomed some five hundred yards ahead. The Maine regiment—easily the largest in the brigade—was "designated as the center of the storming column." Its three battalions formed in three lines. The first line's objective was to clear the obstructions in front of the Confederate works and reach the ditch at the foot of the parapet. The second line would follow, providing covering fire for the men of the first line, then rush in once the obstacles were clear. The third line, Emerson's likely post, would add its weight to the final push to seize the Rebel line. Their entire division was to advance simultaneously in support. The undertaking seemed impossible to Lt. Shaw and many others, "but the First Maine officers and men were soldiers. The first duty of a soldier is obedience to orders."

At the signal, Emerson and his comrades stepped off with vigor. The other regiments of the brigade—veterans of Fredericksburg, Gettysburg, and the month of battles leading up to this day—advanced, too, but intense enemy fire sent them back to the shelter of the road. With their supports running for cover, the Mainers—still advancing amidst the tempest of lead—became the focus of Rebel musketry and artillery. "The earth was literally torn up with iron and lead," wrote Shaw. "The field became a burning seething, crashing, hissing hell. . . . So in ten minutes those who were not slaughtered had returned to the road or were lying prostrate upon that awful field of carnage."

Among the prostrate was James Emerson, who had fallen with wounds to the left arm, right thigh, chest, penis, testicles, and buttocks. Comrades managed to bring him off the field alive. His arm was amputated at a field hospital the following day, and he was subsequently sent to Campbell Hospital in Washington City where his other wounds were treated and additional amputations made. None of these measures were successful, however, and James S. Emerson died on June 30, 1864, at the age of 30.

And what of Lydia Emerson, the supposedly discontented spouse? Unfortunately, little is known of her life beyond what is contained in her application for a widow's pension. The most revealing document is the aforementioned testimony of one of Emerson's parents. This was only a fragment of a letter, though, the remainder of which has apparently been lost. It's important to remember, however, that parents of deceased soldiers were also entitled to a pension if they could prove their sons were supporting them financially. It is quite possible, therefore, that the unnamed parents' letter was at least partially motivated by self-interest. In any event, Lydia Emerson's application for a widow's pension was granted, and she received $8 a month until she remarried in 1868. She resumed receiving her pension upon her second husband's death in 1901, and she died in 1902.

Visitors to Petersburg National Battlefield can find James Emerson's name among the list of killed on the regiment's monument near Colquitt's Salient, the objective of their doomed charge. Emerson himself is buried in Section 13 of Arlington National Cemetery. His grave marker lists his date of death as June 18, 1864, the day he received his fatal wounds at Petersburg.

"That Crater During That Day I Shall Never Forget"

by Sarah Kay Bierle

Point of Interest #5 on the map on pg. xv.

Originally published as a blog post at Emerging Civil War on July 30, 2021

"We storm the works tomorrow at daylight. Our Division leads. I hardly dare hope to live through it. God have mercy. . . If I could only ride, or had two legs, so I could lead my brigade, I believe they would follow me anywhere. I will try as it is. God have pity on dear mother, Agnes, and all loved ones."

William Francis Bartlett penned those words in his diary on July 29, 1864. He had spent part of his afternoon at the division headquarters and knew what was planned for the following day. His journal entries and published letters from late July have a desperation and almost a belief that it will be impossible to survive.

He had returned to front about ten days previous, after recovering from injuries sustained at the Battle of The Wilderness. It was a typical pattern in Bartlett's war service: wounded, recuperate, return. The 21-year-old had enlisted in 1861 in the 20th Massachusetts Regiment. The slaughter and confusion at the Battle of Ball's Bluff in October 1861 forged his leadership and also left him as one of the few unscathed officers in the regiment. In the coming months, many of the men and other officers in the 20th Massachusetts credited Bartlett with holding the unit together and readying them the spring campaign, believing they would follow the young captain anywhere. On April 24, 1862, while waiting near Yorktown, Virginia, Bartlett went to a forward observation post; there, a Confederate sharpshooter's bullet struck him while in crouched in a kneeling position. The bullet hit the knee and splintered the lower bones of the left leg. Doctors amputated the limb and sent Bartlett home where he spent the summer recovering and completing his degree from Harvard.

William Francis Bartlett joined the 20th Massachusetts Regiment as a captain in 1861. By June 1864, he had been promoted to brigadier general, been wounded four times, and fought in both the eastern and western theaters. *Emerging Civil War*

Fitted with a prosthetic leg, Bartlett returned to the army, readying the 49th Massachusetts for action. He became their colonel and took them to battle in Louisiana. At the Battle of Port Hudson on May 27, 1863, Bartlett decided to lead his regiment into combat on horseback since he could not run the attack distance. He left the field wounded again, this time in the left wrist and right foot. Against the odds, he kept his arm, lived through fever and infection, and decided to return to active military service.

As the Overland Campaign opened in May 1864, Bartlett rode at the head of the 57th Regiment. His time with the Army of Potomac ended quickly on May 6 in The Wilderness. A head wound and a bad fall that injured the left leg's stump forced him from active campaigning until mid-

July. Bartlett returned to the siege lines around Petersburg just in time to take command of a brigade and pleased with his promotion to brigadier general which he had received in June.

Arriving in Petersburg that July, the newly-promoted brigadier general walked into a scene that others had been staging for weeks. The previous month Henry Pleasants of the 48th Pennsylvania Infantry had taken a look at the Confederate lines and at the Virginia soil, devising a scheme to dig a mine and blow up a portion of the enemy's fortifications. Eventually, Generals Burnside and Meade gave their stamp of approval for the project, though the details of the detonation and any following attacks seemed unclear.

Vague rumors ran through the Federal corps, but very few soldiers actually knew the truth. By July 23, the mine's chambers were completed, removing an estimated 18,000 cubic feet of dirt. The request for 12,000 pounds of black powder followed.

Meanwhile, in the Confederate lines, suspicions ran high. Some officers seriously believed that Union troops were digging mines. Others dismissively disregarded odd observations. Confederate dug counter shafts and tried various methods of locating the Yankee's project, but without success. The listening poles, tooth pegs, and dozens of feet of explorative underground galleries produced no decisive proof that the there were enemy troops beneath their feet. Brigadier General Edward Porter Alexander had advised General Robert E. Lee that he believed Pegram's Salient faced subterranean danger, but throughout July, the Confederates strengthened that position, little realizing that those reinforcements walked on powder kegs.

Bartlett's return coincided with the Union's high command considerations of what to do next to break the Confederate lines at Petersburg. Although he did not take part in the strategic planning, the results of those meetings would directly impact his command and his personal life. While waiting, Bartlett and his men lived under near-constant fire. He wrote about bullets regularly hitting the logs that surrounded his headquarters and his considerations if he would live through the nights or be killed by a stray bullet or shell fragment in his sleep. From his correspondence and journaling, Bartlett did not evidence a fear of death by this point in the war; he seemed to accept that he would not make it out alive. The constant fire played havoc on his mind and he worried how his mother and his fiancée—Agnes—would respond if he was killed or injured again.

General Grant directed his cavalry and the Union II Corps to march east and cross the James River to threaten that portion of the Confederate line and force them to shift troops. The unsuccessful movement resulted in fighting at Deep Bottom and no Union successes. Annoyed by the lack of progress, Grant and Meade turned their attention back to Burnside's tunnel which was already lined with explosives.

The council of war resulted in arguments and literally drawing names out of a hat to determine who would lead the assault. Though regiments of African-American troops had wanted to lead the attack and had possibly even been doing some forms of training, they were moved from the first line into the support waves. Instead, General James H. Ledlie's First Division of the IX Corps would spearhead the attack after the mine's explosion; General William Francis Bartlett commanded the First Brigade in Ledlie's Divison and Colonel Elisha Marshall led the Second. Supporting Ledlie, the other divisions of the IX Corps commanded by Potter, Willcox, and Ferrero would follow. Divisions of the V Corps waited in support and parts of the II Corps could be called upon, if needed. The plans called for the explosives in the mine to detonate, followed by an artillery barrage from General Henry Hunt's massed cannons. Then the infantry would move forward, pushing further into the Confederate lines and ideally breaking them.

Problems existed in the planning and continued as the generals returned to their divisions to explain things to their brigade commanders. Ledlie met with Bartlett and Marshall shortly before dark on July 29. Contradictions occurred that would later be identified, but that the brigade leaders could have no way of recognizing. Meade and Burnside's orders—as they were supported to be relayed through Ledlie—were to secure the edges of the expected crater, but specifically to not enter the yawning hole. Four days after the attack, Ledlie would admit that he told his officers to "move through the breach to be made by the mine and then to press forward and occupy the hill beyond."

Based on what he heard from Ledlie, Bartlett thought he should enter the crater, get to the other side, and secure the top of the deadly hole. He couldn't ride in this type of attack, so he would have to lead on foot and prosthetic limb. The best he could promise was "to try." At some point in the event, he wrote in his diary, then spent the rest of the dark hours getting his troops into position. His brigade would follow Marshall's in the coming attack. The First Brigade had approximately 1,800 men total, the 21st,

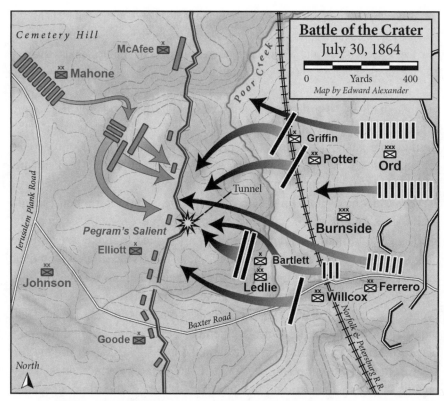

BATTLE OF THE CRATER—Careful advanced planning was all for naught thanks to a last-minute draw-of-the-straw change that left James Ledlie in charge of the lead assault against the Confederate position. After his men flooded into the newly blasted Crater, reinforcements seemed likewise drawn to the gaping hole as they rushed forward. Confederate reinforcements under "Little Billy" Mahone rushed to the scene to help plug the gap.

29th, 56th, 57th, and 59th Massachusetts Infantry, the 100th Pennsylvania Infantry, and the 35th Massachusetts Engineers.

Bartlett and the others waiting to attack knew that the mine explosion was delayed, but they did not know at the time that the fuse had burned out and had to be relit. When it finally detonated, Pegram's Salient exploded high into the air, killing and tearing apart the Confederate soldiers in the direct path of the upheaval. While others took time to marvel at the horrible destruction, Bartlett's diary writings moved directly into his role and attack:

> Mine sprung at 4.40. We rushed across the open field. I got up to the enemy's works about as soon as any one. Got into the crater. Took the first and second lines of the enemy. Held them till after one, when we were

driven back by repeated charges. I fought them for an hour after they held the whole line, excepting the crater where we were, their flag within seven feet of ours across the work. They threw bayonets and bottles on us, and we returned, for we got out of ammunition.

Marshall and Bartlett's brigades did what they thought they were supposed to do, moved into The Crater to cross it and push into the Confederate lines. However, that proved impossible. The Confederates rallied, and led by General William Mahone headed for the broken line. They found Union troops trapped in the debris pit.

Back in the Union lines, Generals Ledlie and Ferrero both sought shelter in a "bomb-proof" and, according to some eye-witness accounts, spent the day drinking while their soldiers struggled to make sense of the orders they had received and adapt the fight as bullets rained down on their exposed position. Bartlett personally tried to keep the Fourth Division with its regiments of African American soldiers from entering The Crater, but eventually many of them joined their other comrades in blue in the death trap. Cries of "No Quarter" and "Remember Fort Pillow" echoed from the black soldiers as Union regiments struggled out of The Crater or tried to fire back from their current positions. As the Confederates counterattacked and regained their position around the large hole blown in their line, desperate fights, panicked retreats, and racial atrocities created a brutal conflict.

According to Bartlett, "At last, to save further slaughter, there being no hope of our being rescued, we gave it up. That crater during that day I shall never forget. A shell knocked down a bowlder of clay on to my wood leg and crushed it to pieces, killing the man next me. I surrendered to General Mahone."

Bartlett had lived through the day, but nearly 3,800 Union soldiers had fallen while Confederate losses totaled around 1,500. The young general did not return to headquarters, and for many weeks, he did not discuss the near-senseless debacle at The Crater with other officers. Still, it weighed on his mind during his imprisonment. In a letter to his mother written from prison at Danville, Virginia, Bartlett confessed, "I hope no blame is given me for the failure of Saturday. I certainly did all in my power. I held the pit with hardly any force after the rest of the line had been retaken. The rebel flag was within six feet of mine, just the ridge of dirt between, for nearly an hour. It was impossible to withdraw without sacrificing all the men, so I held on as

Around 8 a.m. on July 30, 1864, combat artist Alfred R. Waud sketched Union reinforcements advancing toward the Crater at Petersburg. Beyond the outer Federal earthworks, other Union infantrymen swarm on "the mounds of earth thrown up by the explosion," and along "the high ground" extends "the Confederate inner line of works" that the attackers intended to capture, according to a note written by Waud. The attack failed. *Library of Congress*

long as possible in hope of reinforcements. The negroes were crowded into the same pit with us when they retreated in such confusion...."

Bartlett believed that he received exceptionally bad treatment from his Confederate captors because he was taken prisoner with Black soldiers. Though he did not command African American regiments, the Confederates did not particularly differentiate at that point and carried out their harsh treatment of Black men in Union uniform and those white officers who were with them. Immobile without his prosthetic or crutches, Bartlett "slept in a field of stones," was robbed, deprived of food and water, and treated worse than cattle. Shipped by train to Danville, Virginia, he was placed in an open tent for medical care and nearly died of disease before he was transported to Libby Prison in Richmond, Virginia. In the autumn of 1864, Bartlett was exchanged and sent north, but the effects of his prison illnesses and mistreatment lingered for the rest of his life and contributed to his death in 1876 at age 36.

The battle of The Crater on July 30, 1864, was Bartlett's last military combat. Positioned second in line for attack and given faulty orders, he and his men paid the price for the strategists' errors and miscommunications. Clearly perceiving the tactical problems as the morning's battle unfolded, he tried to keep other troops from entering The Crater, but eventually had to surrender in an attempt to save the soldiers still alive.

Bartlett tried, and his hopes for Divine pity were granted. He lived to see his mother and his fiancée again, but ultimately the effects of his imprisonment and harsh treatment from being captured at The Crater would kill him twelve years later. But on that July day, he led his brigade…and they followed anywhere, even into The Crater.

The Crater Sent a Monster Home to Maine

by Brian Swartz

Point of Interest #5 on the map on pg. xv.

Adapted from a series of posts published on the blog Maine at War
on March 20, March 27, and April 3, 2014, it appeared on
Emerging Civil War on July 31, 2021

The massive explosion that created The Crater and stunned James J. Chase followed him home to Maine.[1]

Hailing from Turner in Androscoggin County, the 16-year-old Chase joined the army in August 1863. Showing talent and leadership capabilities, he received a commission and a transfer to the 32nd Maine Infantry Regiment in late winter 1864 as Second Lieutenant, Co. D.

He arrived at Petersburg in July and reported to the 32nd's commander, Col. Mark Wentworth. Guided by a soldier named Peare, Chase navigated the trenches, ran across an open ravine as Confederate bullets whizzed past, and "at about three P.M. we reached the regiment."

He found Capt. H. R. Sargent, who commanded the companies deployed perhaps 60 yards from Confederate positions. Ordered by Sargent "to assume command" of Co. D, Chase "found thirteen privates and three non-

---

1   Sources: Bruce Catton, *Stillness at Appomattox*, (New York, NY, 1953), 242; James J. Chase, *The Charge at Day-Break*, (Lewiston, ME, 1875).

commissioned officers, of the full company of one hundred I left scarcely three months before."

Another regiment relieved the 32nd Maine in the evening on Tuesday, July 26; the Maine boys returned "to our retreat in the pine woods" behind the Union lines, according to Chase. Off to the right he saw Union "sappers and miners carrying powder to the mine (tunnel)" dug from the Federal lines to a point beneath the Confederate fort atop Cemetery Hill.

Excavated by Pennsylvania coal miners, the tunnel ran 511 feet to a gallery excavated about 50 feet beneath the Confederate fort. The miners packed the gallery with four tons of gunpowder.

Only 17 when he joined the 32nd Maine Infantry Regiment as a second lieutenant, James J. Chase participated in the July 30, 1864, at the Crater. After his regiment descended the Crater's explosion-carved sides, Chase was shot in one eye and evacuated. He was so horribly disfigured that a civilian woman later called him "a horrid looking creature!" *Maine State Archives*

Plans called for the mine to blow up at 3:30 a.m., Saturday, July 30, to create a gaping hole in Southern lines. The 32nd Maine Infantry would charge after the mine exploded. "Grasping my sword at my side, I hurriedly took my place in the line now being formed," Chase said. "Silently we marched out of the woods and along the covered way.

"By the light of the full moon we could distinctly see the outlines of the enemy's fort on Cemetery Hill, not 300 yards distant," Chase said. At 3:15 a.m. "our troops were in position." At 3:30 a.m., "contrary to our expectations no explosion took place."

Two Pennsylvania soldiers scurried into the tunnel to splice and light a new fuse. They rushed to safety,

The mine exploded at 4:44 a.m. The detonation "seemed to occur in slow motion," wrote historian Bruce Catton. Soldiers experienced "first a long, deep rumble, like summer thunder rolling along a faraway horizon, then a swaying and swelling of the ground up ahead, with the solid earth rising to form a rounded hill," which "then . . . broke apart, and a prodigious spout of flame and black smoke went up toward the sky. . . ."

"O horrors! was I in the midst of an earthquake?" Chase exclaimed. Looking at Cemetery Hill, "I beheld a huge mass of earth being thrown up, followed by a dark lurid cloud of smoke."

Charging with their brigade, the 32nd Maine boys "found a large hole or crater made by the explosion, shaped like a tunnel, forty feet deep and seventy feet in diameter," Chase said. "We at once took shelter in the deep crater . . . some jumped in, some tumbled in, others rolled in." He jumped into the crater, where "beneath our feet were the torn fragments of men, while upon every side could be seen some portion of a man protruding from the sand."

Chase soon "climbed up a pile of earth . . . thrown up by the explosion" and immediately spotted "a large body of the enemy forming in a deep ravine at the foot of the hill." Sliding into the crater to warn Sargent, who was crawling up "a pile of earth similar to the one I had climbed," Chase stood still too long.

A Confederate "sharpshooter from the pine grove on our left" fired. "The bullet struck me near the left temple and came out through the nose at the inner corner of the right eye, throwing out the left eye in its course." Chase reeled in agony. "Staggering and reeling I walked across the trench, the blood spurting before me from my wound."

Vaguely seeing Capt. Joseph Hammond beside him, Chase said, "Captain, I must die."

"Yes, Chase, you have a death shot," Hammond replied.

As comrades checked on him, Chase begged "for a looking-glass." Gazing into it, "I could see no resemblance to my former self. My left eye lay upon my cheek, while my nose appeared to be shot off."

Sargent administered rudimentary medical care and used a penknife to extract "some loose pieces of bone projecting from my nose into my remaining eye," Chase remembered

"I want to save that eye, for it is a great blessing to have one if you can't have two," Sargent said.

Evacuated to a waiting ambulance, Chase "shrieked with pain" as it jolted and careened toward a field hospital. Passing out on the operating table, he awoke to find his head bandaged "and the blood . . . washed from my face." Evacuated to City Point, he was carried onto a hospital transport. With him went "all my earthly possessions": his sword and "the bloody shirt and trousers I wore."

Chase's father soon arrived at the Washington, D.C., hospital where the wounded lieutenant received excellent medical care. The Chases later left for Maine; after arriving in Auburn by train on Thursday, Aug. 18, they went to board a carriage for the final journey home.

A woman passenger vehemently protested, "Don't let him come in here; I can't ride with such a horrid looking creature!" The Chases shifted to a stagecoach.

The next day, friends gathered around James Chase as he examined his face in a mirror. He saw the same "horrid looking creature" denied transportation by the shrieking passenger—and Chase did not blame her. Swollen and bandaged, his face resembled nothing human.

He recovered and eventually joined the Maine State Guards in January 1865. Mustering out, he married and had children.

But The Crater followed him home. On Tuesday, December 10, 1872, "I was attacked with severe pain in my [right] eye, which increased through the day." Having experienced similar bouts in the past, Chase expected the pain would subside.

"At sunset . . . all objects before me began to fade from my vision," a frightened Chase realized. He called too late for a doctor; "before he reached me all nature was to me a blank.

I had looked upon my wife (Drusilla) and little ones (daughters Jenny and Ella) for the last time." Chase admitted. He groped to find and pick up his 3-year-old daughter (Ella), whom he would never "see" again.

Now permanently blind, "my burden seemed more than I could bear," he commented three years later. "But . . . I now appreciate the many blessings bestowed upon me, which I am permitted to enjoy."

Grant's Lifeline: City Point, Virginia

by Dwight Hughes

Point of Interest #6 on the map on pg. xv.

In the cool dusk of Sunday, April 2, 1865, Abraham Lincoln sat with Rear Admiral David D. Porter, commander of the North Atlantic Blockading Squadron, on the upper deck of the USS *Malvern* at City Point listening to the boom of artillery and rattle of musketry in the Petersburg lines eight miles away. Richmond would be evacuated the next day.

"Can't the Navy do something at this particular moment to make history?" asked the president. "The Navy is doing its best just now," replied Porter, "holding in utter uselessness the rebel navy, consisting of four [three] heavy ironclads. If those should get down to City Point they would commit great havoc. . . ." The iron monsters *Virginia No. 2, Fredericksburg*, and *Richmond* defended the river and Confederate capitol.

Admiral Porter and his sailors had accomplished much more than that to support Lt. Gen. Ulysses S. Grant, and the Armies of the Potomac and the James, as they surrounded and strangled R. E. Lee's Army of Northern Virginia. The admiral and the general continued the interservice partnership so effectively fostered at Vicksburg two years previously. City Point, where the Appomattox meets the James, was one of the busiest ports in the world—and Grant's lifeline.

Before the war, the quiet little peninsula featured modest dockage for exporting tobacco, cotton, and corn. By September 1864, wooden wharfs extended more than a mile along the James, accommodating daily some 40 steamboats, 75 sailing vessels, and 100 barges. Commissary, quartermaster,

As Grant's primary supply hub, City Point, Virginia, became a city unto itself, complete with railroad yards, loading wharfs, and transport vessels with wagons and camp buildings on the bluff.
Library of Congress

and ordnance warehouses stockpiled 3 million pounds of goods including 9 million meals and 12 thousand tons of hay and oats to sustain the army for 30 days and their animals for 20 days. Commissary bakers produced 100,000 bread rations a day.

City Point included a 200-acre tent hospital, medical evacuation pier, U. S. Sanitary Commission headquarters, courthouse, jail, prisoner exchange facility, post office, chaplain corps offices, and telegraph office. Waterborne and telegraphic communications were almost continuous with Fort Monroe and Washington. Bakeries, forges, wagon repair shops, and barracks filled the grounds.

Multiple railroad sidings converged from riverside to a railhead served by an engine roundhouse and repair shed. The Railroad Construction Corps rebuilt the South Side Railroad to Petersburg, then extended it southwest behind Union lines. Twenty-five locomotives and 275 railroad cars brought by barge from Washington, D.C., moved men and material. Manned trenches and batteries surrounded the instillation; the powerful double-turret monitor *Onondaga* and a gaggle of Porter's gunboats patrolled the waters.

Grant relaxes with wife, Julia, and son Jesse before his headquarters cabin at City Point. Julia had an eye condition she was self conscious of and so only let herself be photographed in profile. Grant considered her his rock. *Library of Congress*

The general in chief arrived at City Point on June 15, 1864, after the battle of Cold Harbor and just as Maj. Gen. Benjamin Butler launched the Army of the James in the first major assault on Petersburg. Lieutenant Colonel Horace Porter (no relation to Admiral Porter) recalled that the staff cow—"the rich milk of which went far toward compensating for the shortcomings in other supplies"—had been forgotten on the north bank of the James, the only casualty in the army's crossing of the 2,200-foot pontoon bridge. Grant's reaction? "Well," he said, "it seems that the loss of animals in this movement falls most heavily upon headquarters."

Grant set up with his staff in a tent camp on the east lawn of the abandoned plantation known as Appomattox overlooking the rivers. The stately manor house was assigned to the chief quartermaster. The general later occupied a modest cabin on the site; his wife, Julia, and son, Jesse, joined him for the final three months of the siege. A wooden staircase descended to the steamboat-landing at the foot of the bluff.

For nine and a half months, almost to the end of the war, Grant issued orders and coordinated movements of Federal armies throughout the nation from this site. Maj. Gen. W. T. Sherman marched across Georgia and up through the Carolinas and Maj. Gen. Philip Sheridan swept the Shenandoah Valley while Maj. Gen. George Meade tightened the noose on Petersburg. "The headquarters camp at City Point was destined to become historic and to be the scene of some of the most memorable events of the war," noted Colonel Porter.

*   *   *

In the forenoon of August 9, 1864, Grant was sitting in front of his tent with several officers discussing plans for detecting and capturing spies in the camp. "At twenty minutes to twelve," wrote Colonel Porter, "a terrific explosion shook the earth, accompanied by a sound which vividly recalled the Petersburg mine, still fresh in the memory of every one present. Then there rained down upon the party a terrific shower of shells, bullets, boards, and fragments of timber."

An ammunition barge had exploded at the wharf below the bluff, discharging 30,000 artillery shells and 75,000 small-arms rounds. A mounted orderly and several horses died instantly; a staff member and three orderlies were wounded. Debris flew half a mile in every direction. Hearing the thunderous, 30-second detonation and seeing towering black smoke, observers 30 miles downriver thought Petersburg or Richmond was burning.

Porter: "The general was the only one of the party who remained unmoved; he did not even leave his seat to run to the bluff with the others to see what had happened." Grant composed a telegram to General Halleck in Washington: "Five minutes ago an ordnance boat exploded, carrying lumber, grape, canister, and all kinds of shot over this point. Every part of the yard used as my headquarters is filled with splinters and fragments of shell."

The blast vaporized the barge and all aboard, triggered the next barge, flattened the adjoining warehouse, and destroyed over half of the 400-foot wharf. An estimated $2 million in property was lost. Casualties were noted as 43 killed and 126 wounded, but some accounts put the death toll at 300, with "contraband" workers unaccounted for. An ordnance officer recalled: "From the top of the bluff there lay before me a staggering scene, a mass of overthrown buildings, their timbers tangled into almost impenetrable heaps. In the water were wrecked and sunken barges."

A Union surgeon saw a man lying flat on his back, dead, on the top of a rail car, then, "the lower half of the trunk & about half of the thighs of a man," and along the road, "detached portions of the human body. A foot, hand, pieces of the scalp—large pieces of muscle & flesh lay scattered all around. . . . We dressed some of the most hideous & ghastly wounds which falls to the lot of Surgeons to dress." One account describes eleven barrels holding pieces of collected human flesh. The lemonade vendor expired when hit in the stomach by a flying saddle.

City Point returned to full operation in nine days with tightened security. A board of investigation headed by Colonel Porter could find no revealing evidence. Witnesses attributed the incident to careless ammunition handling, "but there was a suspicion in the minds of many of us that it was the work of some emissaries of the enemy. . . ."

Documents captured post-war revealed that Capt. John Maxwell of the Confederate secret service had crawled on his knees through the picket line, walked in, and placed upon the barge a "horological torpedo"—a time bomb in a candle box packed with 12 pounds of gunpowder, a percussion cap, and clockwork mechanism. Hiding nearby, Maxwell was "terribly shocked by the explosion" but returned safely to Confederate lines.

*   *   *

By December 1864, Admiral Porter had withdrawn most naval vessels from the rivers and departed with them for the massive Fort Fisher expedition. USS *Onondaga* remained, commanded by Navy Captain William A. Parker, along with three or four light gunboats. "There had been so much talk about the formidable character of the double-turreted monitors," wrote Colonel Porter, "that General Grant decided one morning to go up the James and pay a visit. . . ." The ironclad was lying above the pontoon bridge in Trent's Reach.

The general admired the machinery, then asked the range of her 15-inch smoothbores, continued Porter. "About eighteen hundred yards," replied Parker. Grant pointed upriver to an enemy battery about that distance and said, "Suppose you take a shot at it, and see what you can do." The turret revolved; the gun was laid and fired. "There was a tremendous concussion, followed by a deafening roar as the enormous shell passed through the air; and then all eyes were strained to see what execution would be done. . . ."

The round exploded directly within the battery, raising a cloud of smoke; earth and splintered logs flew, and men tumbled over the parapet. With another puff at his cigar, the general nodded and said, "Good shot!" Smiles appeared as the navy officers pretended that this was just routine.

Grant was apprehensive that his depleted naval force would leave City Point vulnerable to the enemy squadron upriver. On the night of January 23, he suggested that a navy officer plant torpedoes in the channel at Trent's Reach, augmenting the sunken boat and boom obstructions and

The USS *Onondaga*, shown at anchor on the James River, was a double-turreted river monitor, 226 ft. long and 52 ft. in beam, manned by 130 officers and men, and armed with two 15-inch smoothbore Dahlgrens and two 50 pdr. Parrott rifles. *Naval History and Heritage Command*

shore batteries already there. On site, the officer spotted the three huge Rebel ironclads quietly descending the dark river with several gunboats and torpedo launches. He alerted headquarters by telegraph.

Grant issued instructions to tow coal schooners up the river, ready to sink in the channel, and to move additional heavy guns to the riverbank. He dispatched Col. Porter and another staff officer by boat to order up all available war vessels. The staff officer "got a little rattled," recalled Porter, and began donning his spurs until persuaded they would not be needed on the water.

"The night was pitch-dark," he wrote, "but our naval vessels were promptly reached by means of steam-tugs; and their commanders, who displayed that cordial spirit of cooperation always manifested by our sister service, expressed an eagerness to obey General Grant's orders as implicitly as if he had been their admiral. Most of these vessels were out of repair and almost unserviceable, but their officers were determined to make the best fight they could." (Even the general in chief could not issue direct orders to a Navy officer.)

Porter returned to the headquarters hut. Soon after one o'clock, a messenger arrived and, with a loud knock on Grant's bedroom door, announced that the enemy force had penetrated river obstructions. "In about two minutes the general came hurriedly into the office. He had drawn on his top-boots over his drawers, and put on his uniform frock-coat, the skirt of which reached about to the tops of the boots and made up for the absence of trousers." He lighted a cigar, sat at his desk, and began writing orders. "The puffs from the cigar were now as rapid as those of the engine of an express-train at full speed."

Mrs. Grant entered and quietly asked: "Ulyss, will those gunboats shell the bluff?" "Well, I think all their time will be occupied in fighting our naval vessels and the batteries ashore," he replied. "The *Onondaga* ought to be able to sink them, but I don't know what they would do if they should get down this far." Then a new report revealed that the Union monitor had disengaged and retired downriver below the pontoon bridge.

Porter recorded the general's reaction: "I have been thrown into close contact with the navy, both on the Mississippi River and upon the Atlantic coast. I entertain the highest regard for the intrepidity of the officers of that service, and it is an inexpressible mortification to think that the captain of so formidable an ironclad, and the only one of its kind we have in the river, should fall back at such a critical moment. Why, it was the great chance of his life to distinguish himself."

Lieutenant Dunn offered to hitch up an ambulance and drive Mrs. Grant into the country. "Oh, their gunboats are not down here yet," answered Grant, "and they must be stopped at all hazards." More dispatches were sent; a fresh cigar was smoked. Two hours later, they learned that only one enemy vessel actually had made it below the obstructions with the rest still above, apparently aground and immobilized under heavy fire. More guns had been placed in the shore batteries. The situation was "greatly relieved." Lieutenant Ingalls quipped: "I've about made up my mind that these boats never intended to come down here anyhow—that they've just been playing it on us to keep us out of bed."

At daylight, *Onondaga* moved up within 900 yards of the Confederate ironclad *Virginia No. 2* and opened fire along with shore guns, striking her some 130 thirty times. The ironclad *Richmond* took numerous hits; a Rebel gunboat and torpedo launch were destroyed. Confederates finally got their vessels afloat at floodtide and withdrew upriver. They tried again that night but under murderous fire retired once more. "This was the last service performed by the enemy's fleet in the James River," concluded Porter. Trent's Reach also was General Grant's last naval battle.

*   *   *

On the morning of January 31, headquarters received a letter from Confederate representatives Alexander H. Stephens, J. A. Campbell, and R. M. T. Hunter asking permission to come through the lines. They were the "Peace Commission" seeking a conference with President Lincoln. Notified to hold the emissaries at City Point pending instructions, Grant greeted them cordially and provided comfortable accommodations aboard a steamer.

"They were treated with every possible courtesy; their movements were not restrained," noted Col. Porter. Confederate Vice President Stephens was about five feet five and of sallow complexion. "His skin seemed shriveled upon his bones. He possessed intellect enough, however, for the whole commission. Many pleasant conversations occurred with him at headquarters. . . ."

Grant felt awkward and uncomfortable playing host while—despite polite prodding— studiously not expressing views on their mission. The general wrote to Secretary of War Stanton: "I will state confidentially, but not officially to become a matter of record, that I am convinced . . . their intentions are good and their desire sincere to restore peace and union." He recognized the difficulties but, "I fear now their going back without any expression from any one in authority will have a bad influence." He would be sorry if the president could not meet with the commissioners in person.

Colonel Porter credited this missive with convincing Lincoln to attend the "Hampton Roads Peace Conference" with Secretary of State Seward on February 2 aboard the steamer *River Queen* at Fort Monroe. The meeting produced no result. Porter recorded a story later related by Lincoln to Grant: Mr. Stephens arrived wrapped in a coarse gray overcoat three sizes too large with a high collar, and—noting the Rebel's yellowish complexion—peeled the coat off "as you would husk an ear of corn." The president couldn't help thinking, "Well, that's the biggest shuck and the littlest nubbin I ever did see." It was one of Grant's favorite anecdotes.

On his return through City Point, Stephens conversed with Col. Porter. The Confederate had developed "certain definite notions" about Grant; he expected only the bluntness of a soldier but was completely surprised upon meeting him. The general's "spare figure, simple manners, lack of all ostentation, extreme politeness, and charm of conversation" were a revelation. "It was plain that he has more brains than tongue. . . . He is one of the most remarkable men I ever met."

*   *   *

After nearly ten months of siege, the end appeared near. Admiral Porter had returned after the fall of Fort Fisher. "Every day was improving our condition and making that of the Confederacy worse," he noted. "All the ports along the coast had been captured; blockade-running was at an end, and the Confederates could no longer depend upon the sea for supplies. . . . How they ever managed to maintain their armies was a mystery to me, and must have astonished the military men of our side who had splendid commissariats to draw from."

Grant telegraphed the president on March 20, 1865: "Can you not visit City Point for a day or two? I would like very much to see you, and I think the rest would do you good." Lincoln's response: "Your kind invitation received. Had already thought of going immediately after the next rain."

At about 9:00 p.m. on the 24th, the sidewheel steamer *River Queen* moved up the James and docked at the wharf with President Lincoln, Mrs. Lincoln, their son Tad, and several ladies. They were greeted by the general and staff including Col. Porter and Capt. Robert Lincoln. This presidential visit would become a two-week sojourn.

Colonel Porter: "Grant, with his usual foresight, had predicted that Lee would make a determined assault at some point on our lines in an endeavor to throw our troops into confusion, and then make his escape. . . ." Grant had notified his commanders in February to be extra vigilant, especially in the center. "No time is to be lost awaiting orders, if an attack is made in bringing all their reserves to the point of danger. With proper alacrity in this respect I would have no objection to seeing the enemy get through."

About six o'clock the next morning, March 25, the camp was awakened with news of the enemy breakthrough near Fort Stedman and a major attack in progress. The telegraph was down; communications to the front depended on couriers. General Meade, commanding the Army of the Potomac, had arrived in City Point the evening before to meet with Mrs. Meade. "Greatly nettled" to be absent from his command, Meade paced back and forth, dictating rapid orders to his chief of staff. The president was aboard the

River Queen anchored in the river; his son Robert (a captain on Grant's staff) kept him informed.

General Grant "did not experience much apprehension," noted Col. Porter. He notified the Army of the James: "This may be a signal for leaving. Be ready to take advantage of it." Finally, about half past eight o'clock, they learned that the whole Union line had been recaptured, many prisoners taken, and that everything was again quiet. "This attack was one of the most dramatic events of the siege of Petersburg," concluded Porter.

Lincoln had come to City Point for rest, recalled Admiral Porter. "He looked much worn out with his responsibilities since I had last seen him. . . . The President was evidently nervous; the enormous expense of the war seemed to weigh upon him like an incubus; he could not keep away from General Grant's tent, and was constantly inquiring when he was going to move; though, if he had looked at the wagons, stuck fast in the thick red mud of the surrounding country, he would have known why no army could operate."

General Sherman arrived and on March 28, he, Grant, and Admiral Porter visited the president on the *River Queen*. "There now occurred in the upper saloon of that vessel the celebrated conference between these four magnates," wrote Col. Porter. "It was in no sense a council of war, but only an informal interchange of views between the four men who, more than any others, held the destiny of the nation in their hands."

General Grant set the armies in motion all along the front and, on the morning of the 29th, began shifting headquarters. Lincoln came ashore to say good-by, continued Col. Porter, looking "more serious than at any other time since he had visited headquarters. The lines in his face seemed deeper, and the rings under his eyes were of a darker hue." Cordial handshakes were exchanged; the general and staff mounted the platform at the rear of the car and raised their hats respectfully. The president returned the salute and said in a broken voice: "Good-by, gentlemen. God bless you all! Remember, your success is my success." The train moved off; Grant's last campaign had begun.

"I attached myself to the President at his own request," wrote Admiral Porter, "and did all I could to interest him by taking him up and down the river in my barge, or driving about the country in General Ingals's buggy with two fine horses." The admiral was alone with the president for several days and heard many Lincoln stories. "To me he was one of the most interesting men I ever met. . . . I saw more to admire in this man, more to reverence, than I had believed possible."

Lincoln invited himself aboard Porter's flagship, USS *Malvern*, a swift, captured blockade-runner, which suited the admiral for getting around in shallow bays and rivers but had poor accommodations. "What pleased [the president] was that he got away from the outer world; no one could get at him but those whom he desired to see. . . . He told me, at parting, that the few days he had spent on board the *Malvern* were among the pleasantest in his life."

"I don't know what his conversations with General Grant were," continued the admiral, "but, from the tenor of his conversations with me, I know that he was determined the Confederacy should have the most liberal terms. 'Get them to plowing once,' Mr. Lincoln said, 'and gathering in their own little crops, eating pop-corn at their own firesides, and you can't get them to shoulder a musket again for half a century.'"

On April 1, Sheridan seized the South Side Railroad at Five Forks. According to Admiral Porter, as they relaxed on *Malvern* that evening of April 2 Lincoln also asked if the Navy couldn't at least make a refreshing noise. Porter telegraphed one of his gunboats upriver to open rapid fire on enemy forts. "The President admitted that the noise was a very respectable one, and listened to it attentively, while the rapid flashes of the guns lit up the whole horizon." Then a loud explosion shook the deck under their feet. Lincoln jumped from his chair. "I hope to Heaven one of them has not blown up!" he exclaimed.

"No, sir," Porter replied. "My ear detects that the sound was at least two miles farther up the river; it is one of the rebel ironclads. You will hear another in a minute." "Well," he said, "our noise has done some good; that's a cheap way of getting rid of ironclads. I am certain Richmond is being evacuated, and that Lee has surrendered, or those fellows would not blow up their ironclads." Just then there was a second and a third explosion. "That is all of them," Porter said; "no doubt the forts are all evacuated, and to-morrow we can go up to Richmond." The admiral ordered the river obstructions removed and torpedoes swept.

At daylight, Federals found the Petersburg fortifications empty; Union troops marched into the city. "Nothing was to be seen of the ironclads but their black hulls partly out of water," wrote Porter. The whole tragedy was

An overlook gives visitors the chance to stand on the bluff and gaze out over the confluence of the Appomattox and James rivers—a fitting metaphor for a place where army and navy came together. *Chris Mackowski*

over. "Thank God," said the President, "that I have lived to see this! It seems to me that I have been dreaming a horrid dream for four years, and now the nightmare is gone. I want to see Richmond." With Admiral Porter on the *Malvern* and the president's party on the *River Queen*, they departed for the former Confederate capital.

*   *   *

Today the site of the City Point facility is a quiet strip of grass on the river bluff nestled in a historic neighborhood on the north side of Hopewell, Virginia. The restored circa 1751 Appomattox Manor plantation house and grounds are managed by the National Park Service. Grant's restored cabin is the Headquarters at City Point Museum, a unit of the Petersburg National Battlefield Park.

*No Bluffing
the King of Spades:
Digging in Along Hatcher's Run*

by Edward Alexander

Point of Interest #7 on the map on pg. xv.

*Originally published as a blog post on Emerging Civil War
on February 3, 2015*

The Army of Northern Virginia had a lengthy front to defend during the early months of 1865. Its commander wanted to guarantee that the earthworks protecting Richmond and Petersburg were up to his standards. "Opinions seem to differ as to Gen. Lee as a tactician or an invader," commented a Union counterpart, "but all agree that when it comes to defensive operations, 'Old Bob' understands his business."[1]

Robert E. Lee took command of the principal Confederate army in the east during the summer of 1862 when the Army of the Potomac had backed it into the capital's defenses. Earlier that year, while serving as a military advisor to President Jefferson Davis, he had overseen the construction of fortifications to bolster the defenses of Richmond—a task that earned him the derisive nickname "the King of Spades". However, now confident

---

1   Don Wickman, ed., *Oscar E. Wait: Three Years with the Tenth Vermont* (Newport, VT: Tony O'Connor Civil War Enterprises, 2006), 147.

that these defenses would safeguard Richmond, Lee executed a series of vicious attacks—the Seven Days Battles—that drove the cautious George B. McClellan's army away from the capital's doorstep.

Two years later, Union forces returned, but this time they would not leave until they had satisfied their objective. After the month-long Overland Campaign did not deliver Richmond as its costly prize, Ulysses S. Grant set his sights on Petersburg to the south. His armies were unwilling and unable to immediately storm their way through the imposing earthworks that ringed the city. Throughout the summer and autumn of 1864, Grant settled upon squeezing the cities and their protective army into submission by slowly chipping away at the supply network where it was more vulnerable outside of the Confederate fortifications. By the winter, Grant's strategy had stretched Lee's army out to where they had to guard thirty-seven miles worth of defenses. Only two supply routes remained—the Boydton Plank Road and the South Side Railroad.

Hatcher's Run—"a very tortuous stream"—marked the furthest point south along the lines.[2] Lee ordered Lt. Gen. A. P. Hill's Third Corps to construct a fort near the creek. "General Hill became ill after the order was received, and the construction of his fort was not pressed," recalled Maj. Gen. John B. Gordon, commanding the Second Corps. "Indeed, the weather was so severe and the roads so nearly impassable that there was no urgent necessity for haste." Major General Henry Heth was to have overseen the construction in Hill's absence.[3]

On a cold January morning in 1865, Lee called both Gordon and Heth to accompany him as the senior general inspected the line. Part of Gordon's command extended the line back from Hatcher's Run to the northwest. "General Gordon, how are you getting along with your fort," asked Lee as the trio rode south from Heth's headquarters at the Pickrell house.

"Very well, sir. It is nearly finished," replied Gordon.

"Well, General Heth, how is the work upon your fort progressing?"

2   Crisfield Johnson, *History of Otsego County, New York, with Illustrations and Biographical Sketches of Some of Its Prominent Men and Pioneers* (Philadelphia, PA: Published by L.H. Everts & Co., 1877), 102.

3   John B. Gordon, *Reminiscences of the Civil War* (New York, NY: Charles Scribner's Sons, 1903), 379.

Artist Andrew W. Warren sketched the Confederate earthworks at Hatcher's Run for this woodcut illustration. *Harper's Weekly*

Heth struggled to find a response. Only temporarily assigned as the Third Corps commander, he had not taken the time to assess the earthworks that far down the line. After a painfully long pause he offered: "I think the fort on my side of the run is also about finished, sir."

The three generals arrived at Hatcher's Run and found construction hardly even begun on the fort. Lee fixed his gaze on the vacant ground before directing his attention on Heth. "General, you say the fort is about finished?"

"I must have misunderstood my engineers, sir," Heth replied.

"But you did not speak of your engineers. You spoke of the fort as nearly completed."[4]

General Heth had been enjoying a pretty good setup that winter at Petersburg. His wife stayed with him at the Pickrell house, and they had a connection that allowed them to host elaborate gatherings there. A friend, Maj. Benjamin F. Ficklin, operated a blockade runner in North Carolina. "During the winter of 1864-5 Ficklin wrote me if I would send a wagon to Wilmington he would load it with good things," Heth recalled in his memoirs. "I did so. The wagon was loaded with canned goods, coffee, tea, sugar, hams, twenty gallons of brandy, and the same amount of whisky, a dozen boxes of fine cigars, etc." Included among the luxury items was a fine black horse "which was the admiration of the army." Heth probably regretted choosing to ride it that morning. The animal had evidently also grown agitated with its rider and began to thrash about under the saddle.[5]

"General, doesn't Mrs. Heth ride that horse occasionally?" asked Lee.

"Yes, sir," came the feeble response.

"Well, general, you know that I am very much interested in Mrs. Heth's safety. I fear that horse is too nervous for her to ride without danger, and I suggest that, in order to make him more quiet, you ride him at least once every day to this fort."

With that subtle reprimand the three continued onward. The scolded general rode considerably in the rear the rest of the way. By the time of the next major Union offensive in February 1865, which culminated in the battle of Hatcher's Run, the fort stood fully functional.[6]

It is not clear precisely where the fortification referenced by Gordon was located. Beginning in August 1864, Confederate engineers laid out six miles of entrenchments parallel to the Boydton Plank Road. In addition to their own work, the soldiers relied on conscripted slave labor and also coerced the local free Black population to complete the construction. It is probable that the fortification is along a stretch currently preserved by the American Battlefield Trust. In 2014, the author helped construct an interpretive walking trail that allows visitors to see the impressive remains of these earthworks.

---

5   James L. Morrison, Jr., ed. *The Memoirs of Henry Heth* (Westport, CT: Greenwood Press, 1974), 192-193.

6   Gordon, *Reminiscences of the Civil War*, 380.

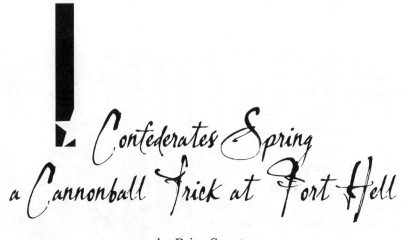

! Confederates Spring a Cannonball Trick at Fort Hell

by Brian Swartz

Point of Interest #8 on the map on pg. xv.

Based on a pair of posts originally published on the blog Maine at War
December 4, 2019, and January 29, 2020, and featured
at Emerging Civil War on January 5, 2020, and February 5, 2020

Perhaps jealous that their Union foes inside Fort Sedgwick were getting more company than they were, Confederate gunners at Fort Mahone across the Jerusalem Plank Road came calling one Sunday morning in early winter 1865.

Senior 1st Lt. William B. Lapham, in civilian attire a doctor from Woodstock in Maine's rural Oxford County, commanded the Union artillery and gunners (including his own 7th Maine Battery) assigned to Sedgwick, also called "Fort Hell."[1] Mahone was called "Fort Damnation." Lapham was never quite sure how the monikers came to be.

"Fort Hell was a spot well known all along the army line, and visitors to the army of the Potomac did not like to return without carrying away some memento from this place," Lapham noticed.

Enclosing roughly an acre, Fort Sedgwick "was somewhat irregular in outline" and "projected as a salient toward the Confederate lines," Lapham

---

1   The account outlined in this story comes from Brevet Maj. William B. Lapham, "With the Seventh Maine Battery," *War Papers Read Before the Commandery of the State of Maine, Military Order of the Loyal Legion of the United States, Vol. 1*, (Portland, ME, 1898), 148-150.

recalled. "It was a closed work and had [cannon] embrasures . . . at the front and rear," but "traverses" to protect "the gunners were erected only against the front parapet.

"The parapets were high and strong" and protected "the garrison from everything except mortar shells," he said. "A deep ditch extended the entire length" of Fort Sedgwick, which "had a commanding position, situated on high ground."

Shaped like a slithering snake, a sunken access road—a "covered way" in army parlance—led to Fort Sedgwick's rear entrance, Excavated "so deep [and wide] that men and artillery" could move without Confederate detection, the road branched right and left to access the adjoining defenses, Lapham observed.

William Berry Lapham, the 7th Maine Battery's senior first lieutenant, commanded the artillery assigned to Fort Sedgwick, also known as "Fort Hell." *Maine State Archives*

Other Union batteries had initially occupied the fort. Then, "one morning in early December," four 12-pound Napoleons from the 7th Maine Battery and a two-gun section of Napoleons from the 3rd New Jersey Battery (under 2nd Lt. Carl Machewsky) went into the fort, Lapham said.

The 7th Maine's remaining two guns rolled into Battery 21, abutting Fort Sedgwick on the right.

Because Sedgwick stood on high ground, the "central bomb-proof" constructed by his men to protect both ammunition and officers thrust above the fort's walls, wrote Lapham.

From this perch, "the rebel lines could be seen for several miles," he reported. Today a Baptist church and its parking lot occupy the Fort Sedgwick site, and development and tree growth have eliminated the views that were available in 1865.

"Also in a clear day . . . the spires of the churches in Petersburg were plainly in view," Lapham further noted.

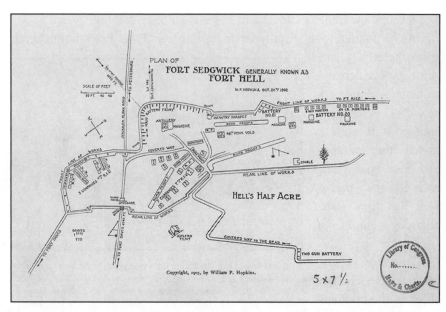

William P. Hopkins of the 7th Rhode Island Infantry Regiment drew a detailed map of Fort Sedgwick, a.k.a. "Fort Hell," for which the Ocean Staters provided infantry support during the Petersburg siege. *Library of Congress*

"The consequence was that we had many visitors," Lapham said, but "as a general thing [they] did not care to remain long after the rebels commenced shelling us."

He noticed that the Confederates usually did not fire "on the Sabbath," and other wartime anecdotes related how soldiers, at least devout Christians, thought that fighting on Sunday was religious sacrilege.

There came a Sunday when "a severe rain . . . converted the Virginia clay in our fort into mortar," Lapham recalled. "A large party" came knocking on Fort Hell's front door "and asked permission to go upon the bomb-proof." Lapham climbed atop the bomb-proof with his civilian guests, "and they were much pleased with the objects that I pointed out."

Among the civilians "was a farmer from the interior of Pennsylvania." The man stood "nearly six feet and a half tall, and wore a tall, stove-pipe hat which made him look like a giant," Lapham said.

Imagine a Confederate officer standing over at Fort Damnation (now an elementary school), glassing with his binoculars. He sees people standing atop Hell's high point—and among them is a very tall gentleman wearing a stove-pipe hat.

Lincoln! the Confederate exclaims. *Abraham Lincoln is over there!*

As he pointed to this Confederate post here and that Petersburg church spire there, Lapham "cast my eye across" to Fort Mahone. "I saw the end of a sponge staff appear above the parapet and then disappear, and I knew pretty well that they were charging a gun."

Surely the Confederates at Damnation would not shoot at the civilians in Hell, would they?

Yes, they would.

A member of the 7th Maine Battery lounges outside the central bomb-proof at Fort Sedgwick in early April 1865. The bomb-proof's details—especially the chimney, door, and window—were described by the post's commander, Senior 1st Lt. William B. Lapham. Other Maine gunners stand on the ramparts. *Maine State Archives*

"In less than a half-minute a rifled gun was discharged, and a shell passed over the bomb-proof, only a few feet above our heads," Lapham recalled. The shell "exploded a little distance to our rear."

With a rifled cannon, the skilled enemy gunners could have nailed the tourists in Fort Hell. Instead the Confederates placed the shell where it would achieve the greatest entertainment value.

"The effect on our visitors was most remarkable," Lapham grunted. The civilians "leaped down the side of the earthwork and rolled, slid or tumbled into the mud below."

The Lincolnesque "Pennsylvanian lost his balance and came down head first, and got up and walked away with a 'shocking bad hat,'" he reported. The 7th Maine boys split their sides in mirth, the Confederates fired "one shot more," and "then we could hear the derisive laughter of the rebels across the way."

"They Did Not Have a Cromwell to Lead Them": Forts Stedman and Haskell and the 100th Pennsylvania

by Dan Welch

Point of Interest #9 on the map on pg. xv.

The attack was over before 9:00 a.m. What had started hours earlier as a complex Confederate assault—layered with many stages and carried out by some of the most hardened, experienced, and devout soldiers of the Army of Northern Virginia—had ended in appalling losses, many of whom were captured. Meticulous planning by Maj. Gen. John B. Gordon over the previous month and the whole-hearted support and belief in its outcome by Gen. Robert E. Lee were not enough to wrest the Federal army out of its position along the Petersburg front. The ultimate failure of the Confederate attack, though, most assuredly rests with those Union soldiers manning that sector of the line. And more so than any other Federal regiment on the morning of March 25, 1865 (save possibly the 3rd Maryland Battalion), the 100th Pennsylvania Volunteer Infantry at every turn rose above their call of duty to turn back the attack. This is the story of the veterans of the Roundhead regiment from western Pennsylvania at the battle of Fort Stedman.

The history of the Roundheads began in the earliest days of the war. Daniel Leasure, a physician from New Castle, Pennsylvania, located in Lawrence County, saw an advertisement in an April 15, 1861, newspaper about President Lincoln's call for 75,000 troops in response to the attack on Fort Sumter. Leasure worked quickly to organize and raise companies

OPPOSITE: Fort Stedman—John Brown Gordon's initial assault successfully punched through the Federal line at Fort Stedman thanks to good planning, speed, and trickery. As the breach widened, Confederates lost their momentum, in part because of stout Federal resistance near Fort Haskell to the south. That bought time for Federal reinforcements to flood into the area and plug the gap.

of men from the surrounding areas. By August, now-Captain Leasure was ready for more, and he met with Secretary of War Simon Cameron in Washington, D.C., about raising an entire regiment. Cameron asked if this regiment would be composed of the same type of men Leasure had already raised, as the secretary had already come to know their reputation. Leasure quipped they would be "of no other brand," referencing the Scotch-Irish lineage that made up most of his previous command and the area in which he recruited. Also in attendance at the meeting was General Winfield Scott, who interjected a suggestion that this new regiment be called the "Roundheads" as a compliment to Cameron, also of Scotch-Irish heritage, and it's deep connection to the seventeenth century Scottish National Covenant and Cromwell. Cameron gave Leasure the authority to raise the regiment. By the end of August, mustering began in Harrisburg, Pennsylvania, and just two months later, the 100th Pennsylvania Volunteer Infantry, the Roundheads, were heading towards the front at Port Royal, South Carolina.

The regiment spent most of the next year involved in southern coastal operations before entering the fighting in Virginia at Second Manassas at the end of August 1862. From there, the regiment fought at Chantilly, South Mountain, Antietam, Fredericksburg, Vicksburg, Wilderness, Spotsylvania Court House, Cold Harbor, and the Crater at Petersburg before finding themselves under attack in the early morning of March 25, 1865.

At approximately 4:00 a.m, Gordon's attack moved forward with a rush, successfully overtaking the Federal pickets with bayonets and clubbed muskets. Then, fifty axemen led the way to Fort Stedman to break a path through the strong outer Union defenses. One witness observed that the "gallant corps of pioneers dashed upon the enemy's obstructions and with their axes chopped and battered them down to make way for the two regiments to enter and take the enemy's line of defense."[1] It was not long before Union positions at Battery Ten north of Fort Stedman and Stedman itself were

---

1   J.D. Barrier, "Breaking Grant's Line," *Confederate Veteran*, Vol. XXXIII, No. 11, November 1925, 417; "Particulars of the Fight at Petersburg, Saturday," *Daily Dispatch*, March 28, 1865, 1.

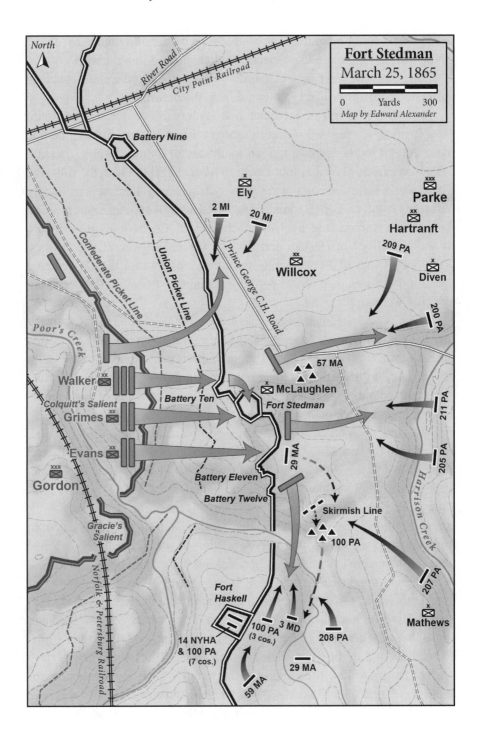

North

River Road

City Point Railroad

Battery Nine

Fort Stedman
March 25, 1865

0   Yards   300
Map by Edward Alexander

Ely
2 MI
20 MI

Parke

Hartranft

209 PA

Willcox

Diven

200 PA

Confederate Picket Line

Union Picket Line

Prince George C.H. Road

Poor's Creek

57 MA

Walker

McLaughlen

211 PA

Colquitt's Salient

Battery Ten

Grimes

Fort Stedman

205 PA

Evans

29 MA

Gordon

Battery Eleven

Battery Twelve

Harrison Creek

Skirmish Line

Gracie's Salient

100 PA

207 PA

Fort
Haskell

Mathews

100 PA
(3 cos.)

3 MD

14 NYHA
& 100 PA
(7 cos.)

208 PA

59 MA

29 MA

Norfolk & Petersburg Railroad

under attack. Both fell to the Confederates in a matter of moments. With the Union line broken, more Confederate soldiers poured into the works.

Following the next part of Gordon's plan, the Confederate attackers pushed both northward and southward from the breach.

Immediately south of Stedman was Battery Eleven, a small redoubt capable of supporting two pieces of artillery. From Battery Eleven, the line of the entrenched Union position ran southward to Battery Twelve, a square redoubt capable of housing four Coehorn mortars. From there, the ridge the Union works followed continued southward again and there, approximately 650 yards south of Fort Stedman, was Fort Haskell, another stout position with six Napoleons and plus a detachment of Coehorn mortars within its walls. In front of Haskell and Battery Eleven, between the two lines, was Poor's Creek. This seemingly miniscule obstacle for the Confederate assaulting column had been partially damnmd, flooding the area and essentially creating a pond.

To its north, Stedman was flanked by other works. Right next to the fort was Battery Ten with four guns mounted, and approximately 800 yards further north was Battery Nine. The line continued to extend to the north until it reached the Appomattox River. To the east of Stedman were two knolls, the heights of which commanded the fort itself. Both of these knolls had artillery emplacements and were partially fortified.

The first division of the IX Corps occupied this portion of the line, commanded by Bvt. Maj. Gen. Orlando Willcox. In the center of Willcox's position rested the third brigade under the command of Bvt. Brig. Gen. Napoleon B. McLaughlen. The brigade included the 3rd Maryland, 29th, 57th, and 59th Massachusetts, 18th New Hampshire, 14th New York Heavy Artillery, and the 100th Pennsylvania. Each of these units had an important role to play in the defense of this sector of the line. They had been in the position since November, making them intimately aware of all of its strengths and weaknesses. With three columns of Confederate soldiers making their way towards this position—one toward the left of Battery Ten, one against Fort Stedman, and one towards a location between Fort Stedman and Battery Eleven, approximately 8,000 men in all—McLaughlen's men and the rest of third brigade would need all the help they could get.

The first area along McLaughlen's line to fall to the Confederate storm of battle was Battery Ten. The attack was so rapid and came upon its objective so quietly that only one round was fired from the two guns in position. This break in the Union line then allowed the Confederates to exploit the rear of Fort Stedman. Attackers charged through the sally-port, and with only one to two rounds fired by the defenders, Stedman fell much the same as Battery Ten.

With this fortification in their hands and a significant breach in the Union

This artillery piece inside Fort Stedman covers the ground Confederates attacked across. Gordon's men began their assault from beyond the far treeline. *Chris Mackowski*

line, a portion of the Confederate attack turned southward. This contingent of Confederate soldiers slammed into the 29th Massachusetts Volunteer Infantry, a small regiment even by 1865 regimental averages. Although they rallied after the initial impact of the Confederate attack into their lines, it was not enough to slow or stop the assault. Despite a severe contest along their rallied lines, within fifteen minutes, the 29th gave way and headed towards the safety of Fort Haskell even farther south along the Union lines. Battery Eleven fell with the retreat of the 29th. The Confederate attack then resumed its push southward.

Standing in their way was the 100th Pennsylvania.

As Confederate infantry moved southward, with their right flank anchored on the Union entrenchments, the center and left of their line moved towards the camp of the Roundheads. When the first real shots of attack rippled through the stillness north of their encampment, Lt. Col. Joseph Pentecost of the 100th Pennsylvania quickly roused the men. "The alarm was sounded at once when one of the most important and decisive battles of the war was fought," wrote Silas Stevenson, a veteran of Company K, in a brief history of the regiment.[2] To stop the approaching onslaught, Pentecost

---

2   Silas Stevenson, "An Epitomized History of the 'Roundheads' or 100th Pennsylvania Veteran Volunteers, Including a Plea for a Complete Publication Thereof in Book Form," Ellwood City, PA.

was able to create little more than a skirmish line, including one company of Roundheads, some 3rd Marylanders, and some of the remnants of the Massachusetts boys. It was the best he could do in the short amount of time he had. An account published near the end of the 1890s by a Roundhead then living in Denver, Colorado, described the moment. "The boys were asleep in their bunks at the first volley, but grabbed guns and cartridge-boxes, not even stopping to dress," J.R. Holibaugh related. "Some were barefooted; some only with shirts and pants on, so that the uniforms were not fully up to the Government standard, but the fighting qualities were above par."[3]

Although heroic, this small and hastily assembled line was soon outflanked and outnumbered. These men retired quickly southwards towards the camp of the 100th to the southeast and Fort Haskell to the south. Meanwhile, Pentecost ordered three more companies of the 100th into a defensive position perpendicular to the main Union line—a position that was parallel to the advancing Confederates. The line formed to the right and rear of Fort Haskell, with the left of the line anchored on Fort Haskell itself. The rest of the regiment was ordered into the fort. Once Pentecost placed the other seven companies, he returned to the skirmish line anchored on the fort where he went down with a mortal wound.

Joseph Henry Pentecost, from West Middletown, Pennsylvania, was just 28 when he died of his wounds on March 26, 1865. Pentecost's role in the defense of Fort Haskell largely set up the success of the Federal repulse and victory on March 25. *The Messick/ Kraus Collection*

The center and left of the advancing Confederate line had now reached the huts and tents of the 100th Pennsylvania encampments in the rear of the main Union line. When the attackers were not firing towards the last line of defense at and perpendicular to Fort Haskell, the Rebels looted as much as possible. J. C. Stevenson, another veteran of the unit who wrote a brief history

---

3   J.R. Holibaugh, "Battle Days of the Roundheads: The Civil War Experience of the Famous 100th Pa., a Fighting Regiment," Part II, Denver, Colorado.

of their service during war, said of the moment, "the victorious but hungry Johnnies, who, finding plenty of sugar, coffee, bread, meat and clothing in our tents, went to plundering."[4] While finding what food they could within the 100th's camp, Confederates also found the first real counterfire and resistance of the morning. All weapons of the Federal soldiers in and outside Fort Haskell poured concentrated fire into the Confederate line. Part of the weight of this counterfire came from the remnants of the 29th and 59th Massachusetts, as well as from the 14th New York Heavy Artillery. They, along with the seven companies of the 100th inside the fort, significantly slowed the Confederate push southwards.

As the fighting raged on this sector of the line, Confederate infantry made a headlong frontal assault against the western side of Fort Haskell. The combined force of units inside Haskell broke the assault as it crested towards the walls.

The sun now broke across the eastern horizon. Targets were no longer necessarily obtained by muzzle flashes and noise alone. Lieutenant John H. Stevenson, in command of Company K of the Roundheads inside the fort, recalled the moment: "Along the parapet of the work stood a line of brave soldiers from different Companies of the 100th Pa., who did the firing, and those who could not get into position, loaded the guns for those who could make effective use of them. The fire soon became so hot that this Confederate Brigade gave it up, taking shelter in our camp, and along our breastworks."[5]

Confederate infantry inside the Union lines continued to press their southward attack. During this phase of the battle, in total, they made three separate assaults against Fort Haskell and the line outside of the fort facing north. Roundhead historian William Gavin wrote in the unit's first full regimental history in 1989, "A lieutenant of the One Hundredth Pennsylvania states that he fired more than one hundred and fifty shots in a few minutes during the assaults."[6]

---

4   J.C. Stevenson, "Condensed History of the One Hundredth Regiment (The Roundheads)," *The Shelby Beacon*, Vol. 4, No. 21, August 31, 1917, 11.

5   Lt. John H. Stevenson, Company K, Manuscript History, McDowell Collection, Historical Collections and Labor Archives, Pattee Library, Pennsylvania State University.

6   William G. Gavin, *Campaigning with the Roundheads: The History of the Hundredth Pennsylvania Veteran Volunteer Infantry in the American Civil War 1861-1865, The Roundhead Regiment* (Dayton: Morningside House, Inc, 1989), 611.

Now help was on the way. Thirty minutes into the fight at Fort Haskell, additional units from other brigades south of the beleaguered Federal position arrived to extend the line of the three Roundhead companies and elements of the 3rd Maryland. The doorway further south for the Confederate attackers was now closed, and the tide had turned. It was approximately 7:30 a.m.

Major General George Gordon Meade, in command of the Army of Potomac, issued orders to division commanders in this sector of the line to retake Stedman. Although some of those officers were working to organize an attack per Meade's orders, Col. Gilbert P. Robinson, now in command of McLaughen's men after McLaughlen's capture earlier in the fight, pushed ahead after the retreating Confederate infantry long before orders arrived to do so. Robinson had "received notice from General Hartranft that he was advancing and would carry the works in fifteen minutes . . . but seeing the demoralized condition of the enemy, and fearful that a large amount of prisoners might be lost by longer delay, it was determined to dash on the enemy at once. . . ."[7] Part of Robinson's command, the 100th Pennsylvania, along with the 3rd Maryland Battalion, 29th and 59th Massachusetts, and the elements of the 14th New York Heavy Artillery, "charged up the line and along the works, carrying the trenches and batteries as far as Fort Stedman."[8] Private James P. Sankey, Company K, 100th Pennsylvania, remembered the charge as well. "Captain Wilson . . . told me to put on my bayonet as they were going to make a charge down the line. I did so," Sankey later wrote, although I felt "at the time if we undertook it, that we would lose a number of brave boys in the attempt."[9]

The counterattack by Robinson's men, joined by reinforcements coming to their aid from the third division from the east, finally drove Confederate soldiers out of the 100th Pennsylvanians' encampment, which had been plundered liberally and now lay in ruins. Lieutenant Stevenson in Company K recalled the moment he, along with several others, pushed far enough

7   United States War Department, *The War of the Rebellion: A Compilation of the Official Records of the Union and Confederate Armies,* 70 vols. in 128 parts (Washington D.C.: Government Printing Office, 1880-1901), Series I, volume 46, part 1, p. 335 (hereafter cited as *O.R.,* I, 46, pt. 1, 335).

8   *O.R.,* I, 46, pt. 1, 335.

9   James P. Sankey, Company K, Letter, No Date, McDowell Collection, Historical Collections and Labor Archives, Pattee Library, Pennsylvania State University.

northward from Fort Haskell to re-enter the encampment. "Passing down the line," Stevenson remembered, "I stopped opposite my own company quarters to see what damage had been done to the tents and here I found dead seven of the enemy and twelve badly wounded, besides quite a number who were uninjured, but who were unwilling to hazard their lives any further. In the company quarters of the other companies, there were also many dead and wounded and many prisoners."[10]

Meanwhile, closing in with Confederate-occupied Fort Stedman, Color Sergeant Charles Oliver of the Roundheads pushed ahead of his line, entered the fort, and planted the colors of the 100th on the fort itself. "[A]bout this time Major Maxwell [in command of the 100th after the mortal wounding of Pentecost] came to me and said he was going to recapture Fort Stedman. I laughed at the idea, but told him to go ahead, if he could risk it, I could," Oliver remembered. "I believe I was the first blue coat in the Fort."[11] General Willcox supported Oliver's statement when he wrote that the "officers and men of the Third Maryland and One hundredth Pennsylvania, seems to be justly due the praise of being the first to re-enter the captured fort. The flag of the One Hundredth Pennsylvania was the first planted on the ramparts."[12]

Oliver's heroics did not stop there as he also "captured a stand of rebel colors, at the same point and at the same time with his own hands."[13] "I captured two rebel Colonels, both of Georgia Regiments and two stands of colors. The officers were taken care of by Captain Book and the colors I turned over to General Willcox," the color sergeant recorded after the war.[14] James P. Sankey, Company K, who was with Oliver, was more descriptive of Oliver's actions. "When Charlie Oliver went up to one of the color bearers (rebel) he told him he would relieve him of the flag," Sankey recalled. "The

10   Lt. John H. Stevenson, Company K, Manuscript History, McDowell Collection, Historical Collections and Labor Archives, Pattee Library, Pennsylvania State University.

11   Sergeant Charles Oliver, Company M, Manuscript Letter, No Date, McDowell Collection, Historical Collections and Labor Archives, Pattee Library, Pennsylvania State University.

12   *O.R.,* I, 46, pt. 3, 264-65.

13   *O.R.,* I, 46, pt. 1, 324.

14   Sergeant Charles Oliver, Company M, Manuscript Letter, No Date, McDowell Collection, Historical Collections and Labor Archives, Pattee Library, Pennsylvania State University.

color bearer said, 'I guess not.' Charlie, who had a gun in his hand at the time said, 'The hell you won't!' and coolly picked up the flag."[15]

Those were not the only colors to occupy the attention of the Roundheads as they fought their way into Stedman. Captain Joseph F. Carter, 3rd Maryland, wrote in his official report of the battle that the Roundheads were responsible for the capture of four Confederate stands of colors, including those of the

This image of the interior of Fort Stedman was one of several captured by photographer Timothy O'Sullivan. *Library of Congress*

1st Virginia, 5th Virginia, and 31st Georgia Infantries, as well as a part of another color and national camp color. The identity of these final two flag parts remains unknown.

With the capture of numerous colors, hundreds of soldiers, and several officers, Robinson's brigade and the newly arrived elements of the third division sealed the breach once and for all. "This ended the Fort Stedman affair with the Roundheads in possession," noted one observer, "and although they did not have a Cromwell to lead them, they had an Oliver, carrying their flag to victory."[16] The battle cost the veteran regiment 21 killed and 57 wounded, as well as a few captured that were almost immediately paroled and returned.

"The accounts which have been given here unequivocalby [sic] prove that the Roundheads played a major and decisive role in the defeat of the

---

15   James P. Sankey, Company K, Letter, No Date, McDowell Collection, Historical Collections and Labor Archives, Pattee Library, Pennsylvania State University.

16   Carter, *History of the Third Brigade, First Division, Ninth Army Corps.*

Confederate attack against Fort Stedman," argued regimental historian Willam Gavin in 1989.[17] Gavin, like veteran Roundheads in the immediate postwar era, had to fight off historical inaccuracies regarding their service during the battle. The 100th's performance during March 25, 1865, was crucial in winning the day, yet Brig. Gen. John Hartranft, commander of the third division, claimed the victory as his own. "The officers and men of my division, composed entirely of new troops, deserve great credit for their promptness in moving forward to the point of attack, to which in a great measure is owing the success of the day, and for their gallant conduct throughout the action," he wrote in his official report. Years later, he followed up his account with a piece in *Century Magazine* that became a standard source about the recapture of the fort.[18]

Hartranft's bold statements have stuck throughout the succeeding generations despite the general not even arriving at the fort until thirty minutes after the Roundheads had taken it back. "History does not always give credit to whom it is due, as the credit of the recapture of Fort Stedman is given to gen. [sic] Hartranft's Division of new troops, or one-year men, who arrived on the ground 20 minutes after the capture, and took charge of the prisoners," J. R. Halibaugh remembered after the war.[19]

In the end, it was Colonel Pentecost in command of the 100th that offered the first real resistance against the Confederate attack when he quickly assembled a skirmish line and sent his men northwards towards Fort Stedman and Battery Ten. It was also Pentecost who had ordered seven companies of the Roundheads into Fort Haskell for its defense, and three companies to form a line perpendicular outside the fort as a further defense. After every turn, the brave veterans of the 100th Pennsylvania followed his commands with alacrity and fought with undeniable ferocity to retake their area of operations. It was the Roundheads, aided by the men from Maryland and Massachusetts, that turned back three separate assaults by the Confederates, holding their position. The time gained by their stubborn

---

17   Gavin, *Campaigning with the Roundheads,* 625.

18   *O.R.,* 1, 46, pt. 1, 346-348. For Hartranft's account in the *Century,* see *Battles and Leaders of the American Civil War,* volume four, 584-589.

19   Holibaugh, "Battle Days of the Roundheads."

John Hartranft, who served as governor of Pennsylvania after the war, did much to influence the memory of Fort Stedman. According to the monument at the fort, erected in 1909, credit for the recapture of the position belongs to "the Third Division IX Corps Army of the Potomac, in whose memory this tablet is erected by the Commonwealth of Pennsylvania." *Chris Mackowski*

defense bought time for reinforcements to be organized and sent towards the scene of the fight. "Then," wrote regimental historian Gavin, "as the Confederates began withdrawing, the Roundheads, under Major Maxwell, were foremost in rushing down on Batteries 11 and 12, and on to Fort Stedman," with two of the Roundheads receiving Medals of Honor for their actions during this rush.[20]

The ultimate failure of the Confederate attack most assuredly rests with those Union soldiers manning this sector of the Union line. "The Roundheads' accomplishments that morning of March 25, 1865," wrote Gavin, "speak for themselves."[21]

20   Gavin, *Campaigning with the Roundheads,* 626.

21   Ibid., 630.

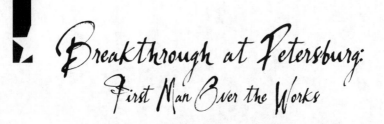

L. Breakthrough at Petersburg:
First Man Over the Works

by Edward Alexander

Point of Interest #10 on the map on pg. xv.

Originally published as a blog post on Emerging Civil War on April 2, 2015

Charlie Gould seemed destined for adventure in his life. While just two years old, he and his family visited his grandparents' house in Windham, Vermont. While the adults talked, young Charlie became infatuated with the tantalizing smell wafting from a boiling pot of applesauce. He crawled over to the cauldron and steadied himself to bend over for an up-close smell. While carefully balancing above the pot, Charlie lost his balance and tumbled in, terribly scalding his legs. He was unable to walk until after his sixth birthday, but his enthusiasm for dangerous deeds remained.

When the war began, Charlie's parents wished their child would remain home. The young lad was determined become a soldier and walked twenty miles to Bellows Falls to enlist in August 1862. He may have fibbed about his age to gain entrance into the army. Some records, including his headstone, show Charlie's birth occurring on May 5, 1845. Others show May 5, 1844, which would place him right at the appropriate age of eighteen for his enlistment. Charlie initially joined the 1st Vermont Heavy Artillery as a private and swiftly rose through the ranks. Upon his promotion to captain in late 1864, Gould was assigned to command of Company H, 5th Vermont Infantry. On April 2, 1865, Brig. Gen. Lewis A. Grant selected that unit to

Lewis Grant directed his Vermont brigade to use this branch of Arthur's Swamp to reach the Confederate lines on the morning of April 2, 1865. *Edward Alexander*

serve as the spearhead for the entire VI Corps attack against the Confederate line protecting the Boydton Plank Road southwest of Petersburg.

That morning the regiment used a branch of Arthur's Swamp to guide their way toward the Confederate earthworks in the darkness. As the Vermonters drew close to the wall, some of the men behind Gould began to drift to the right. Someone in the rear shouted "Bear to the left" to realign the wayward advance. The captain misinterpreted that suggestion as his direct order and led his company across Arthur's Swamp where they found themselves separated from the rest of the brigade.

Despite having only a handful of officers and just fifty men with him, Gould spurred his company forward hoping to capture an artillery piece. With legs fully healed from his applesauce tumble as a toddler, the spry officer raced ahead of his comrades. He found a soft spot in the last line of abatis even as the rest of his company's pace slowed as they filed through a narrow gap in the obstructions. Unaware that his men were no longer at his heels, Gould jumped into the ditch at the base of the enemy works and quickly scrambled up the parapet. "I have heard nothing more daring," recalled a fellow Vermonter:

> The regiment was charging a fort, and as they were delayed a moment getting through the abatis, these officers rushed ahead without looking

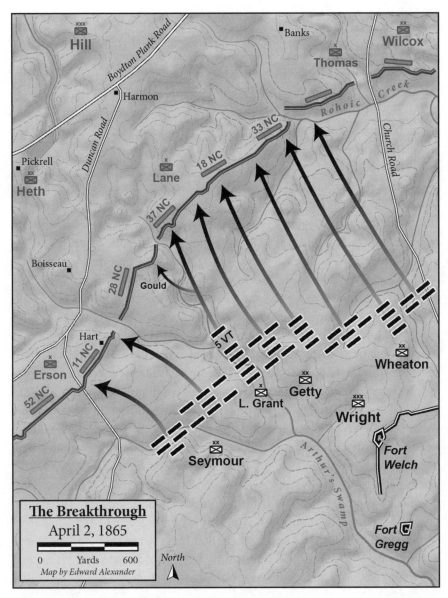

THE BREAKTHROUGH—Horatio Wright amassed an overwhelming force to sweep forward over the open ground in front of the formidable but scantly defended Confederate works. Today, Forts Welch and Gregg fall within Petersburg National Battlefield; the VI Corps attack plain was saved by the American Battlefield Trust; and the breakthrough site is contained within the boundaries of Pamplin Historical Park.

back to see whether the men were following. Capt. Gould rushed into the fort all alone, with nothing but his sword. The rebels came at him with swords, bayonets and clubbed muskets. One bayonet was thrust into his mouth and through his cheek, and while in that position he killed the man with his sword. An officer struck him on the head with a sword, and he was struck in the shoulder by a bayonet and pounded all over with clubbed muskets; but he gave as good as he got, until a corporal rushed in and pulled him out.[1]

Corporal Henry Recor received credit for hauling the officer back into the ditch while Sgt. Jackson Sargent rushed forward to plant the state colors on the works. Spurred by the shouts of their commander and the sight of their flag on the wall, more Vermonters hurried forward to the top of the parapet. A brief but desperate struggle was all it took to establish a foothold on the works as the North Carolinian defenders threw down their muskets to surrender or turned and ran as the bluecoats piled over the wall. Miraculously, the captain regained his consciousness and stumbled the full mile back to the Union works where he asked for reinforcements to support his storming party. After receiving a guarantee that help was on the way for his men, Charlie then asked for some medical assistance for himself.

Though greivous in appearance, Charlie's wounds turned out to be rather slight. He wrote a letter to his parents two days after the battle describing his wounds as "a bayonet wound through the left part of my face which entered near my mouth and came out under the jaw, another bayonet wound in my back between my shoulders and a sabre cut on the right side of my skull." Then, perhaps to assuage his parents' concerns, he wrote: "The wound in my back is nothing at all as it hit the backbone and stopped. The cut on my head is very slight and in fact all my wounds are."[2] Gould separately admitted to his brother, "Am only sorry that I was wounded before I got into Richmond."[3] Meanwhile, he bragged to a fellow comrade that "if he had only had his revolver he could have held the fort alone."[4]

1   "Our Army Correspondence," *Vermont Phoenix*, April 28, 1865.

2   Charles G. Gould to "Dear Parents," April 4, 1865, in Charles G. Gould Letters at Bailey/Howe Library University of Vermont.

3   Charles G. Gould to "Brother Aron," April 5, 1865, University of Vermont.

4   "Our Army Correspondence," *Vermont Phoenix*, April 28, 1865.

Years after the war, a Vermont historian enlisted Charlie's support in chronicling his action that morning. The veteran Gould vividly recalled:

> My appearance upon the parapet was met with a leveled musket, which fortunately missed fire. I immediately jumped into the work, and my part in the engagement was soon over. I was scarcely inside before a bayonet was thrust through my face and a sword-thrust returned for it that fully repaid the wound given me, as I was subsequently informed that it killed my assailant. At almost the same breath an officer—or some one armed with a sword— gave me a severe cut in the head. The remainder of my brief stay in the work was a confused scramble, from which, had my assailants been fewer in number, I should scarcely have escaped. As it was, firing on their part would have been dangerous for their own men; consequently their efforts were apparently restricted to the use of bayonets and clubbed muskets. During the struggle I was once seized and my overcoat partially pulled off, and probably at this time another bayonet wound was given me in the back, as the bayonet passed through my inner coat between the shoulders, while my overcoat remained intact. This was the most severe wound of the three, the bayonet entering the spine and penetrating it nearly to the spinal cord.

> I have no distinct recollection of what followed, until I found myself at the parapet, trying to climb out of the work, but unable to do so. At this time Private Henry H. Recor, Company A., Fifth Vermont, appeared upon the parapet at that point. The brave fellow recognized the situation, and notwithstanding the danger incurred in doing so, pulled me upon the parapet, receiving a gunshot wound himself while saving me. This terminated my part in the assault upon the lines at Petersburg. I must have been assisted out of the ditch without being recognized, as those with me were not aware of my escape, and I made my way to the rear as far as my remaining strength would carry me. Some of this journey is a blank to me.[5]

After an early life full of adventure, Charlie decided to settle down for

---

5   George G. Benedict, *Vermont in the Civil War: A History of the Part Taken by the Vermont Soldiers and Sailors in the War for the Union, 1861-5*, vol. 1 (Burlington, VT: The Free Press Association, 1886), 594-595.

a quieter existence as a clerk in the pension office and later the patent office. Lewis Grant petitioned for Gould to receive some recognition for his involvement during the breakthrough, testifying in 1890: "I think there is no doubt of the fact that Capt. Charles G. Gould, 5th Vt. Vols. was the first upon the rebel works at the time of the breaking of the Confederate lines by the Sixth Corps in front of Petersburg, April 2, '65."[6]

The bayonet wound Charles Gould immediately received in his jaw after mounting the Confederate earthworks is visible in this photograph. *Vermont Historical Society*

On July 30, 1890, Charles Gould finally received a Medal of Honor, which declared: "Among the first to mount the enemy's works in the assault, he received a serious bayonet wound in the face, was struck several times with clubbed muskets, but bravely stood his ground, and with his sword killed the man who bayoneted him."[7]

6   Lewis A. Grant, July 15, 1890 memorandum, in Charles G. Gould Compiled Service Record, National Archives.

7   *Medals of Honor Issued by the War Department, Up to and Including September 1, 1904* (Washington, DC: Government Printing Office, 1904), 55.

Separate Roads to Petersburg: The Fractured Federal High Command, April 1865

by Edward Alexander

Point of Interest #11 on the map on pg. xv.

*Originally published as a blog post on Emerging Civil War
on August 18, 2015*

Ever have a dispute with someone turn so ugly that you don't want to even share the same road? From all appearances, that may have been the case on April 2, 1865 with the damaged relationship between Lt. Gen. Ulysses S. Grant and Maj. Gen. George G. Meade.

In the last days of March 1865, Grant brought his headquarters south of Hatcher's Run to Dabney's Mill. For most of the Petersburg campaign, he had stayed at the Eppes plantation at City Point, but now the Federal commander wanted to be closer to where he had planned his final strike at the Confederate army. There at Dabney's Mill on April 1, Grant received the fateful news of Maj. Gen. Philip Sheridan's victory at Five Forks. While staff officers ecstatically slapped each other's backs in glee, Grant calmly walked into his tent and crafted a dispatch. He reemerged shortly thereafter with the news: "I have ordered a general assault along the lines."[1]

Grant wanted his forces to immediately press the Confederate earthworks along the entire front to prevent Gen. Robert E. Lee from either slipping

---

1   Horace Porter, *Campaigning with Grant* (New York, NY: The Century Co., 1897), 443.

reinforcements out to Five Forks or abandoning the entire line altogether. The various Union corps opposing the main Confederate defenses along the Dimmock Line and the extension protecting Boydton Plank Road were not, however, in position for an immediate attack. Eventually the orders were amended for the VI Corps and IX Corps to stage a direct assault the next morning while the II Corps and the Army of the James felt the Confederate line for weaknesses. "A little after midnight the general tucked himself into his camp-bed and was soon sleeping as peacefully as if the next day was to be devoted to a picnic instead of a decisive battle," recalled Lt. Col. Horace Porter, a member of Grant's staff. "Every one at headquarters had caught as many catnaps as he could, so as to be able to keep both eyes open the next day, in the hope of getting a sight of Petersburg, and possibly Richmond."[2]

Porter was awakened the next morning, April 2, by "the thunder of hundreds of guns" which "shook the ground like an earthquake."[3] The soldiers of the VI Corps and IX Corps rushed boldly at the Confederate earthworks while the II Corps and XXIV Corps cautiously probed the enemy's picket line. At 5:15 a.m., Grant received a message from Maj. Gen. Horatio G. Wright that his VI Corps had carried the Confederate line opposite Fort Welch and was continuing to push forward. Shortly thereafter he learned that Maj. Gen. John G. Parke's IX Corps had captured the outer works southeast of Petersburg, seizing 800 prisoners and 12 pieces of artillery. However, due to the Confederate defense-in-depth around Fort Mahone, Parke was having a harder time following up this initial success.

More dispatches poured in from across the wide front, and Grant waited at his headquarters to maintain correspondence with his various subordinates. He wanted to remain in a position "where he could be easily communicated with, and from which he could give general directions."[4] At 6:40 a.m., Grant wrote to President Abraham Lincoln, who was back at City Point: "Both Wright and Parke got through the enemy's line. The battle now rages furiously. Sheridan, with his cavalry, the Fifth Corps, and [Brig. Gen. Nelson A.] Miles's division of the Second Corps, which was sent to him

2   Ibid.

3   Ibid.

4   Ibid.

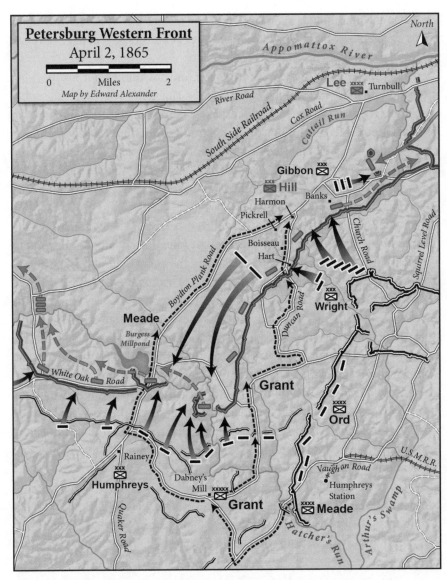

PETERSBURG WESTERN FRONT—Because of tensions between Grant and Meade, the two commanders kept separate headquarters and so, following the Federal breakthrough on April 2, they arrived on the battlefield by different routes. They first met at Dabney's Mill, and after entering the breakthrough at different spots, they again linked up at the Harmon house.

since one this morning, is now sweeping down from the west. All now looks highly favorable. [Major General Edward O.C.] Ord is engaged, but I have not yet heard the result in his front."[5]

Major General George Gordon Meade, meanwhile, began his morning just south of where the Vaughn Road crossed Hatcher's Run, approximately two miles east of Grant's headquarters. Though in early 1864 the two generals seemed to start things off on the right foot after Grant's promotion and arrival to Virginia, their working relationship had quickly soured during the Overland Campaign. "The papers are giving Grant all the credit of what they call successes," grumbled Meade to his wife in early June. "I hope they will remember this if anything goes wrong."[6]

Grant's decision to ride along with the Army of the Potomac during the 1864 campaigns had stripped Meade of much of his autonomy. One of Meade's orders on April 1, 1865 illustrates the point. Though it is usually overshadowed by Porter's dramatic story of riding to Dabney's Mill to deliver Sheridan's news, Meade had played a forgotten role in setting up the attack the following day. At 4 p.m., just as the V Corps attacks at Five Forks were beginning, Meade issued orders for Wright: "You will assault the enemy's works in your front at 4 a.m. tomorrow morning."[7] Aware that the Confederates might shift troops from their center to the right, Meade wanted to exploit that possibility. When Grant merged these existing instructions to the VI Corps into his plan for an attack all along the lines, Wright's men benefitted from their head start in preparing, and their determined attack the following morning proved to be the most consequential in convincing Lee to abandon Petersburg and Richmond.

Despite moments of Meade trying to insert himself into the role of army commander, the sacking of Maj. Gen. Gouverneur Warren on April 1 meant that Grant had all new corps commanders in place compared to those he had inherited the previous spring. Brigadier General Charles Griffin took over

---

5   Ulysses S. Grant to Theodore S. Bowers, April 2, 1865, in *The War of the Rebellion: A Compilation of the Official Records of the Union and Confederate Armies*, 128 vols. (Washington, DC, 1880-1901), Series 1, vol. 46, pt. 3, 448. Hereafter cited as *O.R.*

6   George G. Meade to Margaretta Meade, June 1, 1864, in George Meade, ed., *The Life and Letters of George Gordon Meade*, vol. 2 (New York, NY: Charles Scribners's Sons, 1913), 200.

7   George G. Meade to Horatio G. Wright, April 1, 1865, *O.R.* vol. 46, pt. 3, 422.

command of the V Corps after Five Forks, Wright had stepped up to helm the VI Corps after Maj. Gen. John Sedgwick's death at Spotsylvania, and Maj. Gen. Andrew A. Humphreys had assumed command of the II from the embattled Winfield Scott Hancock in late 1864. Meanwhile in the IX Corps, which Grant had officially attached to Meade's Army of the Potomac after beginning the Overland Campaign as an independent unit, Parke had finally replaced Ambrose Burnside for good. Sheridan's cavalry had also recently rejoined the four infantry corps south of the Appomattox River. Meade detested the brash, aggressive trooper. Sheridan's direct order relieving Warren from command of the V Corps, which Meade had previously led, no doubt rankled the "goggle-eyed snapping turtle."

In addition to these command changes, Grant brought three divisions from Maj. Gen. Edward O.C. Ord's Army of the James south from Richmond to join the Army of the Potomac for the decisive campaign against Petersburg. Meade could not issue orders for those units even though they connected the VI Corps with the II Corps. The ground in between Ord and Maj. Gen. Henry Heth's three Confederate brigades near Hatcher's Run was treacherous for an advance. Grant decided early on April 2 that he did not want Ord to commit his men into a frontal assault and retasked the XXIV Corps with moving up behind the Union fortifications to help exploit Wright's breakthrough. Grant hoped they could sever the South Side Railroad, if not take Petersburg outright. Meanwhile, seven of the VI Corps brigades pivoted south from their initial penetration of the Confederate works near Tudor Hall. They swept down from the north, outflanking Heth's line and rolling them all the way to Hatcher's Run.

After receiving a flurry of dispatches that morning, Meade rode for Grant's headquarters and found the commanding general in an open field in front of Dabney's Mill. The two enjoyed only "a few moments of conversation" before Meade continued along to Humphreys's headquarters near the Rainey house on Boydton Plank Road.[8] The cheers of Maj. Gen. Gershom Mott's division warmed the general's ears as he quickly rode from his brief meeting.

Grant remained at Dabney's Mill, waiting to hear back from Humphreys

---

8   Theodore S. Lyman, Diary, April 2, 1865, in David W. Lowe, ed., *Meade's Army: The Private Notebooks of Lt. Col. Theodore Lyman* (Kent, OH: Kent State University Press, 2008), 357.

and Ord, who were still testing the Confederate defenses south of Hatcher's Run. By 7:30, the II Corps had begun pushing the Confederates from their White Oak Road line, and by 8:00 Grant learned that Brig. Gen. William Hays's division carried an imposing fort near the plank road, capturing three guns and most of its garrison. Half an hour later, Ord reported that Brig. Gen. Thomas M. Harris's brigade had carried the last of the Confederate earthworks south of the stream. "It was all now one battlefield from Petersburg to beyond Five Forks," wrote Lt. Col. Adam Badeau of Grant's staff. "Everywhere the national columns had burst the rebel barriers, and were surging inward towards the railroad and the town that had been their goal for a year. The various corps were becoming confused as they converged, and it needed the chief to disentangle the lines."[9]

Busy maintaining communications with Meade, Sheridan, Humphreys, Ord, Wright, Parke, Lincoln, and Maj. Gen. Godfrey Weitzel, who commanded the Union forces outside of Richmond, Grant began to worry about the cooperation between Wright's VI Corps (Army of the Potomac) and Maj. Gen. John Gibbon's XXIV Corps (Army of the James) as they sought to tamp out the last remaining Confederate resistance. "Thank God, the Lieutenant General has commanded in it himself and not permitted the spirit, or, I might say, the genius of his orders, to be dampened by his subordinate commander," crowed Grant's chief of staff, Brig. Gen. John A. Rawlins, at the end of the day—a clear censure of Meade.[10]

Grant decided to abandon Dabney's Mill once all dispatches had returned and to ride forward to help coordinate the follow-up to the initial stunning success. "Finding at length that they were all in, I mounted my horse to join the troops who were inside the works," Grant recalled as he rode to supervise the final movement to envelop Petersburg.[11] He spurred his black horse, "Jeff Davis," eastward toward Duncan Road where he turned north to cross Hatcher's Run. After riding another three and a half miles, he reached the point where Brig. Gen. Truman Seymour's VI Corps division

9   Adam Badeau, *Military History of Ulysses S. Grant, from April, 1861, to April, 1865*, vol. 3 (New York, NY: D. Appleton and Company, 1882), 515.

10   John A. Rawlins, Diary, April 2, 1865, in James H. Wilson, *The Life of John A. Rawlins: Lawyer* (New York, NY: The Neale Publishing Company, 1916), 316.

11   Ulysses S. Grant, *Personal Memoirs of U.S. Grant*, vol. 2 (New York: Charles L. Webster & Company, 1886), 449.

punched through the Confederate line. It is likely that the general entered the Confederate works at the site of the six-gun battery near John Hart's house.[12] A small detachment of two North Carolina regiments commanded by Lt. Col. Eric Erson garrisoned this part of the works that morning. Like the brigades around them, most of Erson's command were captured by the VI Corps. "When I arrived there I rode my horse over the parapet just as Wright's three thousand prisoners were coming out," recalled Grant.[13]

"His whole attention was for some time riveted upon them, and we knew that he was enjoying his usual satisfaction in seeing so large a capture," claimed Lt. Col. Porter who rode in the long cavalcade with Grant. "Some of the guards told the prisoners who the general was, and they manifested great curiosity to get a good look at him."[14] Captain Lemuel Abbott of the 10th Vermont Infantry was among those rounding up the prisoners and provided a stirring, though probably exaggerated, description of Grant's crossing of the Confederate works at the Hart farm:

He was mounted on a proud-stepping dark charger, dressed with unusual care and never appeared to better advantage. The occasion inspiring it, he was a perfect picture of a conquering hero, but seemed all unconscious of it. The artist who could put Grant and his suite on canvas as he appeared then would win renown. As Grant's eye caught the motley group of prisoners with me, who were regarding him with silent, open-mouthed wonder, he smiled slightly, drew in his horse a little as though to speak or in doubt of his safety, seeing the rebs had guns, but finally dashed on, an impressive picture not only in the midst of war, but surrounded by grand fortifications and the victorious and defeated living, wounded, dying and dead, real heroes of both the blue and the gray, never forgotten by those who were fortunate enough to see it.[15]

---

12   John Hart, a Pennsylvania native, had been conscripted into the Confederate army as a teamster and was taken prisoner on April 2, 1865. He did not return home until the summer. The rest of his family took shelter in the cellar during the Union attack that morning.

13   Grant, *Personal Memoirs of U.S. Grant*, 449.

14   Porter, *Campaigning with Grant*, 446.

15   Lemuel A. Abbott, *Personal Recollections and Civil War Diary, 1864* (Burlington, VT: Free Press Printing Co., 1908), 273-274.

Following the successful attack by the VI Corps on the morning of April 2, 1865, Ulysses S. Grant passed through the Confederate earthworks near the home on John Hart. The outline of a prominent six-gun battery is barely visible in the foreground. *Edward Alexander*

Grant continued riding through Seymour's division, which was "flushed with success, and rushing forward with a dash that was inspiriting beyond description."[16] When they spotted Grant, they began a cheer that spread along the line. "Boys, here's General Grant, three cheers for him," shouted a New Jersey sergeant who claimed the men "cheered him with the wildest enthusiasm." Grant reciprocated their praise with his "head uncovered" and "bowed his thanks for the soldiers' hearty greeting."[17]

"The dead and the wounded showed that the works had not been too easily won," observed Badeau.[18] He "sat on his horse in a plain blouse suit," remembered a Connecticut lieutenant, whose description of Grant is probably more accurate than Captain Abbott's; "if I had not known

16   Porter, *Campaigning with Grant*, 446.

17   J. Newton Terrill, *Campaign of the Fourteenth Regiment New Jersey Volunteers* (New Brunswick, NJ: Daily Home News Press, 1884), 119.

18   Badeau, *Military History of Ulysses S. Grant*, 516.

him by sight I would have said he and his staff were just an ordinary bunch of cavalrymen."[19]

Grant shook hands "with great heartiness" with General Wright and the VI Corps division commanders before galloping along past Tudor Hall "staying neither for prisoners nor cheers" as he continued to send and receive dispatches while on the move.[20] Soon the commander arrived where Duncan Road fed into the Boydton Plank Road and briefly stopped at the home of John W. Harmon.

A local Dinwiddie county sheriff, Harmon had purchased thirty-five acres at this intersection from Athaliah Boisseau, matriarch of Tudor Hall, for $800 in December 1858. By 1860, he had completed construction of his home, likely a simple frame structure.[21] That year's census showed that Harmon owned two female slaves and rented a male slave. Born around 1828, and thus approximately thirty-seven at the time of the breakthrough, the sheriff does not appear in any Confederate enlistment records. If he did stay in his home during the winter encampment of 1864-1865, however, he would have shared it with Confederate officers. Here Grant met with Meade for a second time that morning.

The Army of the Potomac's commander had taken a different path to reach the junction. After a brief stay at Humphreys's headquarters, waiting for the II Corps to finish mopping up what remained of the Confederate brigades along the White Oak Road, Meade rode along the hard-fought Boydton Plank Road.[22] The commander received a similar, hearty greeting from the soldiers along his journey as he crossed Hatcher's Run at Burgess Mill and ascended the plank road. "As we got to the top of a rise, we struck the open country that surrounds the town, for several miles, and here the road was full of troops, who, catching sight of the General trotting briskly

---

19   David E. Soule, "Recollections of the Civil War, LVIII," *New Milford Gazette*, July 19, 1912.

20   Terrill, *Campaign of the Fourteenth Regiment*, 119; Badeau, *Military History of Ulysses S. Grant*, 516.

21   Some campaign maps and accounts refer to Harmon's home as the "Red House."

22   This ground witnessed heavy combat during multiple Union offensives at Petersburg, including at Burgess Mill (or Boydton Plank Road), October 27, 1864; Hatcher's Run, February 5-7, 1865; Lewis Farm, March 29, 1865; White Oak Road, March 31, 1865; and the II Corps attacks on April 2, 1865.

by, began to cheer and wave their caps enthusiastically!" recalled Meade's chief of staff, Lt. Col. Theodore Lyman. "This continued all along the column, each regiment taking it up in turn. It was a goodly ride, I can tell you!"[23] A New Jersey sergeant wrote that when Meade passed along the line, hat in hand, "Cheer after cheer rent the air."[24]

Eventually Meade's ride took him into an unexpected collision with the commanding general at the Harmon house. "Presently we spied General Grant seated on the porch," stated Lyman, "and there too we halted." While the generals once more conversed, the staff officer poked around the empty structure: "It seemed a deserted building and had been occupied by a Rebel ordnance sergeant, whose papers and returns were lying about in admirable confusion. A moral man was this sergeant, and had left behind a diary, in one page of which he lamented the vice and profanity of his fellow soldiers. He was not, however, cleanly, but quite untidy in his domestic arrangements." Lyman walked outside, while Meade and Grant quickly concluded their hasty conversation, and glimpsed around at his surroundings. "From this spot we had an admirable view of our own works, as the Rebels had, for months, been used to look at them. There was that tall signal tower, over against us, and the bastions of Fort Fisher, and here, near at hand, the Rebel line, with its huts and its defenders sorely beleaguered over there in the inner lines against which our batteries were even now playing."[25]

Meanwhile, the XXIV Corps had assumed the lead in the advance toward Petersburg, and Col. Thomas O. Osborn's brigade slowly drove Brig. Gen. Nathaniel H. Harris's four Mississippi regiments back to the two solitary forts—Gregg and Whitworth—that stood in between the Federals and Petersburg's temporarily vacated inner lines. Grant wanted to get a better view of the situation for himself and mounted "Jeff Davis" to depart both the Harmon house and Meade in favor of another humble dwelling half a mile closer to the action. From a slightly elevated knoll at the Banks house, Grant

23   George R. Agassiz, ed., *Meade's Headquarters, 1863-1865: Letters of Colonel Theodore Lyman from the Wilderness to Appomattox* (Boston: The Atlantic Monthly Press, 1922), 338.

24   Samuel B. Fisher to "Dear Sister," April 3, 1865, Wiley Sword Collection at Pamplin Historical Park. Sergeant Fisher also claimed to have seen Grant, writing, "You ought to have heard the boys cheer."

25   Agassiz, *Meade's Headquarters*, 338.

watched as multiple brigades from Gibbon's command hurled themselves at the ramparts of Fort Gregg. Wright's exhausted VI Corps, meanwhile, took up a supporting role, stretching the line up to the Appomattox River.

While the Army of the James sunk the final nail in the Confederate coffin, Grant continued sending and receiving dispatches, coordinating the movements of both major armies in Virginia as well as the operations of Union commanders throughout the various military districts in the south. The lieutenant general briefly came under fire while he hastily scribbled messages to be sent throughout what remained of the Confederacy but shrugged it off to focus on the task at hand. Despite Meade's bitterness at being overshadowed, the last days of the Petersburg campaign illustrated why a strategist like Grant was needed to see the war to its victorious conclusion.

A Poet's Perspective:
Herman Melville on the Fall of Richmond

by Caroline Davis

April 1865 would see the beginning of the end of the American Civil War. Grant had closed in on Lee and, as Petersburg succumbed to the Union, those in Richmond began to evacuate. Confederate President Jefferson Davis, his cabinet, civilians, and soldiers alike all began fleeing the city, knowing the capital would not hold up against a Union attack. This is what the Federal army had sought for four long and grueling years.

Poet and author Herman Melville wrote about the capture of the confederate capital in his poem "The Fall of Richmond":

> The tidings received in the Northern Metropolis.
> (April, 1865.)
> What mean these peals from every tower,
> And crowds like seas that sway?
>
> The cannon reply; they speak the heart
> Of the People impassions, and say—
> A city in flags for a city in flames, Richmond goes Babylon's way—
> Sing and pray.

The poem itself, while about the fall of Richmond, addresses the feelings felt by those in the North. "A city in flags for a city in flames" were powerful

Currier & Ives thought the fall of Richmond worthy enough to deserve the lithograph treatment. *Metropolitan Museum of Art*

words to describe the celebration, relief, and reflection northerners felt. But Melville does not write this with malice; rather, he writes with gratitude that the war has finally ended.

In the next stanza, Melville praises Grant: "Honor to Grant the brave," he says. Grant, of course, is due the credit for defeating General Robert E. Lee following the long siege of Petersburg. "Bless his glaive," Melville ends the verse—translated, this means "bless his sword":

> O weary years and woeful wars,
> And armies in the grave;
> But hearts unquelled at last deter
> The helmed dilated Lucifer--
>
> Honor to Grant the brave,
> Whose three stars now like Orion's rise
> When wreck is on the wave--
> Bless his glaive.

It was a long road to Richmond, and much was sacrificed. The weary years and the armies of men buried in the grave all point to the feelings of despair that came with each passing day the war continued. Yet with Grant, who Melville describes in a comparison with Orion, the Greek God of Hunting, comes victory at last.

With the third stanza, Melville turns his praise to the northern people who never lost faith:

> Well that the faith we firmly kept,
> And never our aim forswore
> For the Terrors that trooped from each recess
> When fainting we fought in the Wilderness,
>
> And Hell made loud hurrah;
> But God is in Heaven, and Grant in the Town,
> And Right through might is Law–
> God's way adore.

Northerners kept their faith firmly intact, despite the gruesome fighting. This final stanza is not only about the north; it is also about the bravery of the soldiers, the might of Grant—who never turned back—and the faith it took to withstand the brutal years of war.

Melville began his series of poems on the Civil War with one entitled "Misgivings." In this, he talks about a storm, a nation divided. He expressively illustrates the feelings of foreboding. "The Fall of Richmond," while not the last poem of the collection, still shows a distinct difference in emotions. Despair versus hope—hope that the war was over and that Grant had accomplished what many had given up on: a Northern victory.

On to Appomattox

by Sarah Kay Bierle

Originally published as a blog post at Emerging Civil War
on April 8, 2019

As the days passed and the armies slogged forward after the breakthrough at Petersburg on April 2, 1865, civilians and soldiers alike sensed a coming end of the Army of Northern Virginia. Through the week, Union cavalry and infantry cut off the Confederate retreat, small battles and constant skirmishing erupted along the route of pursuit, and the promised Southern supply wagons did not survive Sheridan and his Yankee boys.

Distant from the scenes of the final large-scale campaign in Virginia, Mary Chesnut recorded the fall of Richmond in her diary, days after it actually happened. On the muddy roads—lined with the fallen, deserters, and abandoned equipment—Private Edgar Warfield of the 17th Virginia Infantry kept running, trying to stay ahead of the Union soldiers; still, his compassion did not end, and he took time to aid a hurting comrade. On the Federal side, Brig. Gen. Joshua L. Chamberlain pressed his men in the V Corps to exhaustion, following orders. Eventually, he gave in for some rest, until a messenger arrived in the darkness with history-making news.

Those who were there or following the news from afar can give us a better glimpse into the dangers, difficulties, and uncertainty on the road to Appomattox. Here are the accounts of Chesnut, Warfield, and Chamberlain.

Mary Chesnut's Diary

April 7, 1865

Richmond has fallen—and I have no heart to write about it. Grant broke through our lines. Sherman cut through them. Stoneman is this side of Danville.

They are too many for us.

Everything lost in Richmond, even our archives.

Blue-black is our horizon.[1]

Edgar Warfield's Memoirs

No rations were issued to us, the horses and mules faring as badly as the men. On the 7th rations were issued to a portion of the army. We got none, and in consequence we were continually abandoning and destroying artillery wagons to keep them from falling into the hands of the enemy. As soon as the horses gave out from fatigue the pieces were run to the side of the road and cut down.

There was a great deal of straggling, the men falling down by the wayside and being taken prisoner. One poor fellow of my company, who was making great efforts to keep up, finally fell down from complete exhaustion. He said to me as I left him, "I can go no farther, but tell Colonel Herbert that I may be taken prisoner but I will never take the oath." In a few minutes he was in the hands of the enemy. He never lived to reach home. A few weeks later I was called upon to assist in putting his body in the ground at Ivy Hill.

Near Farmville I was delayed a while when I stopped to put my wounded comrade, Hal Appich, in a church which had been converted into a temporary hospital, with the ladies of the town acting as nurses. The enemy was held in check not over two hundred yards off by our rear guard. A portion of this guard had taken position under the church, the rear of which was built on brick piers. While I was in the hospital the bullets were entering the windows, and the cries of the wounded and the screams of the nurses were pitiful to hear.

---

1   Mary Chesnut, *Mary Chesnut's Civil War,* edited by C. Vann Woodward (New Haven: Yale University Press, 1981), 782.

I carried my comrade on my back down the aisle and put him just inside the chancel rail on the floor. I bade him goodbye and ran out as fast as I could and started down the street. I met a mounted officer of my acquaintance who called out to me to look behind. He was directing my attention to a body of Union cavalry who were crossing just back of me. I answered by telling him to look in the opposite direction where a body of Sherman's men were crossing the main street about two blocks from where we were.

I called out to him that they would surely get him. Then I ran across the street and through a gateway into a yard, climbed over the back fence, and finally, after climbing several other fences, reached the fields where the cavalry could not well go. In less than two hours I was up with our troops. My friend was captured immediately and spent some time in a Northern prison before returning home, as he told me after the war. Had he abandoned his horse and followed me he too would have escaped.

The morning of April 9 found us near Appomattox Court House. . . . [2]

Joshua L. Chamberlain's Reminiscence

The 8th of April found the Fifth Corps at Prospect Station, on the South Side Railroad, nearly abreast of the head of Lee's retreating column, while Meade was with his two corps close upon Lee's rear at New Store, ten miles north of us, across the Appomattox. At noon of this day, General Ord, of the Army of the James, joined us with two divisions of the Twenty-fourth Corps under General Gibbon, and Birney's Division of the Twenty-fifth Corps,—colored troops; Ord, by virtue of seniority, becoming commanding officer of the whole. He was a stranger to us all, but his simple and cordial manner toward Sheridan and Griffin, and even to us subordinates, made him welcome. We pushed on,—the cavalry ahead.

The Fifth Corps had a very hard march that day,—made more so in the afternoon and night by the lumbering obstructions of the rear of Ord's tired column, by courtesy given the road before us, the incessant check fretting our men almost to mutiny. We had been rushed all day to keep up with the cavalry, but this constant checking was worse. We did not know that Grant

2   Edgar Warfield, *Manassas to Appomattox: The Civil War Memoirs of Pvt. Edgar Warfield, 17th Virginia Infantry,* (McLean, VA: EPM Publications, 1996), 171-172.

had sent orders for the Fifth Corps to march all night without halting; but it was not necessary for us to know it. After twenty-nine miles of this kind of marching, at the blackest hour of night, human nature called a halt. Dropping by the roadside, right and left, wet or dry, down went the men as in a swoon. Officers slid out of the saddle, loosened the girth, slipped an arm through a loop of bridle-rein, and sunk to sleep. Horses stood with drooping heads just above their masters' faces. All dreaming,—one knows not what, of past, or coming, possible or fated.

Scarcely is the first broken dream begun when a cavalry man comes splashing down the road, and vigorously dismounts, pulling from his jacket front a crumpled note. The sentinel standing watch by his commander, worn in body but alert in every sense, touches you on the shoulder. "Orders, sir, I think!" You rise on elbow, strike a match, and with smarting, streaming eyes read the brief, thrilling note from Sheridan – like this, as I remember: "I have cut across the enemy at Appomattox Station, and captured three of his trains. If you can possibly push your infantry up here tonight, we will have great results in the morning."

Ah, sleep no more! The startling bugle notes ring out "The General"—"To the march!" Word is sent for the men to take a bite of such as they had for food: the promised rations would not be up till noon, and by that time we should be—where? Few try to eat, no matter what. Meanwhile, almost with one foot in the stirrup you take from the hands of the black boy a tin plate of nondescript food and a dipper of miscalled coffee. . . . You eat and drink at a swallow; mount, and away to get to the head of the column before you sound the "Forward." They are there—the men: shivering to their senses as if risen out of the earth, but something in them not of it! Now sounds the "Forward," for the last time in our long-drawn strife; and they move—these men—sleepless, supperless, breakfastless, sore-footed, stiff-jointed, sense-benumbed, but with flushed faces pressing for the front.

By sunrise we have reached Appomattox Station. . . .[3]

---

3   Joshua Lawrence Chamberlain, *"Bayonet! Forward": My Civil War Reminiscences* (Gettysburg: Stan Clark Military Books, 1994), 143-144.

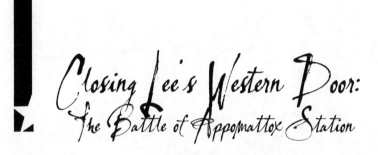

Closing Lee's Western Door: The Battle of Appomattox Station

by Daniel T. Davis

Originally published as a blog post at Emerging Civil War on April 8, 2015

The evacuation of Farmville and subsequent fight at Cumberland Church on April 7, 1865 continued to force Robert E. Lee's retreating Army of Northern Virginia west. By the morning of April 8, Lee decided to head for Appomattox Station. There he hoped to obtain critical supplies for his men while keeping one step ahead of the pursuing Union armies, which would allow him to turn south toward North Carolina and a hoped-for junction with forces commanded by Gen. Joseph E. Johnston.

Appomattox Station also began to loom large in the mind of the commander of the Army of the Shenandoah, Maj. Gen. Philip Sheridan. After his divisions routed the enemy at Sailor's Creek two days earlier, Sheridan directed his blue horsemen to continue their march, arriving at Prospect Station early in the day. While there, Sheridan received intelligence that Confederate supply trains were at Appomattox Station. The race was on as "Little Phil" turned his horsemen toward the station, with Bvt. Maj. Gen. George A. Custer's Third Division leading the advance.

"It was well understood that the command was now in Lee's front, and in consequence, the men were in fine spirits. General Sheridan rode along

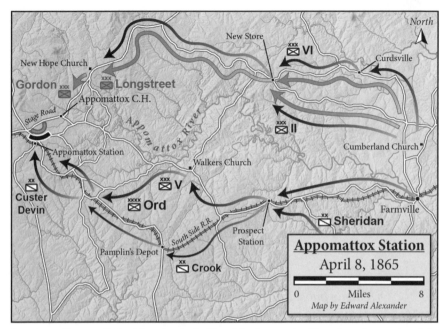

APPOMATTOX STATION—Federal forces on both sides of the Appomattox River drove the remains of the Army of Northern Virginia westward. Lee eyed Appomattox Station as an opportunity to reach much-needed supplies for his depleted force. With enough of a lead, he might also hope to turn the corner on the Federals and start moving south for a junction with Joseph E. Johnston's forces in North Carolina. Custer's cavalry force reached the station first, though, cutting off Lee's access.

the column toward the front, offering words of encouragement," recalled a West Virginia trooper under Custer.[1]

The Confederates, however, won the race to Appomattox Station. The lead elements of Lee's army, Brig. Gen. Reuben L. Walker's artillery battalion, supported by Brig. Gen. Martin Gary's cavalry, arrived early in the afternoon. The exhausted cannoneers slumped to the ground for a much-needed rest, although they had no idea of the mounted juggernaut heading straight for them.

Sometime around 4 p.m., the head of Custer's division, Col. Alexander C.M. Pennington's brigade, rode into view. As the Federal cavalryman moved forward, a surgeon recalled that Custer "directed two regiments of the division to move forward at a trot as advance guard. The balance of the

---

1   J. J. Sutton, *History of the Second Regiment of West Virginia Cavalry Volunteers During the War of the Rebellion* (Huntington, CA: Blue Acorn Press, 2001) 223.

command followed at the same gait. The advance had orders to charge the station the moment they came in sight of it and capture the trains."[2]

Closing in on the station, a curious incident took place. "Two young ladies came running, screaming down the walk leading to the road, from a large and elegant mansion," the [regimental?] surgeon wrote:

> 'They are robbing us! They are robbing and trying to murder us!' they screamed with all of their might. General Custer, without saying a word stopped short and quickly dismounted, ran up the walk just in time to catch a man in United States uniform running from the front door. With his fist, he almost annihilated the miserable scalawag. Then, running through the house, he caught another making his exit from the rear door. Catching up an axe, he threw it, hitting the brute in the back of his head, thus quickly disposing of the two wretches. In a moment he was in the saddle again . . . directing . . . the provost marshal to place a guard on the premises.[3]

Resuming his place at the head of his command, Custer sent his men forward. Capturing the trains, Custer turned his attention to Walker's artillery. After two fruitless attacks by Pennington and Col. Henry Capeheart's brigade, Custer finally ordered up Col. William Wells's brigade about nightfall. Around dark, Custer once again led his men forward, one trooper writing afterwards that the "flashes of the enemy's guns, as reflected against the sky, resembled a furious storm of lighting."[4] This final charge carried the station, driving what was left of Walker's command back down the Stage Road toward Appomattox Court House.

The action slammed the door shut for Lee. Arriving in the Appomattox River Valley, Lee looked west to see Sheridan's cavalry. Close on the heels of the Union cavalry came Maj. Gen. Edward O. C. Ord's Army of the James, along with the V Corps of the Army of the Potomac. To the east, directly in Lee's rear, stood the rest of the Army of the Potomac. To the north lay the James River. The "Old Gray Fox" was finally cornered and the following day, April 9, would be one of the most pivotal for his army.

---

2   Frederick W. Whitaker, *A Complete Life of General George A. Custer* (New York: Sheldon and Company, 1876) 305.

3   Ibid., 306.

4   Sutton, 223.

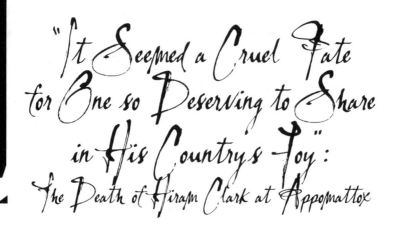

"It Seemed a Cruel Fate
for One so Deserving to Share
in His Country's Joy":
The Death of Hiram Clark at Appomattox

by Ryan Quint

*Adapted and revised from a post originally published
at Emerging Civil War on April 9, 2015*

Since the first engagement between Ulysses S. Grant and Robert E. Lee in the Wilderness on May 5, 1864, 339 days had passed. Now, in the early morning hours of April 9, 1865, the closing moments of the Civil War's Eastern Theater were at hand. But before a white flag would be waved, the last shots had to be fired and, with those, the last deaths had to be incurred.

Realizing that his army's chances to escape were slipping away, Lee ordered one last attack. The remnants of Maj. Gen. John B. Gordon's Second Corps formed up and attacked for the final time. They doggedly pushed Federal cavalry away from the Richmond-Lynchburg Stage Road, but just as it seemed that victory was at hand for the Confederates, Gordon saw column after column of blue-clad infantry arriving on the field to slam the door shut on any such hope. "Tell General Lee that my command has been fought to a frazzle," Gordon had no choice but to admit to a staff officer.

"I cannot long go forward." The Confederate attack died out, and Gordon's men slowly retreated towards the town of Appomattox Court House.[1]

Some of the Federals arriving on the field belonged to Brig. Gen. Joshua Chamberlain's brigade of the Army of the Potomac's V Corps. Chamberlain's two regiments, the 185th New York and the 198th Pennsylvania, arrived on the field to support the U.S. cavalry. Seeing Chamberlain, Maj. Gen. Edward Ord, commanding the Army of the James, advised the Mainer, "Don't expose your lines on that crest. The enemy have massed their guns to give it a raking fire the moment you set foot there." Chamberlain weighed his options for a moment before he decided to press ahead regardless of Ord's warning.[2]

Lt. Hiram Clark, 185th New York Infantry *New York State Military Museum*

Among the 185th New York's ranks stood First Lt. Hiram Clark, commanding the regiment's Company G. Clark, 26 years old, was from Richford, New York, and had enlisted in the regiment the previous September. Commissioned as a lieutenant, Clark served with the regiment through its experiences at Petersburg and most recently at the battle of Five Forks. Respected by his fellow soldiers, Clark was described as "an excellent officer, a perfect gentleman, highly respected by all who knew him, not only for his soldierly qualities but his genial spirit, never dampened—and his kindness to and care for those under his immediate command."[3]

1   John B. Gordon, *Reminiscences of the Civil War* (New York: Charles Scribner's Sons, 1903), 437-438; See Chris M. Calkins, *The Battles of Appomattox Station and Appomattox Court House April 8-9, 1865* (Lynchburg: H.E. Howard, 1987) for the best monograph on the battle of Appomattox Court House.

2   Joshua L. Chamberlain, *The Passing of the Armies: An Account of the Final Campaign of the Army of the Potomac, Based Upon Personal Reminiscences of the Fifth Army Corps* (New York: G.P. Putnam's Sons, 1915), 236.

3   Roster of 185th New York, 575, http://dmna.ny.gov/historic/reghist/civil/rosters/Infantry/185th_Infantry_CW_Roster.pdf (accessed July 22, 2021); "Letter from the 185th Regiment," in Unknown Newspaper Publication, 185th Regiment New York Volunteers Civil War Newspaper Clippings, New York State Military Museum and Veterans Research Center (hereafter "Letter from the 185th Regiment").

The Army of Northern Virginia fired its last artillery shots from George Peers's front yard. *Ryan Quint*

Lieutenant Clark deployed his company as skirmishers ahead of the rest of the 185th New York. Replacing the Federal cavalry, the infantry pushed ahead, but Gordon's Confederates were already falling back. "The whole work of driving the enemy was done by the skirmishers," wrote one Federal correspondent. Chamberlain agreed, describing the fight later: "The disheartened enemy take it easy; our men take them easier. It is a wild, musing fusing—earnest, but not deadly earnest."[4]

There was little left for the Confederates to do. An officer carrying a white flag rode ahead seeking a truce. He made his way towards the closest Federals, who were in Chamberlain's brigade. According to Chamberlain, the Confederate said, "General Lee desires a cessation of hostilities until he can hear from General Grant as to the proposed surrender." The time left

---

4　James Edward Nicholson, "A History of the One Hundred and Eighty-Fifth Regiment of New York State Volunteers," (PhD diss., Canisius College, Buffalo, 1962), 83; *New York Daily Herald,* April 14, 1865; Chamberlain, 239.

remaining in the war in Virginia could now be measured in minutes, not days or weeks.[5]

But before the truce went into effect, before Grant and Lee met in Wilmer McLean's parlor, and right about the time that the Confederate officer rode up to Chamberlain, a last cannon shot roared out. Unlimbered at the edge of town in the front yard of George Peers, a battery of the Richmond Howitzers had been firing in support of Gordon's attack. As the attack gave way, "one by one their guns are withdrawn, until only one remains." The last cannon, "so near Mr. Peers' doorstep that the rebound brings it plumb against it," continued to fire. Manning the piece, the crew, "having already discharged one volley, was loading for another, [when] the order was given to cease firing."[6]

For Hiram Clark, the cease fire came too late. One of, if not the very last, shots from the Confederate artillery arced down the ridge towards the 185th New York's skirmish line. A witness wrote that Clark "was cut in two by a cannon ball just as the white flag was raised." Another added that the shot continued "afterwards taking off a foot of a member of the 198th Pennsylvania." Clark's death was instantaneous—and marked the only casualty suffered by the 185th New York at Appomattox.[7]

Clark's death came almost simultaneously with the cessation of hostilities. Death was to be expected in warfare, but the timing of Clark's left observers horrified. His brigade commander, Joshua Chamberlain, wrote, "Not a strange thing for war, this swift stroke of the mortal; but coming after the truce was in, it seemed a cruel fate for one so deserving to share his country's joy, and a sad peace-offering for us all." In a history of the 185th New York, Clark's death coinciding with the truce was called a "pathetic incident." Clark's disheartened comrades buried him "at the foot of a large cherry tree."[8]

5   Chamberlain, 240.

6   Calkins, 103-104; *Nashville Banner,* Sept. 5, 1881; John C. Gorman, *Lee's Last Campaign* (Raleigh: Wm. B. Smith & Company, 1866), 41.

7   *National Tribune,* Sept. 3, 1887; "Letter from the 185th Regiment"; Frederick Phisterer *New York in the War of the Rebellion: Volume 5* (Albany: J.B. Lyon Company, 1912), 4059.

8   Chamberlain, 242; *The Union Army: A History of Military Affairs in the Loyal States 1861-1865...: Volume 2, New York, Maryland, West Virginia and Ohio* (Madison: Federal Publishing Company, 1908), 178; Nicholson, 85.

As the nation celebrated the end of the war, the sad word made its way back to Tioga County, New York. Hiram Clark had no wife or children, but he had a mother, Elizabeth Clark. Upon his father's death in 1861, Hiram had taken up the mantle of caring for Elizabeth. With Hiram's death, Elizabeth Clark filed for a pension from the government. For the death of her son, the Federal government paid Elizabeth Clark $17 a month, starting in January 1866. Sometime thereafter, Hiram Clark's remains were moved to the Poplar Grove National Cemetery outside Petersburg.[9]

Hiram Clark, though, was not the only person to die at Appomattox. The casualties on April 9 inevitably led to debate between veterans of various units claiming the morbid honor of the last death. Death also came to those not in uniform. Hannah Reynolds, an enslaved woman in town, was mortally wounded by a Confederate shell on April 9; she endured long enough to die a free woman on April 12 after fruitless efforts by Federal surgeons to save her. About the debate of who was last to die, Joshua Chamberlain wrote fittingly, "The honor of this last death is not a proper subject of quarrel."[10]

The "proper subject", instead, was that Hiram Clark, and the others killed at Appomattox, fell not in senseless death but that their sacrifice contributed to the conclusion of the war in Virginia. They were the last in a butcher's list that at some points seemed would never end. But it did end. The nation was one step closer to Lincoln's promise of "a new birth of freedom."

---

9   Elizabeth Clark Pension, Case Files of Approved Pension Applications of Widows and Other Dependents of the Army and Navy Who Served Mainly in the Civil War and the War With Spain, Record Group 15, National Archives and Records Administration (NARA); John Auwaerter, *Cultural Landscape Report for Poplar Grove National Cemetery* (Boston: National Park Service, 2009), 44.

10   See Calkins, 227-234 for a tabulation of casualties; See *Under the Maltese Cross: Antietam to Appomattox Campaigns, 155th Pennsylvania Regiment* (Pittsburgh: 155th Regimental Association, 1910), 360-362 for a biography of William Montgomery, another Federal soldier killed just before the truce; William Marvel, *A Place Called Appomattox* (Chapel Hill: University of North Carolina Press, 2000), 235; Chicago *Tribune*, April 9, 2015.

Picturing Union Victory: Early Images of the Surrender at Appomattox

by Cecily Nelson Zander

Originally published as a blog post on Emerging Civil War on June 18, 2020

The following is a familiar story: On April 9, 1865, generals Ulysses S. Grant and Robert E. Lee met in Wilmer McLean's parlor at Appomattox Courthouse to sign the documents that would dictate the surrender of the most important national institution in the Confederacy: the Army of Northern Virginia. Grant sat at a small wooden table with spindle-turned legs and an

Grant and Lee, with their disproportionately large heads, crisp uniforms, and dainty feet sit down for a refined conversation in this 1873 Currier & Ives print, "Surrender of General Lee." *Library of Congress*

oval top. His aide, Lt. Col. Ely S. Parker, sat at another small wooden table in order to write out copies of the surrender. Lee sat at a much grander table, with a large black wooden base and a marble top. It is very probable that neither general made much of the seating arrangements (Grant, in fact, fails to describe them in his memoirs), but that has not prevented those arrangements from being the subject of much controversy and debate in the fifteen decades since.

I have asked myself why so many early images produced of the scene in Wilmer McLean's parlor seem to get so many details about the war's most important surrender wrong. As a historian, trained to analyze sources and inspect their biases—as well as to understand how history and memory overlap and differ—I formed a hypothesis that images produced closer to April 9, 1865, would be more reliable than those that came long after many of the participants had died or those that were created during the centennial and sesquicentennial celebrations of the event.

A brief test of my hypothesis revealed just how wrong I was, and I had to set off to answer a new question: why are so many early images of the surrender wrong, and what are they trying to tell viewers?

I became particularly concerned by the failure of early artists to assign Grant and Lee to the correct tables. As will be seen below, the earliest images of the surrender take two approaches—they either depict Grant and Lee sharing a single table or they swap the positions of the two most important commanders, putting Grant at the larger, marble-topped table. This phenomenon leads me to believe that many of the earliest images of the Appomattox surrender were created to celebrate the victory of the United States in the Civil War and not to provide accurate historical evidence. Hence, there is a strong pro-Union bias in the first Appomattox imagery.

Early images either strive to make Ulysses S. Grant and the Union cause appear more important by placing him at the grander table and surrounding him with his most important officers (regardless of whether they were actually present at the surrender); or they emphasize Grant's humanity and belief in reconciliation by suggesting that he met Lee and shared a table with the Confederate officer, acting in such a way that would encourage all Union soldiers and Northern citizens to be magnanimous in victory.

I will use three examples to illustrate my hypothesis.

Alonzo Chappel, an American painter whose life spanned the Civil War, made two attempts at portraying the events of Appomattox. Best known today as a painter of scenes from the Revolutionary War, Chappel's first Appomattox painting depicted Lee and Grant sharing a large wooden table. The painting now greets visitors in the Smithsonian American Art Museum. The image makes clear that Grant is the victor but does not overawe the

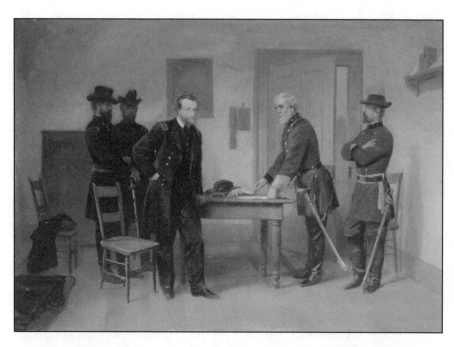

Alonzo Chappel, *Lee Surrendering to Grant at Appomattox*, ca. 1870, oil on paperboard. *Smithsonian American Art Museum*

audience with the superiority of the Union. It is an image that promotes reconciliation—but, critically, reconciliation on Grant's terms.

A second Chappel rendering, which scholars Barbara J. Mitnick and David Meschutt identify as the artist's effort to "paint a new and more accurate version of the surrender," shows the two most famous tables in recognizable form, but places the two principal participants at the wrong ones.[1] Grant still dominates the frame, surrounded by many of the luminaries of the Union high command. Parker sits at a third table—identical to Lee's. The image directs viewers to notice that Grant and his fellow officers are watching Lee intently and Grant appears comfortably in charge of events.

Chappel's painting could also be viewed as the artist's commentary on the success of the army's interventions in watching over the former Confederacy during Reconstruction. The entire focus of the Union high

1   Barbara J. Mitnick and David Meschutt, *The Portraits and History Paintings of Alonzo Chappel* (Brandywine River Museum, 1992), 84.

Postcard ca. 1907 featuring Chappel's 1884 painting *The surrender of Lee, Appomattox C.H., Va., April 9th, 1865. Gary W. Gallagher*

command is on Lee and his aide, Charles Marshall, just as the primary focus of the Regular Army would shift to maintaining peace and order across the Reconstruction South in the decade after the Civil War. Regardless of any Reconstruction commentary, Chappel's contemporary image clearly celebrates the achievements of Grant and his subordinates during the war.

More Americans were likely to have to have seen the illustration that accompanied the Century Publishing Company's *Battles and Leaders* history of the Civil War than any other Appomattox image. That image hews closely to Chappel's second painting and switches the tables for Lee and Grant, placing the Union commander at the more ostentatious of the two. Maj. Gen. Philip Sheridan is given more to do—and points his sword at Lee, perhaps suggesting the superiority of Union arms (as Lee's sword is barely visible) and reminding viewers that Sheridan's army had been critical in pinning Lee's dwindling forces near Appomattox Courthouse (especially at Five Forks) as the Confederate force retreated out of its Petersburg lines.

The choice to include Sheridan is a further indication of the lithograph's pro-Union point of view. Historical accounts differ on whether "Little Phil" was in the McLean parlor on April 9, though Sheridan himself told artist James E. Kelly in 1878 that he was not in the room during the negotiations

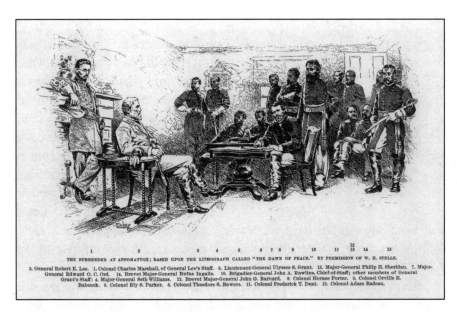

THE SURRENDER AT APPOMATTOX; BASED UPON THE LITHOGRAPH CALLED "THE DAWN OF PEACE." BY PERMISSION OF W. H. STELLE.

2. General Robert E. Lee. 1. Colonel Charles Marshall, of General Lee's Staff. 8. Lieutenant-General Ulysses S. Grant. 15. Major-General Philip H. Sheridan. 7. Major-General Edward O. C. Ord. 14. Brevet Major-General Rufus Ingalls. 10. Brigadier-General John A. Rawlins, Chief-of-Staff; other members of General Grant's Staff: 4. Major-General Seth Williams. 12. Brevet Major-General John G. Barnard. 9. Colonel Horace Porter. 3. Colonel Orville E. Babcock. 5. Colonel Ely S. Parker. 6. Colonel Theodore S. Bowers. 11. Colonel Frederick T. Dent. 13. Colonel Adam Badeau.

The Dawn of Peace by W. H. Steele (1888). *Battles and Leaders of the Civil War, 4:736*

(he claimed in his interview with Kelly to have been napping under a tree in McLean's front yard).[2] In his 1888 memoirs, Sheridan changed his story and explained that he had been in the room for portions of the surrender, but that during the discussion of the surrender conditions only Grant, Lee, Marshall, and Parker were present.[3] By including the full cast of participants alongside the principal players, early Union lithographs emphasized the might of the Union army and the numerical differences between the two major combatants in the war's Eastern Theater.

In viewing Appomattox imagery, it is striking that one of the few historical details the Lost Cause memory of the Civil War got correct is the seating arrangements in the McLean parlor. While not explicitly a Lost Cause document, Tom Lovell's *Surrender at Appomattox* (painted at the culmination of the war's centennial in 1965) depicts Robert E. Lee at the center of the surrender. Light, presumably emanating from a window to the

2   William B. Styple, ed., *Generals in Bronze: Interviewing the Commanders of the Civil War* (Kearny, N.J.: Belle Grove Publishing 2005), 4-5.

3   Phillip H. Sheridan, *Personal Memoirs of P. H. Sheridan*, 2 vols. (New York: Charles H. Webster and Company, 1888), 2:200-1.

Tom Lovell, *Surrender at Appomattox*, (1965).
National Geographic magazine

viewer's left but not visible in the painting, illuminates Lee. The gold sash on his spotless uniform stands out in contrast to the more muted detail of the Union officers present. Grant, meanwhile, correctly hunches over the small table in the shadowy background, his muddy boots offering another point of contrast to Lee's polished footwear. The most noticeable Union officer is arguably Maj. Gen. George Armstrong Custer (who was not present in the room), due to the splash of red on his kerchief.

Despite correcting small details, these Lost Cause-leaning images still celebrate the losing side in the war, and an Appomattox image that properly renders the details of the parlor and emphasizes Union victory would be of great value to historians and visitors to Civil War sites across the country. And while my original hypothesis turned out to be incorrect, my ensuing adventure through Appomattox imagery revealed early celebrations of the Union cause and depictions of Ulysses S. Grant as his contemporaries viewed him. While not particularly useful in crafting a historical narrative, they are potent reminders of how the Civil War generation set about the work of memory making and how the Lost Cause came to displace the robust efforts of Union memorialists in the decades after the Civil War.

Indian Aide: Ely Parker and the Surrender of the Army of Northern Virginia

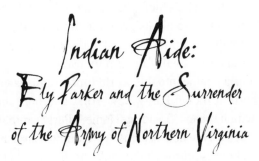

by Kevin Pawlak

*Originally published as a blog post at Emerging Civil War
on April 9, 2019*

Four months before giving birth to her son Ely, expectant mother Elizabeth Johnson Parker ("Gaontguttwus" to the Tonawanda Band of Seneca) awoke one night after experiencing a dream. Her vision had shown a rainbow broken in two. The bottom of one half ended at the home of the local Indian agent in Buffalo, New York, while the other half concluded on the Seneca reservation.

Unsure of its meaning, Elizabeth Parker sought the help of a dream interpreter. "A son will be born to you who will be distinguished among his nation as a peacemaker," began the prophesy. "[H]e will become a white man as well as

Ely Parker of the Tonawanda Band of Senecas became a "leading name" on Grant's staff. *Library of Congress*

an Indian, with great learning; he will be a warrior for the palefaces; he will be a wise white man, but will never desert his Indian people or 'lay down his horns as a great Iroquois chief'; his name will reach from the East to the West–the North to the South, as great among his Indian family and the palefaces. His sun will rise on Indian land and set on the white man's land. Yet the land of his ancestors will fold him in death."[1]

Ely Samuel Parker came into this world four months later with big shoes to fill. He was born in Indian Falls, New York, and bore the Seneca name "Hasanoanda," which means "Leading Name." Parker initially struggled in his schooling, especially when it came to learning English. He persisted, however, and quickly rose through the ranks of the Seneca tribe. At age 18, President James Polk even invited him to dinner at the White House.

Despite his rising star, Parker continued to face obstacles as an American Indian. He was denied the ability to practice law, so he turned his sharp eye to engineering instead and found it a profitable profession. In 1851, at the age of 23, Parker became the Grand Sachem of the Six Nations of the Iroquois Confederacy.

Having been immersed in the two worlds of the Indian and the white man, Parker felt compelled to serve when the Civil War commenced. He unsuccessfully tried three times to tender his talents to the United States. Parker even wrote to Secretary of State William Seward, who rebuffed Parker's entreaty. Seward told Parker that the conflict was "an affair between white men. . . . We will settle our own troubles among ourselves without any Indian aid."[2]

Never one to be deterred, Parker continually searched for ways to serve the United States. Two of his friendships from his time spent in Galena, Illinois, served him well—those with generals Ulysses S. Grant and John E. Smith. The latter placed Parker on his staff with Grant's endorsement. Following exemplary service during the Siege of Vicksburg, Grant plucked Parker away from Smith and appointed the Tonawanda Seneca to his own personal staff.

---

1   Robert Murray Thomas, *Manitou and God: North-American Indian Religions and Christian Culture* (Westport, CT: Praeger, 2007), 23.

2   William H. Armstrong, *Warrior in Two Camps: Ely S. Parker, Union General and Seneca Chief* (Syracuse, NY: Syracuse University Pres, 1978), 77.

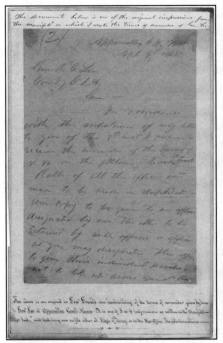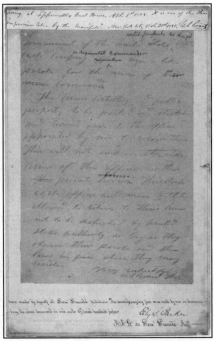

Ely Parker kept this copy of Ulysses S. Grant's handwritten draft of the surrender terms. According to the New York Historical Society, though, the surrender terms were not Parker's most prized possession. That honor belonged to the seven-inch silver medal President George Washington presented in 1792 to Parker's Great, Great Uncle Red Jacket. *New York Historical Society*

In a young life already filled with achievements, Parker's greatest day came on April 9, 1865, at Appomattox Court House. Though Parker had struggled with the English language in his youth, he had become fluent and was known for his immaculate penmanship. As such, Parker personally penned Ulysses S. Grant's reply to Robert E. Lee's request for a meeting between the two generals. Following the conclusion of pleasantries in Wilmer McLean's parlor that afternoon, most of Grant's entourage excused themselves while the surrender proceedings took place. Only a few of Grant's staff remained by the general's side. Lt. Col. Ely Parker was one of them.

"I am glad to see one real American here," Lee reportedly said to Parker as he offered a handshake. Parker accepted, replying, "We are all Americans."[3]

After Grant and Lee agreed to the terms of the Army of Northern Virginia's surrender, Grant put the terms to paper. He scanned them with Parker peering over his shoulder, and the engineer made several amendments to Grant's handwritten terms. When the time came to prepare the official copies of the surrender document, the general turned not to Parker but to his senior adjutant, Col. Theodore Bowers. Unnerved by the momentous occasion, Bowers' hand was too shaky to write the official documents. The task became Parker's, whose penmanship skills churned out the terms of the surrender.

Long after the guns of war fell silent across the former Confederacy, Ely Parker retained one of Grant's handwritten copies on which the general originally drafted the surrender terms. It was one of his prized possessions from the war.

Following Appomattox, Parker and Grant continued their friendship. Grant stood as Parker's best man at his wedding and, under the Grant administration, Parker fittingly led the Bureau of Indian Affairs. He died in 1895 and lies at rest in Forest Lawn Cemetery in Buffalo.

Ultimately, his mother's dream came true: Parker is buried in former Tonawanda Seneca territory. William Seward's prediction that the "affair between white men" could be settled "without any Indian aid" proved grossly false. Parker's pen firmly inked the ceremonial end of the Confederacy and with it the end of the Civil War.

---

3   Arthur C. Parker, *The Life of General Ely S. Parker: Last Grand Sachem of the Iroquois and General Grant's Military Secretary* (Buffalo, New York: Buffalo Historical Society, 1919), 133.

The Appomattox (or Shenandoah) Parole Passes and the Confederate Cavalry After Lee's Surrender

by Jonathan Tracey

*Originally published as a blog post
on Emerging Civil War on July 8, 2021*

Following the combat at Appomattox Court House on the morning of April 9, Gen. Robert E. Lee and the Army of Northern Virginia prepared to surrender. Lee and Union Lt. Gen. Ulysses S. Grant met in the parlor of Wilmer McLean's house in the small town. There they discussed terms that Grant had previously set in messages to Lee, including the provision that enlisted men and officers of the Army of Northern Virginia would be paroled. Lee assented, but also proposed a few additional measures. Grant magnanimously agreed to allow Confederates to retain their personal mounts, as Confederates often owned the horses they used personally, and allowed officers to retain their sidearms and baggage. The terms were copied and signed, and the victorious Union army began distributing rations to their former foes.

However, not all soldiers of the Army of Northern Virginia were among them. Some, including Confederate cavalryman Andrew Gatewood, had fled to avoid surrender. Escaping westward, they held out hope for continued resistance but were eventually compelled to surrender, receiving similar parole passes later.

In the midst of the surrender proceedings, Robert E. Lee issued his farewell address, often described as General Order No. 9. In it, he urged his men to return home peacefully and not to continue the conflict into a bloody guerilla period that the Union army feared. However, his words also proved foundational in the Lost Cause ideology. In part, he wrote:

> After four years of arduous service, marked by unsurpassed courage and fortitude, the Army of Northern Virginia has been compelled to yield to overwhelming numbers and resources. I need not tell the survivors of so many hard-fought battles, who have remained steadfast to the last, that I have consented to this result from no distrust of them; but feeling that valor and devotion could accomplish nothing that could compensate for the loss that would have attended the continuation of the contest, I have determined to avoid the useless sacrifice of those whose past services have endeared them to their countrymen.[1]

Lee had given birth to a key tenet of the Lost Cause - that the Confederate defeat was not due to any shortcomings he may have had as a commander or to inadequacies his men may have had as soldiers, but instead was due to the numbers and resources of the North. These words exempted the soldiers from blame and allowed them to cling to their defeated cause as a glorious and honorable one even if it had been in vain.

Following this first meeting, Lee and Grant had a second conference on the morning of April 10. There, Grant agreed to issue individual paroles to Confederate soldiers. Major General John Gibbon, one of the Union commanders in charge of overseeing the surrender and the parole process, recorded that Grant spoke to him, saying, "Gen. Lee is desirous that his officers and men should have on their persons some evidence that they are paroled prisoners, so that they will not be disturbed. . . . I said I thought that could be arranged, and I had a small printing press and could have blank forms struck off which could be filled in and one given to each officer and

---

1   J. Jones, *Life and Letters of Robert Edward Lee, Soldier and Man* (District of Columbia: Neale Publishing Company, 1906), 486.

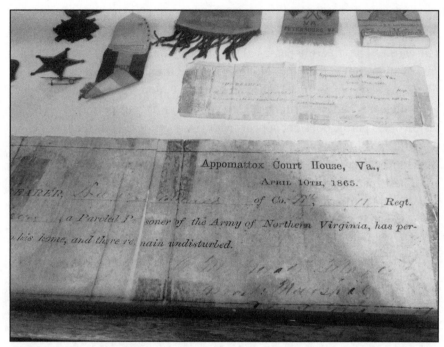

Gatewood's parole pass on display at the Pocahontas County Historical Society in Marlinton, West Virginia. The original parole pass is the smaller of the two versions, while below is an enlarged scan for visitors to see. *Jonathan Tracey*

man of the army."[2] At once, Gibbon brought his command's printing press to the Clover Hill Tavern and sent out a call for all soldiers with printing experience to assist in the herculean task of turning out 30,000 passes. Lee and Grant understood the importance that written parole passes would have, as this paper would provide safety for former solders from execution as deserters or guerillas. Little did they know, however, just *how* important these passes would become to some former Confederates.

Grant took the generosity of his surrender terms even further. On April 10, he issued a special order and distributed it to the commands of both the Union and Confederate armies. It read, "All officers and men of the Confederate service paroled at Appomattox Court House who to reach their

---

2   William G. Nine and Ronald G Wilson, *The Appomattox Paroles, April 9-15, 1865*, 3rd ed. Virginia Civil War Battles and Leaders Series (Lynchburg: H.E. Howard, 1989), 5.

homes are compelled to pass through the lines of the Union armies, will be allowed to do so, and to pass free on all Government transports and military railroads."[3] These parole passes also allowed Confederates to draw rations from Union troops they met along the way. Often, surviving examples of parole passes contain penciled-in writing by Union troops detailing when a Confederate had used this order to gain food or transportation. Trooper Gatewood's parole does not appear to have any of these marks, although the pencilled writing on the front is nearly illegible and it is not possible today to read what may be on the rear of the pass, due to how it is displayed.[4]

These paroles were distributed to the Army of Northern Virginia's cavalry and artillery on April 11 although, as previously mentioned, many cavalrymen had fled rather than surrender. The infantry received their paroles following the formal surrender and stacking of arms on April 12. Almost immediately, Confederate soldiers grasped the importance of the papers. To them, "the paroles represented the promise that they would not be treated dishonorably."[5] Instead, they could travel home without fear of being accosted and could even draw food or transportation from Union garrisons they passed. These papers were fervently sought "as a shield against 'punishment and vengeance,'" and a Union officer recorded, "It was very noticeable how greedily the Confederates, rank and file especially, clutched at their 'protection papers' provided for them by the terms of the treaty."[6]

Things became more complicated for the Army of Northern Virginia's cavalry. For example, no members of the 11th Virginia Cavalry, including Andrew Gatewood, received parole passes printed at Appomattox Court House between April 10 and April 13. One artillerist who avoided surrender and capture wrote home explaining his choice. "I am by no means conquered yet," wrote Ham Chamberlayne. "We refused to take part in the funeral at Appomattox C.H. & cut or crept our way out."[7] One can imagine that

---

3   Ibid., 5.

4   Gatewood's pass can be viewed at the Pocahontas County Historical Society in Marlinton, WV (http://www.pocahontashistorical.org/).

5   Elizabeth R. Varon, *Appomattox: Victory, Defeat, and Freedom at the End of the Civil War* (Oxford: Oxford University Press, 2014), 72.

6   Varon, 73.

7   Caroline E. Janney, "Free to Go Where We Liked: The Army of Northern Virginia after Appomattox," *The Journal of the Civil War Era* 9, no. 1 (2019), 10.

Gatewood felt similarly. Hoping to bring these stragglers in to surrender rather than allowing them to form pockets of resistance, Grant offered the same parole terms to any scattered Confederate holdouts to turn themselves in. Major General Fitzhugh Lee and most of the cavalry returned to be paroled, but many horsemen in the division under Maj. Gen. Thomas Rosser, including Gatewood, did not.[8]

When Rosser finally saw the inevitable, however, he arranged for the surrender of his command. Though he intended a mass surrender on May 10, his dispersed command actually surrendered in a much less synchronized fashion. On May 4, the 11th Pennsylvania Cavalry received orders to travel to Staunton and receive the surrender of Rosser's command. The orders stated, "By agreement with the authorities here he is to have his command collected and necessary steps taken for their parole on the 10th instant. The general terms are the same as those agreed upon between Gens. Grant and Lee."[9] Franklin Stratton, lieutenant colonel of the 11th Pennsylvania, wrote that when his regiment arrived, he found other Union troops had begun to parole the Confederates. He wrote to his commanders, complaining that Rosser "had made no visible preparation for paroling the remainder of his men, nor was there any tangible evidence of his intention to turn over any rebel government property whatever. After several interviews with him I ascertained that the men of his command were entirely dispersed, and would only come in in small detachments, or singly, to be paroled."[10] Doing little to ameliorate fears of guerilla warfare, Rosser admitted that he had hidden several pieces of artillery that he had no intention of turning in. Slowly but surely, however, Gatewood and others made their way to surrender and be paroled.

The parole passes printed in the Shenandoah Valley look extremely similar to those issued the month prior, and as such it is difficult to conduct extensive research on their specifics. One obvious key difference is the decorative design on the left which differs from those printed at Appomattox. This can be seen by comparing Gatewood's pass to the reproduction pass. Additionally, examining the detailed returns and records kept by both

8   Varon, 73-75.

9   Henry Wilson Storey, *History of Cambria County Pennsylvania,* Vol. 2 (New York: Lewis Publishing Company, 1907), 202.

10   Ibid., 203.

armies during the parole distribution reveals that no members of the 11th Virginia Cavalry received passes at Appomattox. This same decorative left-side design is shown on the parole pass issued to Sergeant Benjamin H. Woodford of the 62nd Virginia Mounted Infantry and published in "A Priceless Legacy" in the March 2006 issue of *Civil War Times*. Like the 11th, the 62nd was not at Appomattox. Although the location of issue is unknown, many other soldiers of this unit were paroled by the Middle Military Division headquartered at Winchester, Virginia.[11] Thus, it appears that this design was copied and printed by a military office handling the paroles of straggling Confederate troops in the Shenandoah Valley, and is likely of the same origin as Gatewood's pass. The reason the passes were so similar was that, despite the change in northern attitude in the aftermath of President Lincoln's assassination, Rosser's command was to receive the same terms as those given to the troops that surrendered at Appomattox. As such, the passes retained the same textual design, even to the point of including the original date, and the same privileges.

Unfortunately, Gatewood's diary skips the month of May and never officially records when he received his parole pass. He may have ridden into Staunton to surrender, or he may have received it when elements of the 8th Ohio Cavalry arrived on his farm in early June.[12] Most likely, however, is that he was given the pass in Winchester, since other examples of the same style were issued there. Despite Gatewood's later-expressed pride in his pass, he may have been embarrassed to surrender and therefore decided not to record the event. In any case, by July his diary turned away from the war and politics and towards recording farm business. Gatewood's war was over.

These parole passes, whether gained during those fateful April days at Appomattox Court House or acquired later by men who had broken out of the Union lines, took on great importance. One veteran, Edgar Warfield, kept his parole pass until his death in 1934. He recorded, "I still have it. I have carefully preserved it, valuing it as a priceless relic, as it furnishes official proof that I was present with the army to the last."[13] Over time,

---

11   Coco, "A Priceless Legacy," *Civil War Times*, March 2006, 44.

12   Diary June 1, 1865, A.C.L. Gatewood Papers, WVRHC.

13   Coco, 43.

these passes were transformed from an admission of defeat to a practical tool to ensure food, transportation, and safety and, eventually, to a sign of Lost Cause pride. They symbolized that a soldier had fought for the cause until the last moment, even beyond Appomattox in some cases, and were treasured by those who had them, whether they were an Appomattox design or, instead, the Shenandoah version.

1. Thoughts on Appomattox

by Chris Mackowski

Originally published at Emerging Civil War on April 12, 2015, as the last installment in a five-part series to commemorate the Sesquicentennial of Lee's surrender

On the night of April 12, 1865, as he made his way back to Richmond after leaving the remnants of his Army of Northern Virginia, Gen. Robert E. Lee pitched his camp alongside the road. Today, the spot—along modern Route 60 midway between Dillwyn and Buckingham—is marked by a few historical signs and a small monument. Little Confederate flags flutter around each monument, sign, and marker like daffodils that have sprung up for the surrender.

How did Lee feel that evening, after he'd retired to his tent?

Does the gut punch of defeat keep him awake? Does he feel relief that his desperate flight is over? Disappointment that he failed his men? Has exhaustion finally caught up with him and pulled him into a deep sleep? Or is he restless?

Is he heartbroken? Is he deflated? Is he resigned? Is he embarrassed?

Is he looking forward to just being home, finally, after all these years? Is he anxious to see his wife? Anxious to hide away?

Lee has become so mythologized, so marbleized, over 150 years that it's sometimes hard to remember how human he was. We see him as a military leader—but forget to see him as a man.

So duty-bound was he that he often subsumed his own emotions and opinions. One hundred and fifty years later, it's often hard to discern how he felt at any given time, although his actions always demonstrated what he knew to be right.

But on this April evening, right and wrong had been redefined from the rules in his old world order—decided on the battlefield, a result that the professional soldier in him recognized as absolute. Had he yet started to wonder *Now what?*

He had thrown away his entire career and had turned his back on the opportunity to lead the Federal army in exchange for a cause he felt was right: the defense of his home, Virginia. His duty kept him away from his wife and children for years at a time.

Robert E. Lee Wayside: A monument marks the spot where Lee's tent allegedly stood on the night of April 12, 1865. *Chris Mackowski*

Did it all seem for naught?

In a letter he wrote to Confederate President Jefferson Davis on April 20, Lee revealed that he'd already seen the handwriting on the wall prior to the collapse of the army. "The operations which occurred while the troops were in their entrenchments in front of Richmond and Petersburg were not marked by the boldness and decision which formerly characterized them," he wrote. "Except in particular instances, they were feeble, and a want of confidence seemed to possess officers and men. This condition, I think. was produced by the state of the feeling in the country, and the communications received be the men from their homes, urging their return and the abandonment of the field."[1]

Did he feel embittered? Betrayed? Resigned?

Had these thoughts even gelled by the time he took his leave from the men of his former command?

As he sat in his tent, how did he *feel*?

---

1   Lee to Davis, 20 April 1865, *The Wartime Papers of Robert E. Lee*, Clifford Dowdey, ed. (Boston: Da Capo, 1961), 938.

Contributors' Notes

Emerging Civil War is the collaborative effort of more than thirty historians committed to sharing the story of the Civil War in an accessible way. Founded in 2011 by Chris Mackowski, Jake Struhelka, and Kristopher D. White, Emerging Civil War features public and academic historians of diverse backgrounds and interests, while also providing a platform for emerging voices in the field. Initiatives include the award-winning Emerging Civil War Series of books published by Savas Beatie, LLC; the "Engaging the Civil War" Series published by Southern Illinois University Press; an annual symposium; a speakers bureau; and a daily blog: www.emergingcivilwar.com.

Emerging Civil War is recognized by the I.R.S. as a 501(c)3 not-for-profit corporation.

*   *   *

Edward Alexander is a freelance cartographer at Make Me a Map, LLC. He is a regular contributor for Emerging Civil War and the author of *Dawn of Victory: Breakthrough at Petersburg* in the Emerging Civil War Series. Edward has previously worked at Pamplin Historical Park and Richmond National Battlefield Park. He has written for the Emerging Civil War blog since March 2013.

Sarah Kay Bierle, author, speaker, and researcher focusing on the American Civil War, graduated from Thomas Edison State University with a BA in History, volunteers as the managing editor at Emerging Civil War, and works for a non-profit preserving battlefields and promoting history education. The Overland Campaign battlefields have become particularly meaningful to her, and she can often be found studying the land and comparing it to primary sources.

Sean Michael Chick is a New Orleans native. He holds an undergraduate degree from the University of New Orleans and a Master of Arts from Southeastern Louisiana University. He is currently a New Orleans tour guide, giving one of the only guided tours of the French Quarter concentrating on the American Civil War and slavery. His first book was *The Battle of Petersburg, June 15-18, 1864*. He joined the Emerging Civil War blog in the summer of 2017 after making several guest contributions to the blog.

Caroline Davis grew up in Indiana, with her passion for history starting at a young age. She earned her bachelor's degree in American History from Ball State University and her Master's in Historical Preservation with a concentration in Public History at Georgia State University. She has worked at Fredericksburg and Spotsylvania NMP, Vicksburg NMP, Stones River NB, and C&O Canal NHP. She hopes to continue a career with the National Park Service. Caroline started writing with ECW in June 2013.

Dan Davis is a graduate of Longwood University with a bachelor's degree in Public History. He has worked as a Ranger/Historian at Appomattox Court House National Historic Site and Fredericksburg and Spotsylvania National Military Park. Dan is the author or co-author of numerous books and articles on the Civil War. He is the co-author, with Phillip S. Greenwalt of *Hurricane from the Heavens: The Battle of Cold Harbor, May 26-June 5, 1864* and the author of *Most Desperate Acts of Gallantry: George A. Custer in the Civil War*. Dan is the education manager with the American Battlefield Trust and resides in Fredericksburg, Virginia.

Robert M. Dunkerly (Bert) is a historian, award-winning author, and speaker who is actively involved in historic preservation and research. He holds a degree in History from St. Vincent College and a Masters in Historic Preservation from Middle Tennessee State University. He has worked at 13 historic sites, written 11 books and over 20 articles. Among his books in the ECW series is *No Turning Back: A Guide to the 1864 Overland Campaign*. Dunkerly is currently a Park Ranger at Richmond National Battlefield Park.

Phillip S. Greenwalt is a historian with Emerging CIvil War and the co-founder of Emerging Revolutionary War. He is the author or coauthor of five books on the American Revolution and American Civil War. He is currently a park ranger with the National Park Service.

In 1990, **Chris Heisey** began photographing American battlefields. He has published images in more than 250 worldwide publications and media venues, and his images have garnered numerous awards including four national merit awards. He has collaborated on three previous books: *In the Footsteps of Grant and Lee* with Gordon Rhea; *Gettysburg: This Hallowed Ground*; and *Gettysburg: The Living and The Dead* with Kent Gramm. He started writing and contributing photography with Emerging Civil War in June 2020.

Steward Henderson is currently a park ranger/historian with the Fredericksburg and Spotsylvania National Military Park after having retired from a 35 year career in the financial services field. He has had a life-long interest in the Civil War and is a co-founder of the 23rd Regiment United States Colored Troops. Steward is also a member of the 54th Massachusetts Volunteers Co. B, the Civil War Trust, and the Central Virginia Battlefield Trust.

Dwight Hughes is a retired U. S. Navy officer, Vietnam War veteran, and public historian who speaks and writes on Civil War naval history. He is author of two books and a contributing author at the Emerging Civil War blog. His essay "The Soldier and the Sailor at Vicksburg: Grant and Porter" was published in *The Summer of '63, Vicksburg and Tullahoma* (Savas Beatie, 2021). Dwight has presented at numerous Civil War roundtables, historical conferences, and other venues. You can find out more about Dwight's works at https://civilwarnavyhistory.com. His first guest post on the ECW blog was in December 2014, and since that time has contributed more than 70 posts.

Christopher L. Kolakowski has spent his career interpreting and preserving American military history, and is currently Director of the Wisconsin Veterans Museum in Madison, Wisconsin. He has written and spoken on various aspects of military history from 1775 to the present, including four books on the Civil War and World War II. He started blogging for Emerging Civil War in May 2013, and most recently served as its Chief Historian.

Chris Mackowski, Ph.D., is the editor in chief and a co-founder of Emerging Civil War, and he's the managing editor of the Emerging Civil War Series published by Savas Beatie. Chris is a writing professor in the Jandoli School of Communication at St. Bonaventure University, where he also serves as the associate dean for undergraduate programs, and is the historian-in-residence at Stevenson Ridge, a historic property on the Spotsylvania Court House battlefield. He serves as the vice president of the Central Virginia Battlefields Trust and serves on the advisory board for the Civil War Roundtable Congress.

Rob Orrison, co-founder of Emerging Revolutionary War, serves as the Division Manager for the Prince William County Office of Historic Preservation, which operates 12 historic sites, museums, and parks in Prince William County. He is the author or coauthor of four books and is currently working on a book on the Battle of Camden. He lives in Dumfries, Virginia with his wife Jamie and sons Carter and Grayson.

Kevin Pawlak is a Historic Site Manager for Prince William County's Historic Preservation Division and serves as a Certified Battlefield Guide at Antietam National Battlefield and Harpers Ferry National Historical Park. Kevin is the author or co-author of five books. He has been a member of Emerging Civil War since May 2016.

Nathan Provost is a doctoral candidate at Liberty University in Lynchburg, Virginia. His dissertation topic covers the battle of Cold Harbor and its complex outcome. Nate is under the direction of Civil War historian Dr. Steven Woodworth. In his spare time, Nate enjoys touring battlefields and reading all he can on North American military history. He is working towards publishing books related to the military career of Ulysses Grant and becoming a professor. He works as a U.S History Teacher at Crossroads Preparatory Academy.

Ryan Quint graduated with a BA in History from the University of Mary Washington. He has worked for a number of museums, including the George Washington Foundation, Colonial Williamsburg, Richmond National Battlefield Park, and the Fredericksburg & Spotsylvania National Military Park. His book, *Determined to Stand and Fight: The Battle of Monocacy, July 9, 1864,* was published as part of the Emerging Civil War Series in 2017. Ryan has written for the Emerging Civil War since July 2013.

Terry Rensel is the executive director of the Central Virginia Battlefields Trust in Fredericksburg, Virginia. He's earned a bachelor degree in History/Political Science from the University of Pittsburgh at Bradford and a Master of Public Administration from the University of Alaska Southeast. He served for 6 years in the 1/112th INF. BN of the Pennsylvania National Guard, the direct descendant unit of the 83rd Pennsylvania Volunteer Infantry. He joined the Emerging Civil War Editorial Board in the fall of 2015.

Brian Swartz is a 36-year veteran newspaper journalist and a historian focusing on Maine's and Mainers' involvement in the Civil War. He has published several history books, including a Joshua Chamberlain biography for the Emerging Civil War Series. Besides contributing posts to Emerging Civil War, he writes for a newspaper and other publications in Maine. His own blog posts can be found at www.maineatwar.bdnblogs.com.

Jon Tracey is a public historian focused on soldier experience, medical care, and veteran life in the Civil War era. He holds a BA in History from Gettysburg College and an MA from West Virginia University in Public History with a Certificate in Cultural Resource Management. He has also worked several seasons as a Park Ranger at various sites and is now a Historian with the National Park Service. He began writing for the Emerging Civil War blog in August 2020, and serves as the Editorial Board Chairman.

Douglas Ullman Jr., is an independent scholar who has worked for or with the American Battlefield Trust since 2010. In addition to contributing to Emerging Civil War, his work has been seen in *Hallowed Ground* magazine, and he has been featured in numerous video offerings for the American Battlefield Trust. He is a graduate of New York University's Steinhardt School.

Dan Welch is a public school teacher and seasonal Park Ranger at Gettysburg National Military Park. Dan received his BA in Instrumental Music Education from Youngstown State University and a MA in Military History with a Civil War Era concentration at American Military University. He is the co-author of *The Last Road North: A Guide to the Gettysburg Campaign, 1863* and *Ohio at Antietam: The Buckeye State's Sacrifice on America's Bloodiest Day*. Dan is also the co-editor of *The Summer of '63: Gettysburg* and *The Summer of '63: Vicksburg & Tullahoma*, both part of the Emerging Civil War Tenth Anniversary Series. He has been a contributing member at Emerging Civil War for more than seven years.

Kristopher D. White is the deputy director of education at the American Battlefield Trust, co-founder and chief historian of Emerging Civil War and is also the co-creator of the Engaging the Civil War Series. White is a graduate of Norwich University with an M.A. in Military History, as well as a graduate of California University of Pennsylvania with a B.A. in History. For nearly five years he served as a ranger-historian at Fredericksburg and Spotsylvania National Military Park. White has authored, co-authored, or edited nearly two-dozen books.

Cecily Zander is a postdoctoral fellow at the Center for Presidential History at Southern Methodist University. She received her PhD in History from the Pennsylvania State University in 2021. She has published her work in *Civil War Times* magazine, *The Journal Civil War History*, and has written essays for several edited collections. Her first piece for ECW appeared in June 2020.

Postscript

Dear Faithful Readers:

As Cecily Nelson Zander pointed out in her essay in this volume, more and more people over time seemed to sneak into pictures of Lee's surrender to Grant.

But it's like Woodstock: if everyone who claimed they were there was *actually* there. . . .

Print-makers capitalized on this trend by inserting more people into their prints because, the more celebrities there were basking in the reflected light of the great moment, the more commercially appealing the print would be. The growing population in the McLean parlor over time suggests the more ersatz witnesses, the better.

We are pleased to present, on the following spread, our favorite such picture, created, no-doubt, for maximum commercial appeal.

Sincerely,

The Editors

Index

OPPOSITE: Artillery frozen in the Wilderness. *Chris Heisey*

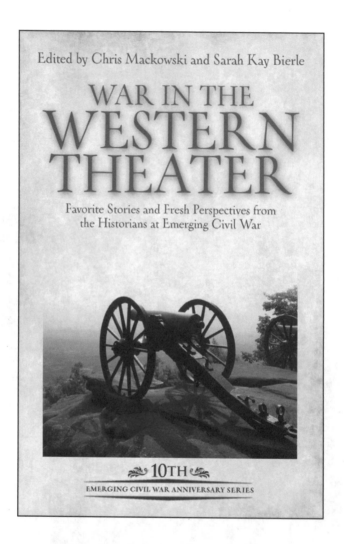

Edited by Chris Mackowski and Sarah Kay Bierle

WAR IN THE WESTERN THEATER

Favorite Stories and Fresh Perspectives from
the Historians at Emerging Civil War

❧ 10TH ❧

EMERGING CIVIL WAR ANNIVERSARY SERIES

Also from the Emerging Civil War 10th Anniversary Series

EMERGING CIVIL WAR

www.emergingcivilwar.com